Tick...Tick...

Hear that clock ticking? It's the countdown to the AP U.S. History Exam, and it'll be here before you know it. Whether you have one year or one day to go, now's the time to start maximizing your score.

The Test Is Just a Few Months Away!

The rest of us are jealous—you're ahead of the game. But you still need to make the most of your time. Start on page 321, where we'll help you devise **long-term strategies** to make the most of your time so you'll be well prepared for the big day.

Actually, I Only Have a Few Weeks!

That's plenty of time for a full review. Turn to the **Comprehensive Strategies and Review** on page 39, where you'll find a **comprehensive guide** to the multiple-choice section and the essays, as well as a review of all the **rhetoric** you'll need to know.

Let's Be Honest. The Test Is Tomorrow and I'm Freaking Out!

No problem. Read through the **Big Ideas in U.S. History** (page 9). Then grab a pencil and take a **practice test** (page 329). Don't worry about the scores—just focus on getting to know the test. Before you go to bed, go through the **Checklist for Test Day** (page 3) and keep it close. It'll walk you through the day ahead.

Relax. Everything you need to know, you've already learned. We're just here to keep it fresh in your mind for test day.

My Max Score

AP U.S. HISTORY

Maximize Your Score in Less Time

Michael Romano

 sourcebooks

Published by Sourcebooks, Inc.
P.O. Box 4410, Naperville, Illinois 60567-4410
(630) 961-3900
Fax: (630) 961-2168
www.sourcebooks.com

Library of Congress Cataloging-in-Publication Data

Romano, Michael J.
  My max score AP U.S. history : maximize your score in less time / by Michael Romano.
     p. cm.
  1. United States—History—Examinations—Study guides. 2. United States—History—Examinations, questions, etc. 3. Advanced placement programs (Education)—Examinations—Study guides. I. Title. II. Title: AP U.S. history. III. Title: Advanced placement United States history. IV. Title: Advanced placement U.S. history.
  E178.25.R66 2011
  973—dc22
                                        2010039352

Printed and bound in the United States of America.
                VP 10 9 8 7 6 5 4 3 2 1

Contents

Introduction

Everybody comes to an AP test from a different place. For some, it's the one AP test of their high-school career, while for others, it's just one of many. Some students have been focused on it all year, supplementing their classwork with extra practice at home. Other students haven't been able to devote the time they would like—perhaps other classes, extracurricular activities, after-school jobs, or other obligations have gotten in the way. Wherever you're coming from, this book can help. It's divided into three sections: a last-minute study guide to use the week before, a comprehensive review for those with more than a week to prepare, and a long-term study plan for students preparing well in advance.

Think of these sections as a suggestion rather than a rigid prescription. Feel free to pick and choose the pieces from each section that you find most helpful. If you have time, review everything—and take as many practice tests as you can.

Whether you have a day or a year to study, there are a few things you need to know before diving in. Let's start by getting to know the AP U.S. History Exam.

About the Exam

The AP U.S. History Exam lasts for three hours and five minutes and consists of two sections, a multiple-choice section and an essay section. The essay section is divided into three parts: the first part asks you to answer a document-based question, testing your ability to respond to primary sources, and the second and third parts ask you to write essays based on prompts.

The multiple-choice section contains eighty questions, and you are given fifty-five minutes to answer them. There is no longer any penalty to guessing incorrectly, so it's always better to guess than to leave an item blank. This section is worth half of your final grade.

For the document-based question (affectionately called the DBQ), you will work with a set of primary source documents that may include political cartoons, photographs, charts, and maps to analyze an issue in U.S. History. The DBQ is worth 22.5 percent of your total exam score, and your response is scored on how effectively and accurately you incorporate the documents into your analysis, and how well you incorporate your knowledge of the topic into the response. You will have fifteen minutes to read the documents and plan your response, then forty-five minutes to write your response.

For the essay section, you will be given two groups of questions. Each section will have two questions and you must select one question from each group. The first group (Part B) will contain questions about the United States pre-Civil War, and the second group (Part C) will have questions on events after the Civil War. These questions test your ability to synthesize information about U.S. History into thoughtful analysis. They comprise 27.5 percent of your total exam score. You will have seventy minutes for this section. The two essays are graded on the same scale of 0 to 9.

Scoring

The multiple-choice section is worth half of the total score. The document-based question is worth 22.5 percent of the score, and the two essays together are worth 27.5 percent.

Each essay is graded on a scale of 1 to 9, with a 9 being an exceptional essay and a 0 or 1 being incoherent, off topic, or otherwise unacceptable. These scores are combined to give you an AP grade:

5 Extremely well qualified

4 Well qualified

3 Qualified

2 Possibly qualified

1 Not recommended for AP credit

To earn a 3, a rough guide is that you will need to answer at least 60 percent of the multiple choice questions correctly and earn at least a 5 on each essay.

What's on the Exam

The AP U.S. History Exam covers the history of the United States from pre-Columbian times (before it was the United States) to modern times. Of course, some topics receive greater emphasis than others. Here is how the College Board breaks it down:

PERIOD	PERCENT OF QUESTIONS
Pre-Columbian to 1789	20 percent
1790 to 1914	45 percent
1915 to present	35 percent

Here's another way of looking at it:

MATERIAL COVERED	PERCENT OF QUESTIONS
Political institutions, behavior, and public policy	35 percent
Social change and cultural and intellectual developments	40 percent
Diplomacy and international relations	15 percent
Economic developments	10 percent

Piece of cake, right? Don't worry—while you technically are responsible for knowing all of U.S. history (an impossible task), there are many topics that come up again and again. And you don't need to get every question right, just most of them. So focus on the key facts and ideas, and how it all fits together, and you should do fine.

Visit mymaxscore.com for an additional practice test for the AP U.S. History Exam, as well as practice tests for other AP subjects.

THE ESSENTIALS: A LAST-MINUTE STUDY GUIDE

Okay, so it's a night or two before the exam and you just don't feel ready. Is it time to panic? No, it's time to prepare. If you've been taking an AP U.S. History class, or preparing in other ways throughout the year, then you're nearly there. All you need now is to settle your nerves, review a few strategies to refresh your mind, and line everything up for test day. It's not too late to maximize your score.

Get focused. You don't have much time, so you'll want to make the most of the time you have. Turn off all your electronics and technological gadgetry. No texting or web-surfing. Ask your family not to bother you unless it's really important. Close the door. Ready? Then let's get started.

Review the Test-Taking Tips

Start by getting to know the test. The speedy way is to review the **Quick Test-Taking Tips** in this section. If you have more time, you can get more detail in the Strategies chapters in the next section.

Review the Big Ideas in U.S. History

If you don't have time for a full review, go over the basics by reading over the Big Ideas section that begins on page 9. This section covers some of the broad themes and key events you are likely to encounter in both the multiple-choice and essay sections of the test.

Take a Practice Test

The only way to really get to know the test—and to try your test-taking strategies—is to take a practice test. Time yourself as if it were a real exam, moving on to the next section when the time runs out. When you finish, go over your answers, looking particularly for areas where you struggled. If you still have time, go over the sections that cover those problem areas in the comprehensive review later in the book.

Checklist for the Night Before

Put together a backpack or small bag with everything you'll need for the test. Have it ready the night before so that you can grab it and go, knowing you're properly equipped. Listed are some things you might put inside your backpack, as well as other suggestions to help you prepare for test day.

- Several pencils, a good eraser (test it first to make sure it erases without marking the paper), and several black or blue pens. Use erasable pens if you want, but make sure they don't smudge.

- A small, easy-to-eat snack. Avoid chocolate, which could melt and get all over your hands and your desk. Avoid nuts, which could trigger allergies in other testers. An energy bar, an easy-to-eat piece of fruit, or some crackers would be good choices.

- A bottle of water. Avoid drinks with sugar or caffeine. You may think they'll give you energy, but they're more likely to make you jittery.

- Don't stay up all night studying. Get a good night's sleep so you will be alert and ready for the test.

- Eat a light but satisfying meal before the test. Protein-rich foods like eggs, nuts, and yogurt are a good choice. Don't eat too heavily—you don't want to be sleepy or uncomfortably full. If you must have coffee, don't overdo it.

- Dress in layers. You'll want to be able to adjust if the testing room is too warm or too cool. Wear comfortable clothes.

Checklist for Test Day

- Don't bring anything you don't need. Cell phones, pagers, and anything else that might let you communicate outside the test room will be prohibited.
- Do bring a photo ID and your school code.
- Wear or bring a watch. If your watch has any alarms, buzzers, or beepers, turn them off.

Once you get to the testing room, take a few deep breaths and relax. Remind yourself that you're well prepared. It's natural to be nervous. Channel your nervousness into alertness and energy for the long test ahead. When the test begins, set all worries aside. You've done all you can to prepare. Time to make that preparation pay off!

Quick Test-Taking Tips

Your score on the AP U.S. History Exam depends on your knowledge of history. But even if you don't know all the content, you can improve your score by knowing the best way to attack the test. Here are a few easy tips.

I. Strategies for the Multiple-Choice Questions

You have just fifty-five minutes to answer the eighty multiple-choice questions, so your time will be limited. Here's how to make the most of it:

1. **Answer the easy questions first.** The questions are organized in random order; you won't come to the easy questions first and get the hard ones at the end. You don't want to waste time agonizing over a tough question until you've gone through the easier ones. Besides, later on in the test you may come to a question or answer choice that jogs your memory and helps you identify the answer to the question you skipped.

2. **Be careful on the answer sheet.** There is nothing that can lower your score as much as mistakes in using the answer sheet. Be sure you are marking the answers in the correct row, and keep checking it as you go, especially when you skip questions. Also, be sure you have

penciled in the answer space completely and have no stray pencil marks in other spaces.

3. **Mark up your test booklet.** While the answer sheet needs to be kept clean and free from any stray markings, the test booklet can be marked up as much as you want. Circle questions you skip. Put an asterisk by any questions you answer but want to come back to if you have more time.

4. **Answer the question before you look at the choices.** It's easy to get distracted by an incorrect answer choice. If you think of the answer to the question, then find it among the answer choices, then you don't have to worry about the other options.

5. **If you don't know an answer, start by eliminating answer choices.** If you don't know an answer, don't give up. See if you can eliminate one or more of the choices. Once you've eliminated the wrong answer choices, guess among the ones remaining. The more answer choices you eliminate, the better your chances of getting the correct answer.

6. **Take a guess, any guess.** If you get lost on a question or don't have time for it, just take a wild guess. Fill in an oval at random if you must. There's no penalty for guessing, and you just might get lucky.

II. Strategies for the Essay Questions

Section II of the exam contains three essay questions, including the document-based question. You have fifteen minutes to read the documents for the DBQ, forty-five minutes to write the DBQ essay, and seventy minutes to write each of the remaining essay questions.

1. **Start with a laundry list.** Once you've read the question, take a few minutes to jot down whatever comes to mind about the topic. Don't worry about structuring the essay first, just get those juices flowing.

2. **DBQ: Analyze and categorize.** Before reading each document for the Document-Based Question, look at who the author is. Consider the author's point of view, the time period in which it was written, and the purpose of the document. As you read, mark any part of the document that sheds light on the author's purpose or how the document relates to the prompt. When you have read all the documents, organize them by which viewpoint or idea they support.

3. **DBQ: Go beyond the documents.** The AP readers don't want you to regurgitate what the documents say. They want you to analyze the documents, evaluate the evidence they provide, and bolster it with your own knowledge of the time period. The document should be fodder for your analysis, but the analysis itself should come from you.

4. **Create a coherent thesis.** Your thesis statement should be a clear and focused response to the prompt. Each of the ideas you provide in your essay should support your thesis. If you can't sum up your argument in a single thesis, then you probably don't have a clear argument.

5. **Outline your ideas.** It's a good idea to draw up a brief outline of your essay before you dig into it. Don't worry about how it looks or how detailed it is—it should be just enough to guide you in writing the essay. Organize your ideas so that one flows to the next, allowing for smooth transitions.

6. **Write legibly and coherently.** While the exam is not a test of writing ability, you need to write clearly enough that your answers are understandable, or you won't get all the points you deserve. So even if it slows you down a bit, write clearly enough so that your essays can be read without too much difficulty. Think of the human graders; you won't score well if you leave them frustrated and confused because they can't read your handwriting or understand your sentences.

Big Ideas in U.S. History

In preparing for the AP test, the rote memorization of names and dates is not likely to improve your score. The best way to maximize your score is to identify the thematic threads running throughout U.S. History. Understanding the following twenty "big ideas" will help you to make connections that will benefit you on all parts of the AP exam, including answering multiple-choice questions, writing strong essays, and responding to document-based questions. Each theme has a summary with a brief explanation of its importance, and some milestone dates, events, or writings associated with it.

1. The Growth of Democracy

Beginning in the early 1600s, the English who arrived in the New World brought with them a tradition of representative government colonial assemblies, and the protection of the rights of Englishmen. These rights included trial by jury, free speech, and freedom from unreasonable arrest.

Key Dates

1620

Mayflower Compact—the Pilgrims' written agreement to create a political community based on the principle of government by mutual consent

1776

Declaration of Independence—affirms that government is based on the consent of the governed

1791

Bill of Rights—first Ten Amendments to the U.S. Constitution, guaranteeing freedom of speech, press, religion, trial by jury, and other basic rights of citizens

1848

Seneca Falls Declaration of Rights and Sentiments—expresses women's demand for the right to vote

2. The Divisions of Slavery

Sectional differences over slavery created tensions throughout the nineteenth century. In 1819, Missouri applied for admission to the Union as a slave state. Northerners and Southerners knew that admitting Missouri would shift the balance of power between the Southern slave states and the Northern free states. In 1854, armed clashes erupted in Kansas between pro-slavery forces and anti-slavery forces. "Bleeding Kansas," as it was known, foreshadowed the national war that began a few years later. The issue of slavery would dominate the presidential election of 1860. Lincoln emerged the winner in a four-way race, though he received only 40 percent of the popular vote. He was elected President without one electoral vote from the South. His election triggered the South's secession from the Union and the start of the Civil War in 1861.

Key Dates

1820

Congress passes the Missouri Compromise. Missouri is admitted as a slave state, and Maine is admitted as a free state.

1850

Sectional differences emerge over what to do with the territory acquired in the Mexican War. The South is alarmed because admitting California will upset the balance of power established by the Missouri Compromise. To settle the dispute, Congress passes the Compromise of 1850:

- California admitted as a free state

- Strict fugitive slave laws

- Southwest territories submit the slavery question to the vote of the people (popular sovereignty)

1861

Following the election of Abraham Lincoln, the South secedes from the Union and the Civil War begins.

3. The Church and the State

When Puritans settled the Massachusetts Bay Colony in 1629, they saw it as a "city upon a hill"—an example to the whole world. They believed religion should play the dominant role in the life of the colony, and the colony quickly developed into a theocracy in which the church was paramount in all political and religious decisions. As the United States developed, a growing number of people advocated for the separation of church and state. In the eighteenth century, the Enlightenment in Europe and the Great Awakening in America changed people's relationship with religion and their understanding of the role it should play in government—an issue that remains relevant in modern America.

Key Dates

1663

Parliament granted the colony of Rhode Island a charter guaranteeing religious freedom. The colony's founder, Roger Williams, advocated for separation of church and state and was banished from the Massachusetts Bay Colony.

1730s

The Great Awakening spread throughout the colonies. It was characterized by fervent expressions of religious feelings among the people, and it helped to democratize religion by changing how people felt about authority. If common people could make their own religious decisions without relying on the authority of ministers, they could also make political decisions without deferring to the upper classes.

1791

The Bill of Rights included protection for freedom of religion and individual liberties.

Twentieth Century

In the presidential election of 1928, many Americans voted against the Democrat, Al Smith, because he was a Catholic. In 1960, John F. Kennedy faced similar resistance to his Catholicism. In recent years, presidential candidates have highlighted their religious practices to appeal to voters, and the religious right has gained influence.

4. The Role of the United States in Foreign Policy

The United States has alternated between engagement and disengagement from foreign affairs. Since World War II, when the United States emerged as the world's most powerful nation, the nation has played an active role in foreign affairs. One recurring conflict in our foreign policy is the question of whether the United States should intervene for humanitarian purposes, or act only in cases that serve its self-interest.

Key Time Periods

Early U.S. History

In his Farewell Address, George Washington warned that the United States should remain neutral and stay out of world affairs that were not its immediate concern. In 1823, James Monroe reaffirmed these ideas in the Monroe Doctrine, but he also asserted that the Western Hemisphere was closed to any further colonization by European powers, and that the United States would oppose attempts by European powers to intervene in the Western Hemisphere. Washington's and Monroe's ideas would influence American foreign policy throughout the nineteenth century.

Early Twentieth Century

The emergence of Theodore Roosevelt and Woodrow Wilson in American politics forced the United States to reevaluate its traditional policies. President Theodore Roosevelt, a Republican, believed that the United States had a responsibility to act like a world leader in order to become a great power like Great Britain. Woodrow Wilson, a Democrat, believed that the United States had a responsibility to promote democracy in the world. He supported American intervention in World War I to make the world "safe for democracy" and proposed the creation of the League of Nations to promote international cooperation among nations. Although he supported the Versailles Treaty, which incorporated the ideas of the League of Nations, the U.S. Senate rejected it in 1920. Throughout the 1920s and 1930s, many Americans sought to return to a position of isolationism.

World War II

As Adolf Hitler's army took aggressive steps across Europe in the late 1930s, isolationists prevented President Franklin D. Roosevelt from taking action against the Nazis. From 1935 to 1939, Congress adopted a series of neutrality acts, which Roosevelt reluctantly signed. These acts were designed to prevent American involvement in the war. By 1939, Congress adopted less restrictive measures, such as the "cash and carry principle," which enabled the United States to take a more active role in helping Great Britain fight the Nazis. In the 1940 presidential campaign, Roosevelt promised that American soldiers would not be sent to any foreign wars. The Japanese attack on Pearl Harbor on December 7, 1941, ended the isolationist movement in the country. The United States entered World War II.

Post-World War II

After World War II ended in 1945, the United States took the leads in preventing the spread of communism worldwide. President Harry S. Truman's policy of containment provided economic and military aid to those countries opposing communism in the late 1940s and early 1950s. Policies such as the Truman Doctrine, the implementation of the Marshall Plan, and the establishment of NATO were all signs of the United States' growing leadership in fighting the communist threat throughout the world.

5. Nineteenth-Century Reforms

Throughout U.S. History people have sought to improve society and social conditions for democracy to succeed. In the nineteenth century, the issues of slavery, women's rights, education, prison reform, temperance, and treatment for the mentally ill were prominent in society. For each issue, the work of influential advocates was key in implementing societal reforms.

Key Movements

Slavery

The 1828 election of Andrew Jackson promoted a series of social and political reforms. In the 1830s, members of the abolitionist movement sought to eradicate slavery, believing it to be a sin. William Lloyd

Garrison, a prominent northern abolitionist, founded the *Liberator*, an anti-slavery newspaper. He advocated the immediate abolition of slavery in every state and territory without compensating the slave owners.

Temperance Movement

Members of the Temperance Movement sought to ban the sale and consumption of alcohol, which reformers targeted as the cause of social ills. Many argued that drinking ruined family life and led to spousal and child abuse. By the 1840s, the various temperance societies had more than one million members. The American Temperance Society, formed in 1826, established many chapters nationwide within ten years. By the 1840s, the various temperance societies had over one million members preaching against the ills of alcoholism. Although several states passed laws prohibiting the sale of liquor, there was no federal law until the 1920s.

Women's Rights

Prominent leaders of the women's right movement included Lucretia Mott, Elizabeth Cady Stanton, and Susan B. Anthony, who led the campaign for equal voting and legal and property rights for women. In their 1848 meeting at Seneca Falls, New York, the first women's rights convention, the feminists issued the Seneca Falls Declaration of Rights and Sentiments, which listed their grievances against the laws discriminating against them. They demanded the right to vote and to hold public office. The struggle for women's rights was soon overshadowed by the rise of slavery, and women would not gain the right to vote until the passage of the Nineteenth Amendment in 1920. The women's movement resurfaced in the 1960s, when they campaigned for greater social, economic, and educational equality.

Public Education

Reformers also focused on the need to establish free public schools for children of all social classes. Many reformers feared that an uneducated public, especially among the newly-arrived immigrants, posed a threat to the republic. Cities increasingly believed that the expansion of public education would expand democracy and make better citizens. As the Secretary of the Board of Education in Massachusetts, Horace Mann led the common public-school movement. He fought for better pay and better preparation for teachers, longer school years, and new school buildings. The movement for tax-supported public education spread to many other states throughout the nineteenth century, and it became the basis of our educational system.

Prison and Mental-Health Reforms

Reformers also sought to improve prison conditions. Physical abuse, humiliation, and neglect were common practices used to maintain order and discipline in prisons. Reformers convinced more and more states to prohibit the use of cruel and inhuman punishment. Their efforts were successful in convincing state legislatures that governments should use prisons to reform criminals, not just imprison them. At the same time, reformers worked for better treatment for the mentally ill, who were often chained, beaten, and abused. Dorothea Dix of Massachusetts worked to call public attention to these conditions, publishing a comprehensive report on the state of the mentally ill in Massachusetts. Her writings persuaded state legislators to establish asylums devoted solely to the mentally ill.

6. Supreme Court and Federalism

Throughout U.S. History, the Supreme Court has played a major role in defining the relationship between state governments and the federal government. In 1800, the Federalist President John Adams appointed John Marshall as Chief Justice of the Supreme Court. He served from 1801 to 1832. His decisions helped to establish the prestige of the federal government, and his rulings favored the central government and the rights of property against the advocates of states' rights. Marshall's decisions increased the power of the federal (or national) government in relation to the states, and they also expanded the influence of the Supreme Court.

Key Decisions

Marbury v. Madison (1803)

Just before leaving office, President John Adams appointed several judges. Thomas Jefferson, the newly elected president, wanted to block the appointment of these judges and ordered Secretary of State James Madison to not complete the appointment process. One Federalist appointee, William Marbury, was so outraged that he appealed to the Supreme Court, arguing that the Judiciary Act of 1780 gave the Supreme Court the power to force Madison to honor the appointment. Chief Justice John Marshall sympathized with his fellow Federalists and wrote the majority opinion, noting that Marbury had the right to his appointment according to the Judiciary Act of 1780—but that the law was unconstitutional, so the Supreme Court had no power to force Madison to act. Thus, Marshall established the principle of judicial review, which is the power of the Supreme Court to rule on the constitutionality of federal and state laws. This principle made the judiciary an equal branch of government alongside the legislative and executive branches.

Dartmouth College v. Woodward (1819)

This case involved the state of New Hampshire's right to change the privately owned Dartmouth College into a public institution. The Court ruled that the state could not change or alter a public contract.

McCulloch v. Maryland (1819)

The issue was whether the state of Maryland had the power to tax a bank created by the United States Congress, and whether Congress had the power to create a bank. Marshall asserted that a state could not tax the bank, which was a federally chartered agency. Marshall argued that the power to tax is the power to destroy, and federal laws are superior to state laws. Using a loose interpretation of the Constitution, Marshall ruled that the government had the implied power to create a bank under the power to coin money. This case also established the idea that a state law can be overturned if it conflicts with a federal law.

Gibbons v. Ogden (1824)

The issue in this case was whether the state of New York could grant a monopoly to a steamboat company to operate on an interstate waterway (Hudson River). Marshall ruled that only Congress had the authority to regulate interstate commerce, so the New York State law was invalid. In this ruling, Marshall established the federal government's broad control over interstate commerce.

7. Supreme Court and Racial Changes

The Civil War formally ended in 1865, but in some ways it was an unfinished battle. Reconstruction, segregation, and the civil rights movement all followed in its wake, and all had major political, social, and economic impacts. In the nineteenth and twentieth centuries, the Supreme Court issued a series of decisions that had important consequences for African Americans, and thus for race relations in the United States.

Key Decisions

Plessy v. Ferguson (1896)

Homer Plessy, a thirty-year-old shoemaker from New Orleans who is one-eighth black, was classified as black by the state of Louisiana. Louisiana had established a law that required separate railroad cars for blacks and whites. Plessy, who refused to sit in the black section, sued the railroad company for violating his rights under the Fourteenth Amendment. The Supreme Court upheld the Louisiana law requiring separate but equal facilities for blacks and whites. The Court ruled that Louisiana did not violate the equal protection clause of the Fourteenth Amendment. The decision was handed down by a vote of 7 to 1. The majority of the Court also rejected the view that the Louisiana law implied any inferiority of blacks. The Supreme Court thus upheld the constitutionality of racial segregation in public accommodations under the doctrine of "separate but equal." The Plessy decision led to a wave of Jim Crow laws throughout the South, which remained in effect until the mid-twentieth century.

Brown v. Board of Education (1954)

Linda Brown's father sought to enroll his third grader in a white elementary school only a few blocks from his home, rather than the all-black school about a mile away. School officials in Topeka, Kansas, turned down his request. He sued the Board of Education. Aided by a team of NAACP lawyers led by Thurgood Marshall, Brown appealed to the Supreme Court, which, by a unanimous vote, reversed its previous decision in the Plessy case. Chief Justice Earl Warren argued that segregation based on race deprived children of equal treatment. The Court concluded that the Topeka school system and others with race-based restrictions violated the Fourteenth Amendment's equal protection clause. Warren concluded that segregation should end as quickly as possible. The Supreme Court's decision did not abolish segregation in other public areas, but it began to pave the way for the civil rights movement.

8. Immigration

Immigrants populated the country's growing cities and metropolitan centers from the very beginning. As the country grew and the United States became more involved in foreign affairs, the nation's views on immigration changed. Some people wanted stricter regulations that would restrict immigrants from entering the country, often due to prejudices and fears that they would change society. Others recognized their ability to positively contribute to society. This conflict continues today.

Key Milestones

First Wave of Immigration or Old Immigration (1830–1890)

Most immigrants were from Great Britain, Germany, and Ireland. The largest immigrant group in the four decades before the Civil War was the Irish—there were nearly two million of them. Most of the Irish immigrants settled in northern cities (Boston, Philadelphia, New York). Many Irish immigrants earned their wages by building canals and roads.

Reaction to First-Wave Immigration

German Protestants distrusted the Irish Roman Catholics and organized anti-foreign societies like the Order of the Star Spangled Banner. This society turned to politics in the early 1850s and formed the American Party, also known as the Know-Nothing Party, whose platform was designed to restrict or limit immigration. The anti-foreign movement faded in the North as the issue of slavery dominated politics in the years leading up to the Civil War.

Second Wave of Immigration or New Immigration (1850–1920)

From the 1890s until 1914, the new immigrants came from southern and eastern Europe. These immigrants were primarily Italian, Greek, Croatian, Polish, and Russian. They were called "new immigrants" because their cultures were different from those of the older groups from Western Europe. These newcomers were Roman Catholics, Greek Orthodox, Russian Orthodox, and Jewish.

During the 1850s, large groups of Chinese immigrants came to the United States, many of whom were attracted by the prospect of finding gold. The Chinese were the first non-Europeans who came of their own free will. The Chinese, like the new immigrants from Europe, were met with suspicion and hostility.

Reaction to Second Wave of Immigration

The Chinese Exclusion Act (1882) was a turning point in U.S. immigration policy. It was the first major restriction on immigrations to America and was not repealed until 1943. This act halted any further Chinese immigration to America. The anti-foreign attitude of many native Americans led to demands for restrictions of the new immigrants from Eastern Europe, who were viewed as intellectually inferior to the old immigrants from northern and Western Europe. The Immigration Act of 1917 required a literacy test for all immigrants entering the United States. The National Origins Act (1924) established a quota for immigrants from each country. The law restricted the immigration of all Chinese, Japanese, and other Asians. The traditional policy of unlimited immigration ended.

Third Wave of Immigration (1965–present)

The Immigration and Nationality Act of 1965 eliminated the national quota system. As a result, the number of immigrants from East Asia increased. Before the 1960s, most immigrants came from Europe and Canada. By 1975, a majority of immigrants came from Latin America and Asia. In addition to millions of new immigrants admitted to the United States, millions entered illegally. In the mid-1970s, an immigration commission concluded that as many as twelve million foreigners were here illegally, primarily from Latin America and Asia.

Reaction to Third Wave of Immigration

In 1986, Congress passed the Immigration Reform and Control Act of 1986. It placed heavy fines on employers who hired illegal immigrants and granted amnesty to illegal immigrants arriving before 1982. However, Americans continued to insist on stronger measures, such as building fences along the Mexican border. These cries to restrict immigration echoed the congressional debates of the 1920s, when some politicians wanted to send immigrants back to southern and central Europe.

9. Expanding Role of Federal Government

Before the Great Depression started in 1929, the federal government had a modest impact on the lives of its citizens. However, Franklin D. Roosevelt's New Deal, which began in 1933, created a radically new role for the federal government. The series of proposals were designed to use the government to overcome economic hardship and reform and correct the abuses of capitalism. Unlike President Herbert Hoover, Roosevelt felt that the federal government should provide jobs for people. Federally funded projects not only gave people a paycheck but also pumped money back into the economy, Roosevelt argued, because people would have the resources to buy more products, which would spur economic growth.

Key Programs

New Deal Agencies

- **Public Works Administration** (PWA) (1933) Provided relief for the unemployed using federal money and put people to work on public-construction projects such as roads, bridges, and libraries

- **Agricultural Adjustment Administration** (AAA) (1933) Used government funds to encourage farmers to limit production of crops and livestock, which increased the price they could charge for those goods

- **Federal Deposit Insurance Corporation** (FDIC) (1933) Government insured that depositors would not have to worry about losing their money if their bank failed.

- **Social Security Act** (1935) Provided compensation for unemployed workers and the elderly

Impact on Future Policies

The New Deal established the principle that the federal government had a responsibility to take care of those who could not take care of themselves. The Great Society followed in the spirit of the New Deal. In 1964, President Lyndon B. Johnson announced his "War on Poverty" and

Congress passed the Economic Opportunity Act to eliminate poverty and deal with other social issues.

Great Society Programs

- **The Jobs Corps** offered vocational training to inner-city young black men.

- **Medicare** provided public health insurance to help senior citizens pay for health care. Under the Medicare program, persons over 65 were insured for a large part of their health costs.

- **Medicaid** provided funds for medical care for people with low incomes.

- **Project Head Start** provided educational funds for pre-school children from disadvantaged backgrounds.

10. Individual Rights and War

During war, the tension between individual rights and government powers heightens. In some instances, the government has rescinded certain individual rights for the greater purpose of winning a war. However, this creates conflict between supporters of individual rights and those who feel a country's wartime interests are the highest priority.

Key Periods

Early U.S. History

During the presidency of John Adams (1797–1801), the United States fought an undeclared war with France. To silence critics of his administration and to help the Federalists undermine the opposing Democratic Republic party, Adams passed the Alien and Sedition acts.

- **Naturalization Act** (1798) Required aliens to live in the United States for 14 years before they were eligible for citizenship

- **Alien Friends Act** (1798) Empowered the president to deport or imprison any foreigner residing in the United States who was considered a threat to national security

- **Alien Enemies Act** (1798) Empowered the president to deport or imprison resident aliens whose home country was at war with the United States

- **Sedition Act** (1798) Empowered the government to imprison or fine newspaper editors who criticized the government

These acts, except the Alien Enemies Act, have either expired or been repealed.

Civil War

President Abraham Lincoln was more concerned with executing the war than protecting the rights of citizens. He suspended the Writ of Habeas Corpus in Maryland and other border states where he believed southern sentiment was strong enough to overthrow the government. As a result, people could be arrested without being informed of the charges against them and placed under martial law for much of the war. Some Democrats in the North who opposed the war, known as Copperheads, were sometimes arrested and banished from the United States for pro-Confederate speeches.

Federal officials also ordered the suspension of certain newspapers and the arrest of their editors for obstructing the war.

World War I

During World Wars I and II, individual rights were again curtailed. In 1917, Congress passed the Espionage Act, making it illegal to obstruct the draft. Any material sent through the mail that was believed to incite treason could be seized. The Sedition Act of 1918 made it illegal to criticize the government. Under these laws, about two thousand people were prosecuted and about one-half of them were found guilty. Among them was Socialist leader Eugene Debs, who was sentenced to ten years in jail.

World War II

At the outbreak of World War II, the fear of Japanese invaders on the West Coast prompted the United States to order the internment of over one hundred thousand Japanese Americans. President Franklin D. Roosevelt signed Executive Order 9006, ordering them to leave their homes and live in barracks. In a 1944 decision, *Korematsu v. the United States*, the Supreme Court ruled that the internment camps were justified during wartime.

11. Industrialization in the Late Nineteenth Century

Between 1864 and 1914, the United States experienced a second Industrial Revolution, transforming the nation into one of the world's leading countries. In many ways, the results of industrialization shaped the relationships between businesses, workers, and farmers. As industry expanded, the role of hard work gained currency as a key American value. The concept of the "American Dream"—working hard to achieve economic success—gained prominence. Entrepreneurs such as Cornelius Vanderbilt and John D. Rockefeller grew large businesses, and a fundamental tension between big business and government grew. Labor unions were organized in reaction to big business. Farming was also affected by changes to the economy during the Industrial Revolution, and the Populist Party and labor unions arose in response.

Key Milestones

The Assembly Line

The United States surpassed Britain as the leading producer of coal and iron and revolutionized the automobile industry by developing the assembly line, which was later adopted by other industries.

Populist Party

Farmers were affected by the development of the railroad because they were dependent on rail transportation to move supplies and products.

They formed the Populist Party, dedicated to protecting their interests through the government ownership and regulation of railroads. Although the Populist movement declined after 1896, many of their ideas—such as graduated income tax and the direct election of senators by popular vote—eventually became law.

Labor Unions

To protect their interests, industrial laborers joined together to form unions such as the Knights of Labor and the American Federation of Labor. Most labor unions did not seek help from the government, instead looking to solve their own issues.

12. The Expansion of Presidential Power

Throughout U.S. History, presidents have interpreted the scope of their powers differently. The question of presidential power came into play in the nation's early decades, when land purchases and Native American relations were key issues. It resurfaced in several nineteenth- and twentieth- century conflicts. Efforts such as the War Power Act of 1973 sought to limit presidential power in entering foreign conflicts, but the struggle to establish balance remains.

Key Milestones

Land Purchases

In 1803, President Thomas Jefferson unilaterally purchased New Orleans and the Louisiana Territory. He did so by loosely interpreting the Constitution's allocation of power. He refused to wait for Congress to grant permission, fearing he would miss the opportunity to double the size of the newly formed United States at a cost of only $15 million.

Native American Rights

In 1832, the Supreme Court ruled that the Cherokee nation had a right to remain on its land in Georgia, despite attempts to force them to move. Andrew Jackson did not enforce the decision, and the Cherokee were forced to move to what is now Oklahoma, resulting in thousands of deaths on the "Trail of Tears."

War Powers

When the Civil War broke out in 1861, Abraham Lincoln called up seventy-five thousand troops and authorized war spending without Congressional approval. During the Vietnam War in the 1960s, Lyndon Johnson ordered more than five hundred thousand men into battle without a declaration of war. In 1973, Congress overrode a presidential veto and passed the War Power Act, which required its approval before a president could order the armed forces into action.

New Deal and Congress

During Franklin Roosevelt's presidency, the legislative branch ceded power to the executive branch, and Congress was criticized for passing laws without understanding their implications. In 1937, Franklin D. Roosevelt was so angry at Supreme Court decisions overturning his New Deal laws that he proposed expanding the Court to include fifteen justices, which would allow him to pick new justices. The idea was defeated.

13. Transformational Elections

As the leader of the executive branch, the president plays a pivotal role in American politics. The election of a new president affects all aspects of government, and at certain points in history, elections have changed the American political landscape.

Key Milestones

Election of 1800

Historians often refer to this election as the Revolution of 1800 because the Federalists peacefully ceded power to the Democrats. This election also changed the electoral college with the passage of the Twelfth Amendment, which required that electors specifically cast one ballot for the president and one for the vice president, rather than casting two ballots for president. Historians believe this change contributed to the decline of the importance of the vice presidency until the middle of the twentieth century.

Election of 1828

To many citizens, Andrew Jackson's victory represented the triumph of the common man in American politics. Jackson, who was from Tennessee, was only the second president who did not have a college education, and he was the first president from the West.

Election of 1860

When Lincoln, the Republican candidate, won the electoral vote with a minority of the popular vote, his election triggered the South's decision to leave the Union, igniting the Civil War. The election guaranteed that Republicans would dominate the American presidency until the late nineteenth century. Anti-slavery voters once associated with the Democratic or Whig parties joined the Republicans. Those who were pro-slavery joined the Democratic Party, which remained a regional party until the twentieth century.

Election of 1896

Republican William McKinley's victory over William Jennings Bryan, a Democrat, highlighted the shift from America as primarily an agrarian nation to one of urban interests.

Election of 1932

The Democratic Party of Franklin Roosevelt came to power by forming the New Deal coalition, which united groups that had not previously been associated with the party. The coalition included urban ethnic workers, African Americans who had previously supported the Republican Party, southern whites, and Jewish voters. This coalition and the realignment of American politics would shape the political landscape to the present day.

Election of 1960

John F. Kennedy's victory over Republican Richard Nixon defied the common wisdom that a Catholic could not be elected president. This was the first election that was greatly influenced by television, and some historians believe that the image projected by Nixon during the four debates cost him the election. Televised debates have been part of presidential campaigns ever since.

Election of 1980

Ronald Reagan's election was referred to as the Reagan Revolution. As a die-hard conservative, he promised to reduce the size of government and shift the balance of power away from the federal government. Although the size of government expanded on his watch, resulting in large deficits, Reagan's conservative philosophy dominated the Republican Party for the next decade. It even influenced Bill Clinton, a Democrat, who pushed his party to the center of the political spectrum in the 1990s.

14. The Media and Foreign Policy

As media evolved, so did its impact on society. Early in U.S. History, newspapers were instrumental in forming public opinion about conflicts. As the media expanded to include radio, television, Internet, and other technologies, its power to reach citizens and influence decisions about foreign policy expanded.

Key Milestones

Spanish-American War

In the 1890s, the American press called for an aggressive foreign policy. Prior to the Spanish-American War, two New York newspapers—Joseph Pulitzer's *New York World* and William Randolph Hearst's *New York Journal*—printed exaggerated and false accounts of Spanish atrocities in Cuba. As a result, Americans urged President McKinley and Congress to intervene in Cuba. In 1898, Hearst leaked a private letter written by the Spanish diplomat that was highly critical of President William McKinley. Less than a week after this "Deplume letter" was published, the U.S. battleship Maine exploded in the harbor of Havana, and 260 Americans died. Despite a lack of evidence, newspapers accused Spain of blowing up the ship. Although McKinley was on the verge of peaceful negotiations with Spain, the public outcry stirred by the press forced him to demand war.

World War I

Journalist George Creel headed the Committee on Public Information, whose job was to "sell" the war to the public. Creel's propaganda took varied forms—for example, millions of leaflets and pamphlets were distributed to promote the war effort. Creel also organized the Four Minute Men, who gave four-minute speeches in favor of the war wherever they could find an audience.

World War II

President Roosevelt recognized the value of the media and took steps to regulate it. The Office of Censorship worked with the media to suppress any information that might be damaging to the war effort. The Office of War Information was set up to counter enemy propaganda, glorify patriotism, and vilify the enemy soldiers. Hollywood directors like Frank Capra created films that were war-oriented and designed to improve the morale of the people. Music, radio, and magazines all supported the war and reflected a positive attitude about it. Americans received more news about the war through radio broadcasts, which were carefully censored by the government and by the media itself.

Vietnam War

The Vietnam War became known as the living-room war because television provided immediate access to images of the war. The dramatic figures of American and Vietnamese casualties revealed the destruction caused by the war. Television dramatically changed the public's perception of the war. The media's coverage contradicted the government's claims that the war was a success. For example, despite the government's claim that its counterattacks were effective against the Viet Cong in the Tet offensive of 1968, millions who saw the destruction on television considered it a setback for the United States. The very fact that a counterattack was necessary meant, to them, that the United States' policy was ineffective. The media was thus instrumental in eroding support for the war, which forced the government to reevaluate its long-term commitment to the war effort.

15. Writers and Social Reformers between 1880 and 1914

Industrialization created a widening gap between the wealthy and the poor in the United States. This gap spurred a generation of writers and social reformers to criticize the government's laissez-faire economic theory. The popularity of these writings and reform movements would wane by 1919, but they had a lasting impact on the country—most notably through the Pure Food and Drug Act and the Seventeenth Amendment.

Key Figures

Henry George

Henry George, a San Francisco journalist, wrote *Progress and Poverty* in 1879. It became an instant best-seller, selling more than 3 million copies. George proposes a single tax on property as a solution to poverty.

The book was successful because it brought attention to the growing economic inequalities created by industrialization.

Edward Bellamy

Bellamy's novel *Looking Backward* was published in 1888. It was about a hero who fell asleep and awakened in the year 2000. He found that the injustices of his era had disappeared and a cooperative society had emerged. Crime and poverty had disappeared. Nationalized by the government, big business served the public rather than private good.

Muckrakers

Exposing injustice became a flourishing industry among magazine publishers in the early twentieth century. *McClure's Magazine*, founded by an Irish immigrant, was famous for running articles about the evils within industrial society. The term *muckrakers* was used to describe journalists and crusading writers who exposed corruption in politics, greed in business, and scandalous conditions in the workplace. Famous muckrakers and their works included:

- Henry Lloyd, *Wealth Against Commonwealth* (1894)—attacked the monopolistic practices of the Standard Oil Company and the railroads

- Ida Tarbell, *History of the Standard Oil Company* (1904)—earned a national audience for its scathing history of the Standard Oil Company, which Tarbell called the "Mother of Trusts"

- Lincoln Steffens, *The Shame of the Cities* (1904)—described in detail the corruption of big-city politics.

- Upton Sinclair, *The Jungle* (1906)—depicted unsanitary conditions in the meatpacking industry. It also attacked the capitalist system that destroyed the dreams of immigrants and the poor. For Sinclair, socialism was the only hope.

16. War and Social Changes in the Twentieth Century

The world wars resulted in significant social changes for African Americans and women. Labor shortages during World War I meant that women were needed in the work force, accelerating the women's suffrage movement. During World War II, the number of women in the workforce rose from fourteen million to nineteen million. At the conclusion of the war, many stayed in their jobs, which created changes in the labor force that gave rise to the second wave of feminism in the 1960s.

In World War I, nearly four hundred thousand African Americans served in the segregated military, which remained segregated during World War II. This continued segregation, combined with unequal and often unfair treatment in the workplace, led to race riots in major northern cities and the start of the civil rights movement.

Key Milestones

Nineteenth Amendment

Ratified in 1920, it gave women the right to vote.

Great African American Migration

As a result of increased demand for workers in the North, waves of blacks began migrating to northern cities in the 1910s. About 2.5 million black southerners relocated to the North, sparking race riots in major cities.

Fair Employment

Philip Randolph, the leader of the Brotherhood of Sleeping Car Porters, organized a massive march on Washington to force government defense contractors to integrate their workforces and open up more skilled jobs to African Americans. Randolph canceled the march when Franklin D. Roosevelt promised to create a Fair Employment Practice Commission, which successfully reduced unemployment for blacks.

Congress of Racial Equality

Founded in 1942, this group was dedicated to ending segregation in the military.

17. Controversy over Segregation between 1890 and 1910

Racial segregation was an accepted policy in the United States for many years. The debate over how to end it in the late nineteenth and early twentieth centuries framed the civil rights movement of the twentieth century.

Between 1890 and 1910, African American leaders disagreed on how to deal with legalized segregation, also known as "Jim Crow" laws. The Supreme Court's *Plessy v. Ferguson* decision in 1896 upheld segregation laws using a doctrine of "separate but equal." There were two approaches: accept it and work to improve economic and educational resources for blacks, or demand full and immediate equal rights. This tension continued through the early part of the twentieth century, and it shaped the civil rights movement of the mid-century decades.

Key Milestones

The Atlanta Compromise

Booker T. Washington, president of the all-black Tuskegee Institute in Alabama, was dedicated to making African Americans economically self-sufficient by training and educating them. Once they improved their economic and social conditions, he believed, blacks would be able to challenge whites on social issues. He felt they should accept segregation until they were ready to challenge whites.

The Niagara Movement

W. E. B. Du Bois believed blacks should not stand back and accept segregation. He believed Washington's stance relegated blacks to second-class status for their entire lives. Du Bois helped found the National Association for the Advancement of Colored People (NAACP), whose goal was to abolish all forms of segregation and increase educational opportunities. The NAACP defended blacks who may have been accused of crimes based on their race.

18. The Frontier and American Identity

The western frontier, many believed, created a society of men and women who were democratic, socially mobile, and committed to self-improvement. People on the frontier were judged by how they handled adversity, not their social status. Frontiersmen were not tied to the land but were free to go where they believed they had the best opportunity to create a successful life. The frontier symbolized the American ideal and positioned the United States as a land of opportunity. Although often romanticized, the reality of the frontier was both positive and negative. It allowed for expansion and mobility, but mainly for whites, and often at the cost of annihilating the Native Americans who had settled the land first.

Key Milestone

The Turner Thesis

In 1893 Frederick Turner Jackson wrote "The Significance of the Frontier in American History," asserting that the frontier created the freedom to expand and develop new institutions. He argued that American democracy was unique because of the character developed by people who settled the western frontier. He said that the need for self-reliance on the frontier defined Americans more than anything else. Critics argued that he ignored the British influence on American democracy, as well as other important factors. Nevertheless, his thesis influenced all aspects of society, including literature.

19. Urbanization in the Late Nineteenth and Early Twentieth Centuries

Cities in the late nineteenth and early twentieth centuries were crowded and impersonal places devoted largely to making money. Corruption was rampant in city government. High rent, low wages, and poor services produced misery. Although this aspect of urbanization was not positive, the Progressive movement succeeded in reducing some of these issues and established housing codes and public-health measures. As a result, cities flourished and became more populated. The cable car system in San Francisco, elevated trains in Chicago, and subway trains in New York allowed urban residents to live further away from cities and create suburbia.

Key Terms

Suburbanization
This is a term for the growth of towns and cities on the fringes of major cities.

Commuter Towns
These are primarily residential urban communities whose residents drive to urban centers to earn their livelihood.

Megalopolis
This is a chain of roughly adjacent metropolitan areas. Lewis Mumford used the term in his 1938 book, *Culture of Cities*, to describe the first stages of urban overdevelopment and social decline.

20. The Great Depression

The Great Depression, which lasted from 1929 to 1940, had a major impact on the social and political fabric of America. The Depression affected virtually all Americans and all aspects of American life. By 1932, more than 25 percent of the American population was unemployed. Many shared jobs, and some pretended to get dressed for work each morning rather than admit they were unemployed. More than two million people were homeless. Those who did have jobs worked for low wages, and women had few employment opportunities, since they were seen as taking jobs from men. African Americans were the hardest hit. The Depression caused a major shift in political power, with the Republicans losing their hold on the White House for two decades, from 1932 to 1952.

Key Developments

Stock Market Crash

The crash of the stock market in 1929 marked the beginning of the Depression. Although the greatest declines occurred in October 1929, the market did not hit bottom until 1932, after it had lost nearly 90 percent of its value.

Bonus Army

In 1932, about seventeen thousand unemployed World War I veterans from across the United States marched to Washington to pressure the federal government to pay the bonus due them for their war service. At the urging of the President, the Senate rejected this request. Most of the Bonus Army returned home, but several thousand set up make-shift shacks near the Capitol and refuse to leave. Hoover ordered their removal.

Hoovervilles

Americans left homeless by the crippling effects of the Depression assembled in shanty towns and lived in shacks called Hoovervilles. They were named after President Herbert Hoover, who is frequently blamed for the Depression.

Roosevelt's Hundred Days

President Roosevelt assembled Congress for a hundred-day special session. It passed into law the initial legislation of the New Deal.

THE MAIN COURSE: COMPREHENSIVE STRATEGIES AND REVIEW

I f you have a few weeks to go before the exam, there's plenty of time to brush up on your skills. Here's a plan of what you can do to prepare in the weeks ahead.

- Go over the Multiple Choice, DBQ, and Essay Strategies sections in the next few chapters to get familiar with the exam.

- Test out the strategies and assess your knowledge by taking a practice exam. As you go through the answers, note any areas of weakness. Read the answers and their explanations. If you missed a question, find out why so you can avoid doing so in the future.

- Read through this Comprehensive Strategies and Review section. Pay special attention to any areas of weakness you identified in the practice test.

- Review the glossary section. Make flash cards of any terms or concepts that give you particular trouble and review them from time to time.

- Take at least one more practice test before test day. You can download one at www.mymaxscore.com/aptests.

- A few nights before the test, go back over the section on "The Essentials" for a refresher on test-taking tips and the Big Ideas of AP U.S. History.

- Do everything on the checklist on page 2.

Pack your materials for the next day, get a good night's sleep, and you'll be ready to earn a top score on the exam.

Multiple-Choice Strategies

The best strategy for acing the multiple-choice exam is, of course, to know your U.S. History inside and out. Even if you know all the material, however, you can still get tripped up if you're not careful. And if you don't know the answer to a question, using the following strategies can give you the best chance to answer the questions correctly anyway. Remember that there is no penalty for guessing, so it's always in your best interest to answer a question rather than leave it blank.

Strategy 1: Know the Question Types

The AP examination asks questions in particular formats. Understanding what they are will help you distill the main point of the question and help you focus on what sort of answer you are looking at. Following are descriptions and examples of the question types you are likely to encounter in the exam.

Identification Questions

> Which of the following men was an important Transcendentalist writer?
>
> (A) Ernest Hemingway
>
> (B) F. Scott Fitzgerald
>
> (C) William Faulkner
>
> (D) John Steinbeck
>
> (E) Ralph Waldo Emerson

This type of question requires you to recall the basic facts and select the correct answer. The correct answer is (E). This is a very straightforward question and requires you to know that Ralph Waldo Emerson was a Transcendentalist writer in the 1830s. If you knew that Transcendentalism was a nineteenth-century literary movement, it would help you eliminate choices (A), (B), (C), and (D) because all of these choices are twentieth century writers.

Analysis Questions

> One result of the National Origin Act of 1924 was that
>
> (A) immigration from China was banned
>
> (B) the United States adopted a literacy test for new immigrants
>
> (C) immigrants from northern and western Europe were directly discriminated against
>
> (D) paupers were denied admission to the United States
>
> (E) quotas were established that specifically limited the number of immigrants from eastern and southern Europe to the United States

This type of question asks you to draw conclusions or make connections between events. Answering analysis questions correctly requires a broader knowledge of historical periods. The correct answer to the above question is (E). This question requires you to analyze and assess, not simply recall, a historical event. The National Origin Act was directly connected to the quota system and how it limited the number of immigrants from eastern and southern Europe. The reader must put each answer choice into a historical time frame. The key term is 1924. If you recall that (A) Chinese immigrants were excluded in 1882; (B) the United States adopted a literacy test in 1917; (C) in the 1920s there was no discrimination against immigrants from northern and western Europe; and (D) paupers were excluded in the late 1880s, you can arrive at the correct answer.

EXCEPT and NOT Questions

All of the following countries attended the Versailles Conference in January 1919 EXCEPT

(A) Russia

(B) France

(C) Italy

(D) United States

(E) Great Britain

When looking at the sample question above, immediately circle the word *EXCEPT*. Remember that 4 of the 5 choices match the question stem. Cross out each choice that would be correct if you left out *EXCEPT*. Now you are left with one choice, which is answer (A). Communism had been established in Russia in 1917. Communist leaders signed a separate treaty with Germany in 1918, which ended Russian participation in World War I. Choices B through E were the countries that attended the Versailles Conference.

Graph/Chart Questions

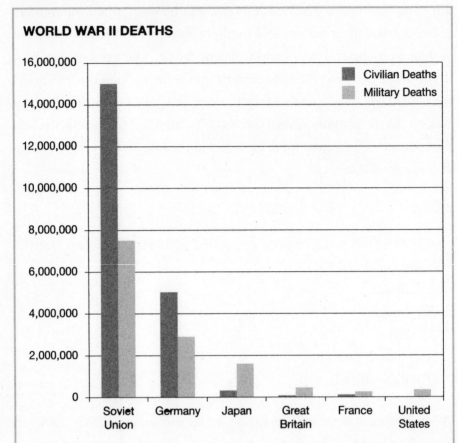

WORLD WAR II DEATHS

Which of the following statements is best supported by the graph above?

(A) All countries experienced both civilian and military deaths during World War II.

(B) The British lost the least number of civilians during World War II.

(C) The United States suffered the least number of military casualties in World War II.

(D) The Japanese civilian deaths were the second largest after Soviet losses.

(E) The Soviets suffered the largest number of civilian and military deaths during World War II.

This type of question requires little outside knowledge or information. They are not difficult because the chart or graph contains all the data you need to answer the question. First read the entire question with the choices, as well as the title or any keys to the chart or graph so that you know what you are looking for. Avoid overanalyzing or interpreting the data by bringing in too much outside information which can bog you down and create unnecessary tension. Focus only on the question and the choices. You can eliminate Choices A and B because the United States did not suffer any civilian casualties. Choice C is wrong because France, not the United States, had the fewest military casualties. Choice D is incorrect because Germany, not Japan, had the second largest number of civilian deaths. Choice E is correct because the Soviets suffered the largest number of military deaths (15 million) and civilian deaths (7.5 million).

Reading/Quotation Questions

"This, then is held to be the duty of the man of wealth;...to set an example of modest...living,...to consider all surplus revenues which come to him simply as trust funds, which he is called upon to administer...in the manner which, in his judgment, is best calculated to produce the most beneficial results for the community... the man of wealth thus becoming a trustee...for his poorer brethren."

The ideas in this passage are most closely associated with
(A) Andrew Carnegie
(B) John D. Rockefeller
(C) James Hill
(D) James Fiske
(E) Cornelius Vanderbilt

For this type of question, underline the words that will help you understand the main idea of the reading passage or quotation. You will be required to give the author or the key idea of the reading sample. The main idea of the above passage is the responsibility of the wealthy in society. The key words are "duty" and "trustee." If you do not recognize the passage you can begin to eliminate Choices B, C, and E because these people are usually referred to as the Robber Barons who were unscrupulous in building their industrial empires. Choice D was a Wall Street stock broker connected to the financial panic in the United States in 1869. Thus the correct answer is Choice A because in 1889 Andrew Carnegie wrote an essay entitled "The Gospel of Wealth," which describes the responsibility of the wealthy to administer their money in order to improve the lives of the less fortunate in society. For Carnegie, the wealthy had an obligation to improve society.

Political Cartoon/Poster Questions

Courtesy of the Library of Congress

Which viewpoint is expressed in the above cartoon?

(A) Congress and Jackson worked closely together to enact legislation.

(B) Jackson sought a return to British traditions.

(C) Jackson was a weak president.

(D) Jackson had monarchical ambitions.

(E) The wealthy class in America supported Jackson.

This type of question requires the reader to interpret the point of view or message of a political cartoon or poster. As with the chart/graph, examine the cartoon carefully, focusing on the title, captions, or any symbolism in the image. Taking this approach before you read the question can help you eliminate choices that do not represent the viewpoint of the cartoon. The example above depicts Andrew Jackson as King Andrew, who is dressed as a monarch and born to rule. Jackson is depicted as a king, a symbol of someone with excessive power. He holds a veto in his hand and is standing on the Constitution and a bank charter, a sign of disrespect to these documents. The image suggests that Jackson abused his power and trampled the constitution when he vetoed the bill rechartering the United States banks.

Choices A, C, and E are incorrect because the image does not indicate that he worked with Congress, nor does it show that he was a weak president or represented the wealthy class. Though British tradition includes the monarchy, Choice B is incorrect because the Constitution and bank charter suggest a different meaning. Choice D is correct because the image suggests that Jackson's veto of the bank charter was a sign that he wanted complete control over the country, like a monarch.

Interpreting a Map

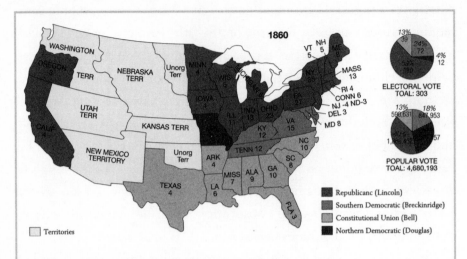

The Electoral Map of 1860 shows that

(A) Lincoln was a national candidate who won votes in all sections of the country.

(B) Breckinridge's popular vote exceeded that of Douglas.

(C) The Northern working class supported Lincoln.

(D) Lincoln won a minority of the popular vote but a majority of the electoral vote.

(E) Bell received the least amount of electoral votes.

Maps are used to describe geographic developments or to present information about social, political, or economic issues. The key to a map question is to look at the map carefully, particularly the legend or other keys which provides you with information that will help you answer the question more effectively. The correct answer is Choice D.

Lincoln was considered a minority president because he received only 40 percent of the popular vote but 59 percent of the electoral vote. By examining the pie graph you can arrive at this correct choice. Choice A is incorrect because the map clearly shows that Lincoln won no states in the South. Choice B is incorrect because the pie chart shows that Douglas had a larger popular vote. Choice C is incorrect because there is no information on the map to determine how the working class voted. Answer E is incorrect because the pie chart shows Douglas, not Bell, received the fewest electoral votes.

Strategy 2: Answer the Easy Questions First

In the multiple-choice section, you have to answer 80 questions in 55 minutes—that's less than a minute per question. Budgeting your time is extremely important, and if you spend too much time on a challenging question early on in the test, you can miss the chance to answer questions you know at the end.

When you begin the section, briefly scan all of the multiple-choice questions to determine which ones you are confident you know, and which ones you are less sure of. Address the easier questions first, and then use the remaining time to tackle the more challenging questions. If you find yourself strapped for time, put a time limit on each question so that you have time to attempt all of them. This strategy helps you assess where you need to spend more time and allows you to plan out the section strategically.

If you use this strategy, make sure to skip the lines on the answer sheet of the questions that you plan to answer later. Make sure you're answering the correct question on your answer sheet! On your test booklet, mark the questions you skipped so you can quickly find them later.

Strategy 3: Underline Key Words and Phrases

When you read a multiple-choice question, underline key words and phrases that illustrate the main point of the question. This will allow you to sort out necessary from unnecessary information to more quickly answer the question.

At which of the following World War II conferences did the "Big Three" meet for the first time?

(a) Yalta

(b) Casablanca

(c) Teheran

(d) Potsdam

(e) Dumbarton Oaks

This is an identification question. By underlining the key words "World War II conferences," "first time," and "Big Three" you are focusing on the main points of the question. You know that all the answer choices will be a World War II conference. However, you need to ensure that the "Big Three" attended it and that it was the first one they attended. Thus this becomes a very direct question requiring specific knowledge about these events. You have to know the identity of the Big Three (Roosevelt, Churchill, and Stalin) and that they had only met twice, first in Teheran in 1943 and the second time at the controversial Yalta conference in February 1945. Only Churchill and Roosevelt met at Casablanca. Potsdam and Dumbarton Oaks took place after Roosevelt's death in April 1945. The correct answer is C.

Strategy 4: Rewrite the Question and Answer

If a multiple-choice question seems particularly challenging, read through the question and answers and rewrite them in your own words. This will help you distill the most important information and figure out exactly what the question is asking. Using this strategy, you will be able to put the questions and answers into language that is easier and faster to comprehend. It is not recommended to use this strategy if you feel you understand what the question is asking, and how to obtain the answer. This is a strategy for when you are having difficulty understanding a question.

> According to Frederick Jackson Turner's Frontier thesis, the impact of the frontier on American society was that
> (a) it limited economic opportunity for most Americans
> (b) women were denied political rights
> (c) abundant free land enabled European countries to get rid of their excess population
> (d) it promoted the growth of democracy
> (e) it made Americans more aware of the need for environmental conservation

This question becomes easier to answer by rewording it in the following way: What did the Turner thesis say about how the frontier affected American life? Next, we can rewrite the choices to address these concerns: Did the frontier limit the chances to be successful in America? Did it hinder women's rights? Did it allow European countries to get rid of their excess population? Did it promote democracy? Did it make Americans more aware of the environment? We can come to the conclusion that D is the best choice. Turner believed that the frontier promoted political democracy because people judged one another not according to rank and social status but on their abilities and that everyone had an equal chance. The frontier was a place for economic opportunity, and the western state of Wyoming was the first to grant women unrestricted suffrage. Conservation was never a major concern of the settlers on the frontier.

Strategy 5: Use the Process of Elimination

Which of the following was a result of the Spanish-American War of 1898?
(a) The United States annexed Cuba.
(b) The United States granted the Philippines its independence.
(c) The United States gained control of the Panama Canal.
(d) Civil War broke out in Mexico.
(e) Spain gave two islands to the United States, Puerto Rico in the Caribbean and Guam in the Pacific.

Although you may not be familiar with all aspects of the Spanish-American War, you can use your knowledge of U.S. History to eliminate choices about Mexico, which was not impacted by this war, and the Panama Canal, which was not built until 1914. The United States did not grant the Philippines its independence until the end of World War II. That leaves you with choices A and E. You can eliminate A if you know that Spain granted Cuba its independence. That leaves the correct choice of E.

Strategy 6: Check for Clues or Key Vocabulary

The Revisionist historians of the 1960s and '70s who wrote on Reconstruction would support the idea that
(A) reconstruction was a blackout of honest government
(B) the Black Codes were necessary to establish control and order for the free slaves in the South
(C) corruption was rampant because the newly enfranchised slaves dominated state legislature in the South
(D) reconstruction was a noble but failed attempt to extend the American principle of equity and justice
(E) radical Reconstruction efforts to enfranchise Blacks were really an excuse to ensure Republican political dominance in the South

Sometimes key words can help you eliminate incorrect answers or help you arrive at the correct one. In the example above, the key word is *Revisionist*, which is a hint that these historians are reinterpreting the traditional view of this era. This would help you to eliminate choices A, B, C, and E because they reinforce the traditional view that was popular in the United States at the beginning of the twentieth century. This leaves you with Choice D, which stands out because it presents a revised view of Reconstruction in U.S. History, which was influenced by the civil rights movement in the 1960s.

Strategy 7: Watch for Choices that Mislead

> Which of the following is an important political slogan that was used by a Democratic presidential candidate in the nineteenth century?
>
> (A) Tippecanoe & Tyler Too
>
> (B) 54–40 or Fight
>
> (C) Don't Swap Horses in Midstream
>
> (D) Vote as You Shot
>
> (E) Rum, Romanism, and Rebellion

Be sure to read all the answer choices before you make your decision. Your initial choice may be correct but sometimes a more careful reading will help you realize that another choice is more appropriate. In the example above, the correct choice is B. It is the only choice that applies to the *Democratic* presidential candidate James K. Polk, who in 1844 promised 54–40 which meant he would force Great Britain to give up all of Oregon. All of the other choices are presidential slogans, but choice A refers to the Whig candidate and choices C, D, and E were Republican presidential candidate slogans.

Strategy 8: Think of an Answer Before Reading the Choices

What was one result of the Kellogg Briand Pact of 1928?

(A) It outlawed war as an instrument of foreign policy in solving disputes among nations.

(B) It enabled Adolf Hitler to gain power in Germany.

(C) It condemned the Japanese invasion of China.

(D) The United States agreed to join the League of Nations.

(E) The United States recognized the Soviet Union.

Thinking about possible answers before reading the answer choices can help you avoid being distracted by wrong answer choices. It will help you make connections or associations with a particular history event or time period that can make it easier for you to select the correct answer. Remember to focus on the big picture and avoid trivial facts.

As you look at the question above, you should begin to make associations or try to recall the main ideas connected to the Kellogg-Briand Pact and how it sought to denounce war as a way to solve international problems. The Pact had nothing to do with Hitler's rise to power (B), the Japanese invasion of China (C), or the United States joining the League of Nations (D) or its recognition of the Soviet Union (E). By quickly making the association about the Pact denouncing war, you will come to the right choice of A.

Strategy 9: Select the *Best* Answer

A major achievement of Dr. Martin Luther King in U.S. History
was

(A) his opposition to the Great Society Program

(B) the winning of the Nobel Peace Prize

(C) his leadership in the Montgomery, Alabama, boycott and
march on Washington in 1963

(D) his efforts to integrate college athletes

(E) the formation of the Urban National League

To choose between two reasonable choices, you must look for the
choice that is more precise or more fully answers the question. Often,
the choice that is more encompassing than the others will be correct.
In the example above, you can use the process of elimination to eliminate choices A, D, and E. Kifng supported the social program of the
Great Society, had no role in the integration of college athletes, and was
not the founder of the Urban National League. Although winning the
Nobel Peace Prize was a major *personal* achievement (B), his leadership
in the Montgomery Bus Boycott and his role in the 1963 March on
Washington (C) is a better answer because these events had a greater
impact on U.S. History.

Document-Based Question Strategies

For the document-based question, you will be asked to combine information from several documents with your own knowledge of a topic and use them to write an essay responding to the prompt. To complete this section, you will have fifteen minutes to read the documents before you can begin writing. After this reading period, you will have 45 minutes of writing time. The following list of strategies will help you make the most of this time and write a strong essay that responds to the prompt.

Strategy 1: Make a Laundry List First

For many, the Articles of Confederation that governed the United States from 1781 to 1789 formed a weak government that could have resulted in the breakup of the newly formed United States. Explain whether the Articles of Confederation provided an effective or weak national government for the United States from 1781 to 1789.

Before you even read the documents that follow this sample DBQ prompt, make a list of everything you can recall about the topic.

Remember that you are expected to infuse your knowledge of the topic to explain an issue. Your ability to weave and incorporate outside information with the data contained in the documents will help you write a quality essay. You might create the following list about the Articles of Confederation:

- critical period
- loose central government
- no power to levy taxes
- Shays' Rebellion
- Northwest Ordinance
- Annapolis Convention

This short list of ideas and events will guide you as you read the DBQ. Categorizing the information might help to formulate your essay as you read the documents.

Strategy 2: Focus Your Reading

Before you begin reading the documents, first underline key words in the prompt that tell you how to approach the essay. Words such as *Analyze, Discuss, Evaluate, Refute,* or *Explain* can help you know what to look for in the documents. In the prompt on the Articles of Confederation above, the key word to underline is *Explain*. You will determine and make clear which documents support the idea that the Articles of Confederation led to either an effective government or a weak government. As you read, focus on the arguments you will use in answering the question.

DOCUMENT A

Source: **The Articles of Confederation**

Article 2. Each state retains its sovereignty, freedom, and independence, and every power, jurisdiction, and right, which is not by this confederation expressly delegated to the United States, in Congress assembled.

Article 3. The said states hereby severally enter into a firm league of friendship with each other for their common defense, the security of their liberties, and their mutual and general welfare.

Article 9. The United States in Congress assembled shall never engage in a war, nor grant letters of marque and reprisal in time of peace, nor enter into any treaties or alliances, nor coin money, nor regulate the value thereof,...nor borrow money on the credit of the United States, nor appropriate money,...nor appoint a commander in chief of the army or navy unless nine states assent to the same.

This document relates to the theme that the Articles created a loose confederation of states (Article 1 and 3). Article 9 shows that Congress could not tax or borrow money without the consent of the states. You would use this document to support the idea that the Articles of Confederation resulted in an ineffective government.

DOCUMENT B

Source: **The Northwest Ordinance of 1785**

...the territory ceded by individual states to the United States, which has been purchased from the Indian inhabitants, shall be disposed of in the following manner:

...The plats (maps) of the townships, respectively, shall be marked by subdivisions into lots of one mile square, or 640 acres...

There shall be reserved for the United States out of every township... four lots...there shall be reserved the lot No. 16 of every township for the maintenance of public schools within the said township...

This document shows that Congress, under the Articles of Confederation, set a pattern for the systematic development of the western lands, which was a problem dividing the states from 1783 to 1787. You could use this document to support the idea that the Articles of Confederation was an effective government. Keep in mind that you were asked to evaluate, which means you must assess how each document addressed the theme of the question.

Strategy 3: Analyze Each Document Carefully

Analyzing each document carefully will help you understand the meaning of the documents and sources. The source provides clues for the idea or position of the document. In analyzing documents it is important to know who the author is, such as a farmer, merchant, lawyer, or political leader. You should also take note of the date and origin of the document.

DOCUMENT C

Source: **Alexander Hamilton, 1787**

We may...be said to have reached almost the last stage of national humiliation. There is scarcely any thing that can wound the pride or degrade the character of an independent nation which we do not experience... Do we owe debts to foreigners and to our own citizens...? These remain without any proper or satisfactory provision for their discharge. Have we valuable territories and power which, by express stipulations, ought long since to have been surrendered? These are still retained...Are we in a condition to resent or to repel the aggression? We have neither troops, nor treasury, nor government.

In analyzing the above document, focus on the fact that Hamilton was a strong supporter of the Constitution of 1789 and thus thought the Articles needed to be completely changed with a strong central government. You can also tell from the date that Hamilton made this statement during the time when the decision was made to create a new constitution.

DOCUMENT D

Source: **Patrick Henry, 1789**

...You are not to inquire how your trade may be increased, nor how you are to become a great and powerful people, but how your liberties can be secured; for liberty ought to be the direct end of your government...

The Confederation...carried us through a long and dangerous war, it rendered us victorious in that bloody conflict with a powerful nation; it has secured us a territory greater than any European monarch possesses: and shall a government which has been thus strong and vigorous, be accused of imbecility and want of energy?

Knowing that Patrick Henry was a strong supporter of states' rights and a fierce advocate of personal liberties can help you in evaluating this document. The document also indicates that Henry opposed the Constitution of 1789 and believed in a loose, not a strong, central government.

Strategy 4: Categorize Each DBQ Document

Charting key ideas can be helpful as you plan your essay. If documents present opposing sides of an issue, you can list them in separate charts. You can refer to the chart of the documents to support your position.

The chart below uses Documents A, B, C, and D to show this strategy.

WEAK GOVERNMENT	EFFECTIVE GOVERNMENT
Doc. A – Provisions of Articles	Doc. B – Northwest Ordinance
Summarizes the key weaknesses re: taxation, printing money, and a loose central government	Systematic development of western land
Doc. C – Ideas of Alexander Hamilton	Doc. D – Patrick Henry
Lack of respect for government	Positive accomplishments of the Confederation

Applying this approach to the eight or more documents in the actual test will give you a quick checklist of documents that can guide you as you begin to write your essay.

Strategy 5: Write a Thesis Statement

The thesis statement provides the foundation for your response to the document-based question. It relates directly to the prompt and provides a focus for your essay. Once you have established the thesis, you can refer to your chart of the individual documents to prove your thesis.

Remember that you are to analyze and synthesize the information in the document. Do not merely summarize the documents to support your thesis. Follow these steps as you write:

1. Establish the thesis.

2. Write an introductory paragraph leading up the thesis.

3. Analyze the documents and weave their ideas into the essay.

4. Write a conclusion supporting your thesis.

Let's try this approach in our abbreviated DBQ on the Articles of Confederation. We will use 2 out of 4 documents to support our thesis statement that the Articles of Confederation was an effective national government.

The Articles of Confederation, the first Constitution of the United States, has been a source of controversy. The traditional view coined by the historian John Fiske was that the government of the United States and the Articles of Confederation was a "critical period" because the central government was too weak and unable to deal with the disputes among the states over control of the western lands. The central government was also held in disdain by foreign powers. Fiske asserted that these conditions threatened the very existence of the newly formed United States. However, it would be more accurate to argue that the Articles of Confederation formed an effective government that sought to put into practice the ideas of the Declaration of Independence. The passage of the Northwest Ordinance provided a model on how to address the problems with the western lands.

Patrick Henry, the revolutionary leader and former governor of Virginia, believed that the Articles of Confederation were strong enough to successfully guide the thirteen colonies during their struggle for independence against Great Britain (Doc. D4). Henry, who would later oppose the Constitution of the United States in 1789, which created a strong central government, claimed that the states could best be governed without the intervention of a strong central government. Henry asserted that the purpose of government was not solely an economic function. He believed that the direct purpose of government was to protect the liberty of its people (Doc. D4). He also pointed out that the new government controlled more territory than any European government (Doc. D4). The historian Merrill Jensen noted that leaders who supported the Articles of Confederation believed that the greatest gain of the American Revolution was the independence of the states and the creation of a central government that was subservient to the state governments.

The Treaty of Paris (1784), which formally ended the Revolutionary War, turned over the Northwest to the United

States, which was the area west of Pennsylvania, north of the Ohio River, east of the Mississippi River, and south of the Great Lakes. The problem was that numerous states claimed these lands. When these states were colonies they were given charters from the king to control all the lands between the Atlantic and Pacific Ocean. Furthermore, Native American tribes did not agree that these lands belonged to the United States. It is also important to recall that the Articles of Confederation did not allow Congress to tax its citizens. Thus, the government hoped to sell the land in the Ohio Valley to raise money. After extensive negotiations the Government adopted the Northwest Ordinance of 1785, which provided a systematic development of western lands. The land ordinance provided that each township be divided into six-mile squares each of which was to be split into thirty-six sections of one square mile or 640 acres (Doc. B). One section had to be put aside for public education (Doc. B). The government would auction off the land to the highest bidder and the money would be used to pay off the national debt.

The Northwest Ordinance of 1785 was significant because it laid the foundation of land policy in the United States until the passage of the Homestead Act of 1862 and also established the mechanism for the funding of public education. Later, the government would pass the Northwest Ordinance of 1787 which would outline how the western territories could apply for statehood and that they would be accepted on the same basis as the original thirteen colonies and all citizens in these territories would have the same rights as the citizens of the states. This achievement was even more noteworthy because it guaranteed that as the United States expanded westward these territories would not become part of an empire but would be guaranteed equality with the original thirteen colonies.

The Articles of Confederation proved to be a landmark in government. It is important to remember that important revolutionaries such as Benjamin Franklin, John Dickerson, and John Sherman initially signed the Articles of Confederation. Thomas Jefferson hailed the new structure as the best that ever existed. It kept the states together and provided the leadership that enabled the United States to effectively conduct the Revolutionary War against Great Britain. The Confederation Congress clearly outlined the general powers of the central government, such as making treaties and establishing the postal service, and effectively addressed the thorny problem of western lands. The Articles of Confederation allowed the Americans to enjoy the fruits of their freedom within the structure of government that built consensus within the state governments, not centralization by Congress.

This essay might earn an 8 or a 9. Here's why:

- The thesis statement is clearly stated in the introduction, and the conclusion reinforces it.

- Each document/viewpoint is clearly identified.

- Relevant outside information, such as John Fiske's theories and Merrill Jensen's viewpoint of Jefferson, are woven into the essay.

- Strong arguments are used to support the idea that the Articles of Confederation was a strong government.

The essay will be judged on the strength and organization of your arguments rather than on factual information. Remember the essay may contain a minor error—for example, the Treaty of Paris was signed in 1783, not 1784. Keep in mind the strategies that we have outlined for the DBQ section and you will be successful.

Essay Question Strategies

The final—and the longest—section of the AP U.S. History Exam is the essay section. You will have seventy minutes to complete the two essays. It is suggested that you allow five minutes of planning and thirty minutes of writing time for each essay, but how you allocate your seventy minutes is ultimately up to you. However, it makes sense to adhere reasonably closely to these guidelines, to ensure that you do not run out of time to write the second essay question.

Here are some basic strategies for tackling the two essays.

Strategy 1: Analyze Carefully and Choose Wisely

For the essay section, you have the freedom to choose one of two questions, and to respond to the questions in the order that best suits you. Here's how to take advantage of that freedom:

- Choose the options that you know the most specific information about. There may be one of the two choices from each part that you discussed recently in class or reviewed specifically in your preparation.

- Watch out for questions that are very general. You might have a lot of general information about a wide-ranging topic, but choosing a narrower topic on which you have more detailed and specific knowledge is probably a better bet.

• Write the essays in the order that feels most comfortable. In most cases, this means answering the question that you are most familiar with first. See if you can answer this question a few minutes early to give you more time with the other question.

• If a question confuses you, rewrite it in your own words. This will help you get to the heart of the question and formulate a thesis.

• As with the document-based question, underline key words such as *assess*, *explain*, *evaluate*, *compare*, *contrast*, *support*, or *refute*. Be sure to use these words when you craft your argument.

Strategy 2: Brainstorm and Outline

As you gather your thoughts about the essay prompt, begin by jotting down any important ideas that come to mind. This "laundry list" might look similar to the one created for the DBQ prompt on page 57. Once you've gotten down several big ideas, create a thesis statement that responds directly to the prompt and is supported by your main ideas. Then, using your ideas and your thesis statement, choose the ideas that support your thesis and organize them into an outline. Take the following essay prompt:

Compare and contrast Alexander Hamilton's and Thomas Jefferson's visions of the United States in 1789.

Based on your brainstorming, your thesis might be:

Alexander Hamilton and Thomas Jefferson had radically different views of America.

Here's an outline you could make to support this thesis:

HAMILTON	JEFFERSON
Encouraged development of industry	Encouraged development of agriculture
Supported high tariffs on foreign goods	Promoted free trade

HAMILTON	JEFFERSON
Loose interpretation of Constitution	Strict interpretation of Constitution
Strong national government	Strong states' rights
Ideas most popular in Northeast	Ideas most popular in the South and among western farmers
Supported alliance with Great Britain	Supported alliance with France

Strategy 3: Use the Outline to Craft Your Essay

Now that you have your outline, your essay should be easier to write. All the information in your outline should now support your thesis. As you write, continually refer back to your outline as a blueprint for your essay. Your essay should include the following:

- A brief introductory paragraph that states your thesis

- Specific facts and details that support your thesis

- Analysis that explains how your information relates to the thesis

- A conclusion that summarizes your argument

Using the outline above, we can contrast Alexander Hamilton's and Thomas Jefferson's views of America regarding industry v. agriculture, the role of government, and other ideas. We can also check off each part of the outline fact to correspond to the views of each leader.

Now using all our essay strategies, let's work on three essays, Excellent (8-9), Good (5-7), and Fair (2-4), to help us understand the grading process.

8–9: Excellent

Alexander Hamilton and Thomas Jefferson were two of the most important Founding Fathers of the United States. Both were members of President George Washington's Cabinet. Hamilton served as the first Secretary of the Treasury and Jefferson was the first

Secretary of State. Each of them held radically different views on the economy, the role of government, and the foreign policy of the newly formed government. The conflict that took place between the two men would have a profound impact on U.S. History.

Hamilton admired the British economic system and wanted to turn the United States, which was an agrarian society in the eighteenth century, into a manufacturing society like Great Britain. He believed that a strong central government was necessary to provide the order that business and industry needed to prosper. He supported a loose interpretation of the Constitution in order to achieve this goal. Hamilton argued that under the loose interpretation or the elastic clause of the Constitution the government had many powers not specifically mentioned in the Constitution that allowed the government to pass all laws which "shall be deemed necessary and proper." As a loose constructionist, Hamilton generally believed that the Constitution permitted everything it did not expressly forbid.

Jefferson had a radically different view. He believed that the nation's strength lay in its agricultural roots. He proposed an America that would remain largely agricultural with industry serving as "the handmaiden of agriculture." He was opposed to a strong central government and supported a decentralized agricultural republic with most powers reserved to the states. Jefferson supported a strict interpretation of the Constitution by which he meant the federal government only had the powers specifically enumerated in the Constitution.

As Secretary of the Treasury, Hamilton sought to turn the United States into a manufacturing power. In his Report on Public Credit, Hamilton proposed that the United States should honor the debts it incurred under the government of the Articles of Confederation. He argued that the United States should pay off a sum close to $51 million as soon as possible. He also wanted the central government to assume the war debts of the state. To raise money to pay off the debt, Hamilton suggested an excise tax on liquor. He also created a privately funded national bank which would safely store government funds and provide loans to developing industries. Hamilton realized that these steps would tie wealthy American interests to the stability of the federal government. He also asked Congress to issue protective tariffs on goods and provide subsidies to encourage the formation of new business.

Jefferson opposed these plans on practical and philosophical terms. He feared that the states would lose power to the extent that the central government would gain. As a strict interpreter or strict constructionist, Jefferson believed that the Constitution did not specifically give the federal government the power to charter a national bank. This view was opposed to Hamilton's which argued that since the central government had the power to print money it was implied that it had the power to start a national bank.

Jefferson also believed that the formation of the National Bank would benefit only the wealthy or commercial elite at the expense of the farmer. He argued against the excise tax because it unfairly punished his southern and western farmers who supported Jefferson's vision of America. Jefferson and his southern supporters like James Madison opposed having the central government assume the state debts at face value because most of it had been incurred by the northern states. However, in return for Jefferson's support on this aspect of his plan, Hamilton agreed to Jefferson's idea to establish the nation's capital in the South along the Potomac River. After considerable squabbling and with the support of President Washington, Congress adopted Hamilton's financial program.

Foreign policy in the 1790s also led to a difference between Hamilton and Jefferson. The United States was tied to France by the Franco Alliance of 1778. Jefferson praised the democratic ideal of the French Revolution and wanted to support the French in its war against Great Britain. Hamilton condemned the French Revolution and supported an alliance that favored England in its war against France. President Washington supported Hamilton's financial plan and issued a Proclamation of Neutrality, where he stated that the United States would stay neutral throughout France's war with Great Britain.

Jefferson and Hamilton had opposing visions for the United States. Jefferson believed in a self-sufficient agricultural nation consisting of small farmers and thought that the cities were dens of corruption and inequality and would destroy the fabric of the American republic. Hamilton wanted a diversified and industrial economy and admired the large cities of Europe, especially London. These philosophical differences between them would have a lasting impact on American politics. Eventually, Jefferson would resign from Washington's Cabinet and two distinct political parties would emerge from this dispute. By 1796 two major political parties were taking shape: the Hamiltonian Federalist Party and the Jeffersonian Democratic-Republicans.

This essay is excellent and scores between 8 and 9 because

- The thesis is clearly stated and effectively outlines the opposing views of Hamilton and Jefferson

- All aspects of the topic are covered in depth, especially Hamilton's financial plan

- Different viewpoints are analyzed and evaluated, such as philosophical and practical reasons why Hamilton and Jefferson opposed each other

- The conclusion summarizes the key points and shows the impact of the feud on the history of the United States—the rise of political parties

5–7: Good

Both Thomas Jefferson and Alexander Hamilton played pivotal roles in the development of the United States, although their perspectives were completely different. Their differences were most pronounced in the areas of the role of the government and how banking should be handled. Although they had differences, they were still key figures in helping America develop into the nation it is today.

Alexander Hamilton had a strong appreciation for the British system of government, which was reflected in his views towards the way he thought government should help society move forward. Above all, Hamilton saw great opportunity for the United States to develop as an industrial and business power. In order for industry to succeed, it was necessary to have a strong, centralized system of government that was able to pass whatever laws it needed to help society move forward. He believed this was possible due to the Constitution's "elastic clause," which gave the government the power to pass laws that the framers had not yet thought of.

Thomas Jefferson vehemently disagreed with Hamilton's view on the centralization of power in the government. First and foremost, Jefferson differed from Hamilton in wanting to move towards a more industry-based society. He truly believed that the farmers that had made the United States an agricultural power were the backbone of society, and that industry would stifle the ability of agriculture to grow. Industry should grow only in as much as it needed to support agriculture. In addition, Jefferson believed the Constitution was a fixed entity, and that the federal government could only do the things that were explicitly listed in the Constitution. Anything not listed in the Constitution was left to the discretion of the states.

Another large difference was in economic policy. Hamilton, in keeping with his desire to make the United States an industrial power, felt that the government should take an active role in establishing the country's economic stability. This meant settling debts, and establishing a national bank that was privately funded by wealthy Americans. This meant that wealthy Americans needed the government to succeed, and would be motivated to help industry expand and grow. Jefferson had major policy issues with this. First of all, in keeping with his views on the Constitution, he believed that the Constitution did not explicitly say that a government could do things like start a bank. Thus, he opposed the national bank. Second of all, Jefferson didn't like that a national bank was tied to wealthy Americans—this would create class issues in society.

Jefferson and Hamilton also disagreed on many aspects of foreign policy. Hamilton admired larger cities that had built up a strong industry; Jefferson did not and more favored France because of its revolutionary ideals and its push to give power to the people. This created friction between the two men when war broke out in Europe. Foreign policy was a large source of disagreement for the two men.

Overall, both Jefferson and Hamilton accomplished great things for the newly formed United States, although they disagreed on almost everything. However, they were able to compromise and because of that, their impacts were felt in political parties for many years to come, and are still felt today.

This essay scores between 5 and 7 for the following reasons:

- The thesis statement is there, but not necessarily that clear.

- It does not fully analyze the difference in viewpoints between Jefferson and Hamilton.

- There are small factual errors throughout.

- The conclusion does not go into enough depth/detail to support the essay as a whole.

- The economic differences are not explored in enough depth.

- The foreign policy stances are not fully explored and analyzed.

2–4: Fair

Alexander Hamilton and Thomas Jefferson had very different views about almost everything. Hamilton and Jefferson got to know each other when they worked under the first President, George Washington. They had different roles for President Adams. Hamilton was the Secretary of the Treasury, while Jefferson was Secretary of State. These jobs were very different, and caused them to have different views on the way government should work. They eventually were responsible for creating two political parties that still have influence in the United States today in many ways.

Hamilton's view was that the United States needed to be more like Great Britain in terms of being more industrial and more reliant on advances in business, and Thomas Jefferson disagreed. He thought the United States was unique in its own way because of farming and not industry, and that Hamilton was wrong. Hamilton wanted the United States to do things like have a national bank, where rich people paid into it and would then want it to do well. This meant that the wealthier members of society would be more likely to want the economy to do well. Jefferson had major problems with this and didn't think it was fair for the rich to have so much control. He thought it was a dangerous system to set up.

They also disagreed about the Constitution. Since Hamilton believed in a strong central government, he believed the Constitution said that the government could do whatever it wanted, including forming a bank, paying off debts, and supporting various taxes on things like cigarettes and alcohol.

Jefferson obviously disagreed, since they disagreed on almost every point. Jefferson believed that the government could only do exactly what was written in the Constitution, nothing more than that. Because of this, he wanted States to have more of the power, to prevent the government from taking over too many parts of life.

In foreign policy, they also agreed. One thing that happened while they were in power was that England and France got into a war, and they disagreed about who to support and tried to get President Washington to take their side. In the end, he didn't take either of their sides, so that was another big disagreement.

As you can see, Hamilton and Jefferson were both really different but also really important. Their impact on history was great.

This essay is fair and scores between 2 and 4 for the following reasons:

- The thesis is confusing and does not fully answer the questions.

- There are major factual errors throughout (the president's name is wrong; the sequence of events is wrong).

- The conclusion is superficial and does not make a clear point.

- The issues are not explored in depth in any way—there is no analysis of their differences in domestic, foreign, or economic policy.

An essay that scores a 0 or 1 either lacks a clear thesis or the thesis is confused. It is not well organized and exhibits weak writing. It does not indicate an understanding of the complexity of the question or topic, and it fails to support a thesis with sufficient historical information and/or analysis. It may contain significant errors.

Review Chapter 1: Colonial America

T he American colonies were established for a variety or reasons, primarily economic and religious.

Northern or New England Colonies
Established primarily for **religious freedom.**

1620: The Pilgrims, who wanted to establish their own church in America, established the Plymouth Colony.

1629: John Winthrop led one thousand Puritans and set up the Massachusetts Bay Colony. Puritans did not want to separate from the Church of England but wanted to purify or cleanse it from any trace of Catholicism. Winthrop wanted to build a "city upon a hill" that would be a model of goodness to the world. His theocratic government would be guided by the religious tenets of Calvinism.

1630s: Religious dissent, which was not tolerated in Massachusetts Bay Colony, led to the founding of other colonies in the region. Roger Williams, Thomas Hooker, and Anne Hutchinson challenged the Puritans' authority in Massachusetts based on the separation of church and state. They established colonies in Rhode Island, and Connecticut.

THE THIRTEEN COLONIES AND THE YEARS FOUNDED

New Hampshire–1623

Massachusetts–1623

NORTHERN COLONIES

New York–1613

Rhode Island–1636

Connecticut–1635
New Jersey–1664

MIDDLE COLONIES

Pennsylvania–1681

Delaware–1638

Maryland–1634

SOUTHERN COLONIES

Virginia–1607

North Carolina–1653

ATLANTIC OCEAN

South Carolina–1670

Georgia–1733

◼ Northern Colonies
☐ Middle Colonies
◼ Southern Colonies

Roger Williams's Rhode Island was the only New England colony to practice religious tolerance.

Economy: Small farming, fishing, and shipbuilding.

Middle Colonies

Established for **economic and religious reasons**. Maryland was set up to provide religious freedom for Catholics, and Pennsylvania was a haven for the Quakers. New York, New Jersey, and Delaware were for trade and profit. Small and medium-sized farms dominated the region.

Economy: Trading contributed to the growth of large cities like New York and Philadelphia.

Southern Colonies

Set up for **economic reasons,** except for Georgia, which was a set up as a buffer state to protect the southern colonies from the threat of invasion from Spanish Florida. A joint stock company for trade and profit founded Virginia, the first permanent colony. Most of the colonies depended on a cash crop for survival; Virginia depended on tobacco, and the Carolinas depended on rice.

Indentured servants usually agreed to work for a period from four to seven years in return for passage to the New World. They were essential to the labor force.

Economy: Large scale or plantation system

Colonial Government

The settlers who came to America brought the "rights of Englishmen," which included the tradition of representative government. In 1619, the settlers of Virginia founded the House of Burgesses, the first representative government in America. In 1620, male Pilgrims aboard the Mayflower signed the Mayflower Compact, agreeing to establish the powers of government. The compact resulted in many New England town meetings to discuss and address local problems.

By the middle of the eighteenth century, the colonies had governments that included a governor as chief executive and an assembly with the power to reject or approve new taxes. However, colonial democracy was limited. The right to vote was usually limited to men who owned property. Participation was generally limited to white male Protestant property owners. Still, colonial society was laying the basis for political democracy in a world still dominated by absolute monarchs.

Colonial Economy

Mercantilism was an economic theory that influenced all the colonies, since its premise was that they existed for the benefit of the mother country. Southern colonies provided crops such as rice and tobacco, and the northern colonies provided raw materials such as lumber. The colonies had to buy European goods from England, and some items had to be transported in English ships. To enforce this system, England passed a series of Navigation Acts beginning in 1650.

Results

- Shipbuilding industry grew in New England.

- Military provided protection from potential attacks by French and Spanish forces.

- Colonial manufacturing was limited.

Throughout the colonial period, the British followed a policy of "salutary neglect." During the period from about 1650 to the end of the French and Indian War in 1763, America was left alone to develop its own economy. The Navigation Laws were not enforced, and the British interfered very little in the political affairs of the colonies.

Colonial Society

Between 1700 and 1775, the American population grew about tenfold. In 1700, the colonies contained less than three hundred thousand people, of which less than thirty thousand were African Americans. By 1775, there were about 2.5 million people in the colonies, of which about five hundred thousand were African Americans. The colonies' population doubled every twenty-five years. Although colonists were mostly from England and Wales, it was the most diverse in the world and was becoming an important melting pot. The pie graph below demonstrates the mixture of the non-Native American nationalities in the thirteen colonies from 1700–1763:

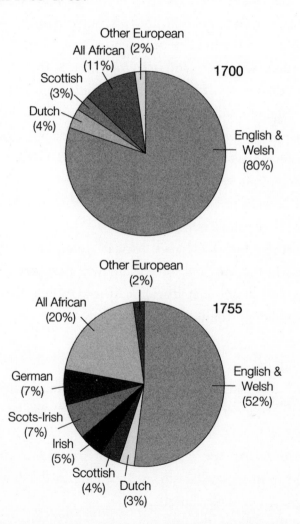

The heavy influx of Irish, Germans, and Africans resulted in a decline of the English and Welsh, from over 80 percent to a slight majority of the population in 1775.

As these groups mingled, they began to lay the foundation for a multicultural society. Hector St. John Crevecoeur, a French settler, saw in this society a "new man," the American.

African Americans

Slavery in British North America was introduced in 1619 at Jamestown. Slaves were the largest single group of non-English immigrants who did not come of their own free will. Initially, some Africans were granted freedom because they had come as indentured servants. As the need for workers to cultivate tobacco and rice crops grew in the late-seventeenth century, and the number of indentured servants from England declined because economic conditions there were improving, the number of Africans slaves imported into the colonies increased. Georgia, which had originally banned slavery, reversed itself in the mid-1700s as the demand for rice grew. About 90 percent of the slaves lived in southern colonies, in a state of permanent bondage. In some states, such as South Carolina and Georgia, they were a majority.

In the northern British colonies, African Americans worked as laborers on large wheat farms, and some even owned property. However, all the colonies, laws discriminated against African Americans and restricted their rights and opportunities.

Role of Religion

Although religion had been a dominant force in the settling of some of the colonies, its power and role in the colonies began to wane by the early 1700s.

The Great Awakening was an attempt by leading churchmen to rekindle the spirit of Puritanism by appealing to the emotions of the masses. It started in Massachusetts.

Jonathan Edwards sparked the Great Awakening. His famous sermon "Sinners in the Hands of an Angry God" described the damnation of those who were not awakened to "true religion." He also argued that people could be saved by expressing deep penitence.

George Whitefield arrived from England and, unlike Edwards, he traveled throughout the colonies. He was a former actor with an electrifying style of preaching. Whitefield's sermons attracted crowds of more than six thousand people.

Impact: The Great Awakening helped to democratize religion. It also had an indirect political effect, because it encouraged people to look at authority differently. People began to take an active role in their religion, rather than following their leaders unquestioningly. Soon, more people believed they could make their own political decisions too. By the middle of the eighteenth century, the American colonies were developing their own distinctive culture and way of life. Some even began to see a future defined by self-governance and independence.

Review

1-1) Between 1720 and 1755 which group in colonial American witnessed the largest growth in population?

A) Africans

B) Dutch and English

C) Scots and Germans

D) Irish and Germans

E) Dutch and English/Welsh

1-2) Two colonies that practiced religious tolerance in colonial America are

A) Pennsylvania and New York

B) Rhode Island and Virginia

C) Connecticut and Georgia

D) Maryland and New Jersey

E) Rhode Island and Pennsylvania

1-3)   The First Great Awakening was designed to

A) rekindle the spirit of Puritanism

B) unite the colonists against strict enforcement of the Navigation Acts

C) counter Catholic attacks against the Massachusetts Bay Colony in Maryland

D) educate the colonists on plans for self-government

E) work with the Quakers in Pennsylvania to end slavery in the colonies

1-4)   New England town meetings and the House of Burgesses in colonial America were

A) efforts to create unity among the colonists

B) colonial meetings to protest the British policy of taxation

C) steps in the development of democracy in the colonies

D) agreements among New England colonies and Virginia to discuss the Native Americans on the frontier

E) a British attempt to end its policy of salutary neglect

Review Chapter 2:
The Revolutionary Era, 1763–1789

The French and Indian War, or Seven Years' War, ended in 1763 and established England as the dominant power on the North American continent. Before the war, the British called for the colonies to meet in Albany, New York, to coordinate their war effort against threats from the French and Native Americans on the frontier. The Albany Plan developed by Benjamin Franklin, of Pennsylvania, and leaders of seven other colonies was an attempt to form a defensive union for the coming war with France. The Albany Plan never took effect because colonial assemblies and the British Crown did not support it.

1763—A Momentous Year

In 1763, Britain ended the policy of **salutary neglect**, which had allowed the colonists to govern themselves without interference. The new British government led by George Greenville decided to exert greater control and tax the colonies. This revenue would offset the administrative costs of overseeing the colonies and help repay the debt the British government had incurred in fighting the French and Indian War.

British Policy

- The Proclamation of 1763 prohibited colonists from settling west of the Appalachian Mountains to prevent further bloodshed between Native Americans and settlers, which infuriated the colonists.

- New regulations enacted between 1763 and 1776.

Below is a chart of the British laws and actions.

BRITISH LAWS/ ACTIONS	COLONIAL RESPONSE	RESULTS
Sugar Tax (1764) Tax on molasses, textiles, wine, sugar, coffee, and other imports	Hated by colonists Solely to produce revenue	Strict enforcement of laws Greater regulation of American shipping to control smuggling
Stamp Act (1765) Tax on printed materials such as newspapers, legal documents, deeds and playing cards	Sons of Liberty, led by Samuel Adams, protest tax Tax collectors are tarred and feathered Stamp Act Congress meets in NY in 1765; 9 colonies attend; delegates assert that only colonial authorities can impose taxes on them	British repeal Stamp Act Declaratory act states that Parliament has authority to set laws for colonies
Townshend Act (1767) Tax on lead, glass, and paper	Renewed boycotts, riots	British troops sent to colonies Boston Massacre: 5 civilians killed by troops Tax repealed except for tax on tea

BRITISH LAWS/ ACTIONS	COLONIAL RESPONSE	RESULTS
Tea Act (1773) Gave British East India Company monopoly on all tea imports to America	Colonists feared that British sought to control all colonial trade Boston Tea Party: Sons of Liberty destroy British tea	British decide to punish the colonists
Coercive or Intolerable Acts (1774) Boston Harbor closed Colonial Charter of Massachusetts annulled Quartering Act: all Bostonians ordered to house and feed British soldiers	First Continental Congress meets in Philadelphia to protest British action Declaration of Rights and Grievances declares that Parliament had no authority over internal matters	King George III orders the arrest of colonial leaders

Fighting Erupts

The escalating conflict between the colonists and the British government resulted in military conflict and rebellion. General Thomas Gage, the military governor of Massachusetts, was ordered by the British to confiscate weapons that rebels had been collecting in Concord and arrest their leaders, Samuel Adams and John Hancock. The Minutemen intercepted the British, and fighting erupted. In the Battles of Lexington and Concord, forty-nine colonial fighters and seventy-three British troops were killed. In July 1775, delegates from the colonies made one last attempt at peace, signing a document called the "Olive Branch Petition" in which they pledged loyalty to the king and asked him to recall the troops in Boston. The king dismissed the petition and declared the colonies in a state of rebellion.

The Declaration of Independence

Thomas Jefferson, who worked with a committee of five men that included Benjamin Franklin and John Adams, was selected to write an official Declaration of Independence. The main ideas were:

- All men are created equal and endowed by their creator with unalienable rights, which include life, liberty, and the pursuit of happiness. Governments are formed to protect these rights.

- Government is a social contract, and when a government violates the rights contained in the contract, the people have the right to revolt or abolish the government. Jefferson was greatly influenced by ideas of the English Enlightenment writer John Locke, whose *Two Treatises of Government*, written in 1689, justified the Glorious Revolution in England.

- Outlined abuses by King George III violating the rights of colonists, such as taxation without their consent.

- Colonists were justified in establishing a new nation in order to preserve the rights that had been violated under the social contract.

Fighting the War

Loyalists (Tories): Colonists who continued to pledge allegiance to the king represented less than 20 percent of the population. Called Tories, many of them were lawyers, royal officials, and Anglican clergymen.

African Americans: Though Washington initially rejected the use of African Americans in the army, eventually about five thousand served in the Patriot cause. Most of them were freemen from the North. The British promise of freedom for slaves convinced Washington to change his mind. African Americans fought on both sides during the war.

Women: Women served as nurses, spied on British troops, and supported the boycott of British goods. They were very effective in running the household while men fought the war. Despite the pleas of Abigail

Adams to her husband to remember the women, the Founding Fathers did not consider equal rights for them.

Native Americans: Most supported the British because they were afraid of future colonist expansion. The British had promised to limit colonial settlement in the west.

Turning Points

The British had a large army and a powerful navy, but George Washington, the American commander, realized that he did not have to defeat them in every battle—he only had to outlast them until they tired of fighting.

Battle of Saratoga (October 1777): This decisive defeat of the British by American troops at Saratoga, New York, convinced the French to give military and economic aid to the colonists. This alliance provided needed relief and help to Washington's army, which was suffering from lack of food and clothing.

Battle of Yorktown (1781): Aided by French naval and military forces, Washington forced General Charles Cornwallis to surrender at Yorktown, Virginia, in this last major battle of the war.

Treaty of Paris (1783): John Adams, Benjamin Franklin, and John Jay negotiated the peace to end the war. These were the major provisions:

- Britain recognized the independence of the United States.

- The Mississippi River was established as the western border.

- The American government had to compensate the Loyalists for property confiscated during the war.

The New Government, 1781–1789

The Articles of Confederation

The Second Continental Congress drafted the Articles of Confederation in 1776 as the first constitution for the new nation, and it was ratified in 1781. It vested most powers with the states and its only governmental body was the Confederation Congress. Following are some of the strengths and weaknesses of the Articles.

Weaknesses

- no national court system

- no authority in Congress to regulate interstate or foreign commerce, levy taxes, or raise an army

- no chief executive, with authority given to a committee of thirteen, with one representative from each of the thirteen states

- unanimity of the thirteen states for an amendment to be ratified

- no provision for uniform currency

Strengths

- brought the Revolutionary War to a successful end.

- passed the Northwest Ordinances of 1785–1787, which regulated the sale of western land and created a plan for governing western lands between the Appalachian Mountains and the Mississippi River. The ordinance stipulated that slavery would be prohibited in the new territories added to the United States.

Problems for the New Government

Economic Distress Since the national government could not tax, it began printing large amounts of paper money to pay off war debts. These "Continentals" became worthless because of inflation. States refused to increase taxes to pay for the national currency, and also printed their own money, thus adding to the inflation.

Shays' Rebellion (1786) Faced with continued economic depression in western Massachusetts, farmers began violent protests against state government. Revolutionary hero Daniel Shays led the most alarming protest. Farmers attacked the local courthouse to prevent judges from foreclosing on farms. State militia put down the rebellion, but it demonstrated the need for a stronger state and national government to maintain law and order.

The Constitutional Convention (1787) Every state but Rhode Island sent delegates to Philadelphia in the summer of 1787 to amend the Articles. Instead, the delegates decided to create a new government. Most delegates believed that a strong central government was necessary to raise taxes, form an army, collect taxes, coin money, and regulate interstate commerce.

Delegates Fifty-five men met in the summer of 1787. They were college educated, a majority were lawyers, about half had fought against the British, and most of the southern delegates were slaveholders. The oldest member was Benjamin Franklin. Other delegates included George Washington, James Madison, and Alexander Hamilton.

Bundle of Compromise The delegates disagreed on three major issues: representation, slavery, and trade.

ISSUE	PROPOSAL	RESULT
Representation	**Virginia Plan** Proposed by James Madison Supported by large states Proportional representation Three branches of government **New Jersey Plan** Proposed by William Patterson Supported by small states Unicameral legislation Every state gets one vote	**Connecticut Plan or Great Compromise** Upper house (Senate)—states get equal representation Lower house—representation based on population
Slavery	**Southern States** Slaves count for representation but not taxation **Northern States** Slaves count for taxation but not representation	**3/5 Compromise** Each slave 3/5 of a person for state level of taxation and representation Congress to pass no laws ending slave trade for 20 years
Trade	**Northern States** Wanted central government to regulate interstate and foreign trade **Southern States** Feared export tax placed on agricultural products like tobacco and rice	**Commercial Compromise** Congress regulates interstate and foreign taxes on imports but not taxes on exports

On September 17, 1787, after 17 weeks of debate, the delegates signed the final a draft of the Constitution that was submitted to the states for ratification. Unlike the Articles of Confederation, only nine out of the thirteen states were needed to approve the Constitution for it to become law.

Struggle over Ratification

After the Constitution was submitted to the states for ratification, a heated debate was waged between the Federalists and the Anti-Federalists.

The **Federalists** were supporters of the Constitution. The Federalist Papers, written by James Madison, John Jay, and Alexander Hamilton, explained the need for a strong central government and stressed that civil liberties would be protected under the new government.

The **Anti-Federalists** were opponents of the Constitution, including revolutionary leaders Samuel Adams and Patrick Henry. They argued that the central government might become too strong, and they stressed the need to protect the rights of the states and individual liberties. The anti-Federalists resented the idea that the Constitution did not contain any mention of specific rights for the people.

By promising to add a Bill of Rights, drawn up by James Madison and officially added to the Constitution in 1791, the Federalists successfully convinced nine states to approve the Constitution by June of 1788. The remaining states of Virginia, New York, North Carolina, and Rhode Island realized that they needed to approve the Constitution in order for the new nation to survive. The United States was ready to launch its new ship of state under a new Constitution.

Review

2-1)   The best description of the Continentals is

A) the volunteer army that fought in the American Revolution

B) the representatives of states that attended the meetings of the Continental Congress

C) settlers who set up townships based on the Northwest Ordinance of 1785 and 1787

D) nearly worthless paper money printed by the Congress under the Articles of Confederation

E) promises that the Congress of the Articles of Confederation would repay its debts to the Continental soldiers

2-2)   Which was one of the results of the Albany Plan of 1754?

A) All thirteen colonies attended, marking the beginning of unity.

B) British and colonial forces united to fight the French in North America.

C) It served as a model for the more revolutionary congresses of the 1770s.

D) Colonists coordinated their efforts against the British efforts to enforce their policy of mercantilism.

E) Benjamin Franklin refused to support the meeting.

2-3)   The Olive Branch Petition

A) convinced Great Britain to repeal the Intolerable Acts except for the tax on tea

B) was an attempt by the British to remove troops from the American colonies as a result of the Quartering Act

C) was an agreement between Great Britain and the colonists to resist French efforts to expand from Canada into the northwest

D) was adopted by the Constitutional Convention in July 1775 to affirm American loyalty to Great Britain to prevent further conflicts

E) was accepted by King George III and Parliament in the hope of avoiding war with the colonists

2-4)   The Battle of Saratoga in the American Revolution is significant because it

A) showed the colonists that they could defeat the British Army

B) convinced the French to provide military support to the American cause

C) convinced many Loyalists to support the Patriots' cause

D) reinforced British determination to end the Revolutionary War as quickly as possible

E) was the last major battle between the Colonial Army and the British

Review Chapter 3:
The Early National Period

The Presidency of George Washington, 1789–1796

Although Washington did not seek the presidency, he was the unanimous choice of the Electoral College. As a revered Revolutionary leader, he had the national stature to lead the country through uncertain times ahead.

The two men who would dominate Washington's first administration were Secretary of State Thomas Jefferson and Secretary of the Treasury Alexander Hamilton. They had conflicting visions of how America should develop.

Economic Views

HAMILTON	JEFFERSON
Favored creation of a national bank to store federal funds and provide loans to businessmen	Opposed the creation of a national bank because he believed it was unconstitutional
Favored a protective tariff for manufacturers	Supported free trade
Believed government should assume state debts and proposed an excise tax to pay off the debt	Opposed the assumption of debts and the use of taxation to pay it off

HAMILTON	JEFFERSON
Supported a commercial society with a large industrial base	Preferred an agrarian society— believed it to be the backbone of America

Political and Social Views

HAMILTON	JEFFERSON
Believed the wealthy should run society. His supporters were mostly merchants bankers, manufacturers, or wealthy farmers.	Believed the masses could run the government. His supporters were mainly artisans, frontier settlers, or small farmers.
Supported a strong central government	Championed a weak central government in favor of strengthening state government
Believed in a loose interpretation of the Constitution, and that it permitted everything that it did not expressly forbid	Held to a strict interpretation of the Constitution, which argued that the federal government had only the powers specifically spelled out
Pro-British	Pro- French

The dispute between Hamilton and Jefferson led to the emergence of the two-party system—the Federalists, led by Hamilton and John Adams; and the Anti-Federalists, or Democratic-Republicans, led by Jefferson and Madison. Jefferson and Madison opposed Hamilton's financial plan, but Washington supported it, and most of Hamilton's plan was accepted. In return for Jefferson's support for the federal government's assumption of state debts, Hamilton agreed to locate the national capital in the South, along the Potomac River. The site would become known as Washington, D.C. The adoption of Hamilton's plan introduced financial stability and promoted economic growth.

In the Whiskey Rebellion of 1794, Pennsylvania farmers opposed Hamilton's excise tax on distilled alcohol, such as whiskey. The rumor that farmers were marching on to Philadelphia to protest the tax re-kindled memories of the government's failure to deal effectively with Shays' Rebellion. Washington was determined to demonstrate the new government's strength, and he raised an army of fifteen thousand men under the command of Alexander Hamilton, who put down the rebellion. Jefferson and western farmers condemned the episode as an excessive use of force against common people.

Foreign Affairs

The French Revolution of 1789 and the continent-wide war that soon engulfed Europe sharply divided Americans on the question of whether to support or give assistance to the French Republic, which was fighting England, Spain, and Austria.

Washington believed that the United States was too weak to get involved in Europe's war. Despite the public sentiment in favor of supporting their revolutionary brothers in France, Washington issued a "proclamation of neutrality" in 1793. This policy allowed American merchants to prosper, because they could trade with both sides. Jefferson resigned his post as secretary of state in protest.

Jay and Pinckney Treaties

In 1794, Washington sent Chief Justice John Jay to London to negotiate a settlement regarding the British search and seizure of American merchant ships and their troops stationed in the Ohio River Valley. The British agreed to withdraw from the frontier post but did not address ending the seizure of American seamen. The treaty was unpopular but narrowly passed after Washington defended it before the Senate. The Democratic-Republicans bitterly opposed the treaty, viewing it as another example of the United States drawing closer to Great Britain.

Unlike the Jay Treaty, the Pinckney Treaty was very popular. Spain, fearing that the United States was becoming too close to the British, granted access to ports along the Mississippi River. Farmers no longer paid taxes to Spain, and their goods got to market quicker. Both sides also agreed on a border between the United States and Spanish Florida.

Washington's Farewell Address (1796)

By 1796, Washington had become tired of the political bickering between Federalists and Democratic-Republicans, and he announced his retirement to his beloved Mount Vernon. In his farewell address, he advised the young nation:

- not to get involved in European affairs

- to avoid permanent alliances

- to avoid factionalism or political parties, which could destroy the country

Washington's advice on foreign policy influenced American politics into the twentieth century, but his hope of avoiding political parties went unheeded, and they became a vital part of the American political system.

The Presidency of John Adams

In 1796 the Democratic-Republican Thomas Jefferson opposed John Adams, Washington's vice president. Adams, who won by three electoral votes, became president. Jefferson, who received the second-highest electoral vote, became vice president, as the Constitution then required.

In 1804, the Twelfth Amendment required that candidates for president and vice president belong to the same political party.

The XYZ Affair

The Proclamation of Neutrality and the Jay Treaty angered the French, who expected the United States to support their revolution. In 1796, France broke off diplomatic relations with the United States and the French navy began seizing American merchant ships. Hoping to avoid war, Adams sent delegates to France to negotiate. French diplomats, known as X, Y, and Z, demanded bribes of about $250,000 before they would talk to the Americans. The American diplomats refused. When the demands were made public, they infuriated Americans, who now insisted on war with France. The popular slogan became "millions for defense but not one cent for tribute." Adams avoided war and in 1800 negotiated an agreement with Napoleon that cancelled the 1778 treaty between them. U.S. merchants promised not to seek compensation for their seized cargo.

Alien and Sedition Acts

Winning a majority in Congress in 1798, the Federalists enacted four laws whose chief purpose was to silence opposition from the Democratic-Republicans and prevent French revolutionaries from entering the United States. These acts empowered the government to deport or imprison aliens or foreigners who the government believed was a threat. It also allowed government to imprison or fine people who criticized the government.

Kentucky and Virginia Resolutions: State legislatures of Kentucky and Virginia passed resolutions protesting these laws because they violated the principles guaranteed by the First Amendment.

The Kentucky resolution, written by Thomas Jefferson, and the Virginia Resolution, written by James Madison, argued that the states had the right to declare any laws null and void. These resolutions set forth an argument that would be at the center of political controversy for more than half a century.

The Election of 1800

In 1800 John Adams ran for re-election. The Democratic-Republican candidate was Thomas Jefferson, and Aaron Burr was his running mate for vice president. Jefferson and Burr both received seventy-three electoral ballots. At the time, the Constitution gave the House of Representatives the power to decide the election in cases of a tie. Though Alexander Hamilton intensely disliked Jefferson, he urged his fellow Federalists to vote for him, because he believed that Burr was unfit to be president, and Jefferson was elected president. It marked the beginning of the Federalist Party's demise and initiated a long era of Democratic-Republic power.

Historians refer to Jefferson's election as the Revolution of 1800 because power passed peacefully from the Federalists to the Democratic-Republicans, who controlled the presidency for the next twenty-four years: Thomas Jefferson, 1801–1809; James Madison, 1809–1817; James Monroe, 1817–1825. All were from Virginia.

The Presidency of Thomas Jefferson

Determined to bring the United States back to its democratic roots, Jefferson walked to his own inauguration and wore an American-made suit to emphasize his rejection of European manufactured goods. In office, his policies were a combination of Federalist and Democratic-Republican ideals. In some ways he carried out the domestic and foreign program of his political opponents—for example, he supported the creation of a national bank and the federal government's assumption of state debts. On the other hand, he reduced the size of the army and navy and slashed the budget to show his belief in limiting the size of government.

Jefferson and the Supreme Court

Although the Federalists lost the election of 1800, they still controlled the federal judiciary. Shortly before Jefferson took office, the Federalist Congress passed the Judiciary Act of 1801, which enlarged the federal court system and allowed John Adams to make a number of last-minute appointments, called "midnight judges." These included Chief Justice John Marshall, who would serve from 1801 to 1835.

Jefferson, determined to repeal all Federalist legislation, instructed James Madison, his secretary of state, to refuse to honor the appointments that were still in process. William Marbury, one of the midnight appointee judges, sued for his commission. Marshall ruled that the basis for Marbury's suit—a statute of the Judiciary Act of 1789—was unconstitutional. Thus Marbury could not be given his appointment. Marshall's rule initiated the principle of judicial review—the power of the Supreme Court to rule on the constitutionality of laws—and made the judicial branch equal with the other branches of government.

Throughout his two terms, Jefferson had an uneasy relationship with the Supreme Court, which he believed was unduly expanding the role of the courts in American society.

The most important events of Jefferson's first term were the Louisiana Purchase and the Lewis and Clark expedition. The Louisiana Purchase came about when western farmers lost the right to use French ports to ship their goods. Jefferson sent ministers to negotiate with the French, with instructions to buy the port of New Orleans for $10 million. Napoleon, who needed money to fight his European wars, and who was confronting a slave rebellion in Haiti, offered to sell the entire Louisiana Territory for $15 million. The ministers accepted the offer. Jefferson, despite his doubts that he had the Constitutional authority to buy the land, saw a unique opportunity to expand the United States as the "empire of liberty." He submitted the agreement to the Senate, which quickly approved it. The purchase doubled the size of the nation and insured continued support among western farmers for the Democratic-Republican Party.

In 1804, Jefferson organized the Lewis and Clark expedition to explore the geography, people, and resources of this newly added territory. It lasted two years and involved forty people, and it opened up the possibility of further exploration and development of the western United States.

The biggest problem of Jefferson's second term was the impact of the Napoleonic Wars (1802–1815) on the nation's foreign policy. The United States was neutral, but the British and the French seized American ships looking for arms and supplies. The British further complicated matters by forcing captured American sailors and citizens to serve in the British Navy.

Hoping to avoid war, Jefferson persuaded Congress to pass the Embargo Act of 1807. It forbade American merchants ships from sailing to foreign ports. The effect on the American economy was disastrous.

Exports fell dramatically, and there were bitter protests, especially among the shipbuilders and merchants of New England. The embargo was lifted in 1809, but trade with England and France was still prohibited.

Madison and the War of 1812

Like Jefferson, his predecessor, James Madison was unable to prevent continued impressments of American sailors and the seizure of ships by the British. In June of 1812, Madison asked for a declaration of war, based on several factors:

- Britain refused to end the impressments of American sailors and to respect America's right of freedom of the seas.

- In the Ohio Valley, settlers believed that the British were inciting Native Americans to attack them. In 1812, Tecumseh of the Shawnee Tribe and his twin brother, a religious leader, sought to unite all tribes east of the Mississippi River against the Americans.

- In 1811, encouraged by settlers to take aggressive action against the Indians, General William Henry Harrison attacked Tecumseh's village at Tippecanoe. Harrison's victory ended any hope among the Indians of preventing the United States from settling their lands.

- Young Democratic-Republicans from the South and West, known as "war hawks," agitated for war, because they believed it would help the United States gain Canada, destroy the threat from Native Americans on the frontier, and establish the nation's honor in a "second war of independence" against Great Britain.

Madison's War

The United States was unprepared for the war, and it went badly. The army consisted of fewer than twelve thousand men and twenty ships. An invasion of Canada failed, and Madison was forced to flee Washington, D.C., in 1814, when the British sacked and burned the city.

The **Treaty of Ghent**, signed on Dec 24, 1814, halted the fighting and restored diplomatic relations between Britain and the United States, but it included nothing about the seizure of men and American ships.

In the **Battle of New Orleans**, General Andrew Jackson defeated the British in early January 1815, two weeks after the peace treaty had been signed. The battle made Jackson a national hero.

At the **Hartford Convention**, New England Federalists, who largely opposed the war, met for about three weeks in December 1814 and January 1815. They rejected the idea of secession but proposed that the Constitution be amended to require a two-thirds majority of both houses for a declaration of war; that the president serve only one term; and that candidates could not come from the same state as the previous president. The last item reflected their frustration with southern dominance of the presidency. No action was taken on this resolution, because news of Jackson's victory and the signing of the peace treaty ended arguments over the war. Still, the Federalists paid a price. They were labeled as traitors by many, and the Federalist Party ceased to be a major influence in American politics.

Another major consequence of the war was its role in intensifying nationalism. Jackson's victory at New Orleans convinced Americans that they could hold their own with the British. This newfound sense of pride was expressed in the poem *The Star Spangled Banner*, written by Francis Scott Key, which eventually became the national anthem. The war also helped the future political careers of several veterans, including Andrew Jackson and William Henry Harrison, both of whom became famous for their military adventures and were later elected presidents.

The Era of Good Feeling

President James Monroe's administration, from 1817 to 1825, was called the "Era of Good Feeling" because it was characterized by domestic tranquility, a lack of partisan bitterness, and a strong sense of nationalism. In the election of 1820, Monroe ran unopposed. He received all but one electoral vote.

The American System

The economic plan known as "the American System," proposed by Henry Clay of Kentucky, John C. Calhoun of South Carolina, and John Quincy Adams of Massachusetts, was designed to unify the country and make it less dependent on Europe and more economically self-sufficient. Its main features were the Tariff of 1816, the Second National Bank, and internal improvements. The tariff, approved by Congress to protect American industries, placed a tax of 20 to 25 percent on foreign goods. This was the first protective tariff in the United States designed to protect industry rather than raise revenue. The Second National Bank was established in 1816 to stabilize the currency and provide easy credit to help the economy run smoothly. Internal improvements included a system of roads and canals that would knit the nation together, built with money raised from the new protective tariff and revenues from the sale of land.

The American system was designed so that the tariffs would benefit the East; internal improvements would help farmers in the West and South ship their goods; and the Bank would help the economies of all sections.

Nationalism in Foreign Policy

The **Monroe Doctrine** of 1823 was conceived by John Quincy Adams and articulated by President James Monroe. It stated that the Western Hemisphere was off limits to European powers. It arose from fear in the United States that Spain and France would send armies to reestablish their control over the colonies that had established their independence during the 1820s.

The Doctrine's key provisions were that Europeans could keep their colonies in the Western Hemisphere but not establish new ones, while the United States would keep out of European affairs.

Britain supported this policy because it wanted to protect its colonies in the West Indies. The Monroe Doctrine became the foundation of U.S. policy toward Europe and Latin America, and it signaled that the United States considered itself a major power.

Judicial Nationalism

Supreme Court Chief Justice John Marshall issued a series of decisions that reflected the young country's rising spirit of nationalism. They included:

- *Dartmouth College v. Woodward* (1819): The Court ruled that state courts could not alter or invalidate a private contract.

- *McCulloch v. Maryland* (1819): The Court ruled that the government possessed the power to create a national bank, and that the state did not have the power to tax federal institutions. Federal law trumped state laws.

- *Gibbons v. Ogden* (1821): The Court ruled that it had the authority to regulate interstate commerce.

These decisions reinforced the Federalist belief in the power of the central government over state governments. They had far-reaching consequences for U.S. History, long after the Federalist Party's demise.

Rise of Sectionalism

As settlers moved westward, the question of whether new territories would be free or slave became a fiercely contested issue. By 1819, there were eleven free states and eleven slave states. Missouri's application for statehood in 1819 threatened to upset this fragile balance of power, tilting it toward the Southern slave states. Debate raged for months. In 1820 Henry Clay proposed the **Missouri Compromise.** According to its provisions,

- Missouri would be admitted as a slave state

- Maine would be admitted as a free state

- slavery was prohibited north of the 36/30 parallel

The Compromise temporarily resolved the controversy but damaged the spirit of unity in the country. Thomas Jefferson referred to the crisis as "the fireball in the night."

In the **Election of 1824**, intraparty politics in the Democratic-Republican Party revealed sectional differences. The four major candidates were William Henry Crawford, secretary of the treasury; Henry Clay, speaker of the House; Secretary of State John Quincy Adams; and Andrew Jackson, the national war hero. All of them ran as Democratic-Republicans. Jackson won the popular vote but not a majority of the electoral votes, and it fell to the House of Representatives to select the new president. After much debate, Henry Clay threw his support to Adams, who then appointed him secretary of state. Outraged, Jackson and his supporters attacked this as a "corrupt bargain," and the cloud of the corruption it created would limit Adams's effectiveness as president. Jackson formed a new political party known simply as the Democrats, thus ending the brief "Era of Good Feeling." Jackson's opponents, led by Henry Clay, formed another party known as the Whigs.

Review

3-1) Which president's administration made it a crime to publish criticism of the president?

A) George Washington

B) John Adams

C) James Madison

D) Thomas Jefferson

E) John Quincy Adams

3-2) Which of these was NOT a result of the Treaty of Ghent that ended the War of 1812?

A) Both sides promised to return prisoners.

B) There was no significant territorial loss for either side.

C) Americans gained fishing rights in the Gulf of Saint Lawrence.

D) The United States and Great Britain agreed to recognize the pre-war boundary between Canada and the United States.

E) Great Britain promised to pay damages for the seizure of American ships and impressments of American seamen.

3-3)   All were accomplishments of Jefferson's presidency EXCEPT

A) repeal of direct taxes

B) cuts in military spending

C) peaceable coercion ending British seizure of American ships to Europe

D) Louisiana Purchase

E) reduction in national debt

3-4)   The "Era of Good Feeling" refers to a period when

A) Americans became a creditor rather than a debtor nation

B) slavery was not an issue in the country

C) the West and North agreed to territorial expansion

D) there was a lack of partisan bitterness and renewed nationalism

E) the Federalists were the dominant party

Review Chapter 4:
The Jacksonian Era

In the **Election of 1828**, Andrew Jackson easily defeated John Quincy Adams, who carried only the New England areas. The campaign was full of vicious personal attacks on both sides. Adams was accused of soliciting prostitutes for the Czar while he was ambassador to Russia, while rumors spread that Jackson's wife, Rachel, was guilty of adultery. Jackson, whose wife died before his inauguration, never forgave his opponents for these attacks.

The Age of Jackson (1829–1837) also became known as the "Era of the Common Man." By the time of Jackson's election, virtually all white men over twenty-one were permitted to vote, and instead of caucuses (meetings among political leaders), political parties held nominating conventions to choose candidates. Three times the number of voters participated in the election of 1828 than previous elections. Jackson, born in a log cabin, was the first president from the West and the first without a college education since Washington. He was popular with common people because he seemed to epitomize the "self-made man," and he believed that political power should rest with the people. He utilized the "spoil system" to reward political supporters with government jobs. Jackson was not the first to utilize this system, but he was the first to justify it.

The following events dominated Jackson's presidency:

ISSUE	REACTION	PRESIDENTIAL ACTION
Tariff of 1828 Increased Duties on imported goods by as much as 50 percent.	In *Exposition and Protest*, John C. Calhoun declared that a state had the right to nullify or defy a national law	Jackson vigorously opposed the doctrine of nullification and asserted that "Our Union must be preserved."
Tariff of 1832 Congress imposed new taxes on imported goods.	South Carolina voted to nullify the laws. The U.S. Congress voted to lower the tariff.	Jackson promised to send troops to South Carolina to prevent secession, and privately threatened to hang Calhoun. Congressional action to lower the tariff prevented a crisis.
Bank Crisis Farmers and westerners disliked the Bank of the United States because they believed it served the interests of the wealthy.	Senator Henry Clay, who was running for president, persuaded Congress to renew the bank charter in 1832 rather than 1836, when it was scheduled to expire. Clay believed he would gain national support for his action.	Jackson vetoed the bill, claiming that it was unconstitutional and benefited only the wealthy. As a result, opponents referred to Jackson as "King Andrew" for his use of Presidential veto, but his action was popular with the people, and he easily defeated Clay in the election of 1832.

In 1833, Jackson killed the National Bank by withdrawing federal funds and investing them in local or "pet" banks. In 1836, to prevent speculation in western lands, Jackson issued the "specie circular," declaring that purchase of all lands had to be in gold and silver. It provoked the panic of 1837 and a depression that lasted until 1840.

Treatment of Native Americans

In 1830, Congress passed the **Indian Removal Act**, authorizing the removal of all Native Americans east of the Mississippi.

In the lawsuit *Worcester v. Georgia* the Cherokee tribes, who lived in Georgia and were assimilated into the white culture, challenged the law in court. Chief Justice Marshall ruled that the Cherokees had a right to remain on their land.

To circumvent this ruling, the government signed a treaty with a small band of Cherokee in which they gave up all their land east of the Mississippi. Even though the rest of the Cherokee protested, the Senate ratified the treaty. In 1838, after Jackson left office, more than fifteen thousand Cherokee were forced to leave Georgia. On the "Trail of Tears," more than four thousand of them died from disease and starvation.

Reform During the Jacksonian Era

Leaders of the reform movement in this era, known as the **antebellum period** (or the years before the Civil War), hoped to improve society through moral and religious persuasion. Much of the impulse for reform came from the Second Great Awakening, which developed during a period of economic and social changes in America at the beginning of the nineteenth century. It was marked by an emphasis on personal piety over schooling and theology. It began as a rural movement, but by the 1820s it had spread to cities across the country. By the 1830s and 1840s, ministers were preaching at revival meetings that lasted for days. Participants were swept up in powerful emotional states. Charles Grandison Finney and other ministers attracted thousands of people. He and other revivalists emphasized the ability of individuals to improve their lives, and they engendered a wide array of reform movements.

Abolitionist movement

In the 1820s and 1830s, abolitionism became the dominant reform movement in the United States Abolitionists believed slavery to be a sin and wanted to end it immediately. Major abolitionist leaders included Theodore Weld, Sojourner Truth, Frederick Douglass, and Elijah Lovejoy. One prominent leader was William Lloyd Garrison, whose newspaper, *The Liberator,* was founded in 1831 and was influential in abolitionist circles. Many considered the abolitionists radical because they demanded immediate emancipation of the slaves. Some Southerners blamed the Nat Turner revolt in 1831 in Virginia, which resulted in the death of sixty whites, on the politics of abolitionists like Garrison. Many Northerners, especially the workers, were critical of the abolitionists because they feared they would have to compete for jobs with free blacks. Abraham Lincoln also considered them too radical.

Temperance Movement

In the 1840s, women took the lead in the campaign against alcohol. They argued that it destroyed family life and led to marital abuse. Their campaign laws against the sale of liquor in several states.

Mental Health

Dorothea Dix, an ex-school teacher, was horrified to discover the conditions of many mental health facilities, where patients were often chained and beaten. She began a campaign for stricter regulations, and by the middle of the 1840s, states began to pass laws improving conditions in mental institutions.

Educational Reform

Horace Mann of Massachusetts advocated a tax-supported public school system to give all children—not just children of the wealthy—the opportunity to get an education. By the 1850s, New York had an extensive public education system serving many children.

Women's Rights

Although women were denied economic and political equality, they were active in reform movements. For example, Sara and Angelina Grimke worked tirelessly in the anti-slavery movement; and Elizabeth Cady Stanton and Lucretia Mott began the campaign for women's

rights. At a meeting at Seneca Falls, New York, in 1848, leading feminists issued a "Declaration of Sentiments," modeled on the Declaration
of Independence, in which they demanded the right of suffrage as well
as property rights. Unfortunately, women would have to wait until the
twentieth century to achieve these goals.

Transcendentalist Movement

The Great Awakening also led to a cultural renaissance that stressed
the importance of the individual and the common man. The best
expression of the importance of intuition over reason was found in the
Transcendentalist Movement of New England. Writers like Ralph Waldo
Emerson and Henry David Thoreau believed that individuals could tran-
scend the limits of the intellectual world by getting in touch with nature.
Although these men were critical of organized institutions, they supported a variety of reform movements, especially the anti-slavery movement. Thoreau's *Walden* and Emerson's *Nature* described their efforts
to improve society.

The Log Cabin Campaign of 1840

Martin Van Buren, Jackson's vice president in 1832, won the presidential election of 1836. However, the Panic of 1837 destroyed his hope
for re-election and provided an opportunity for the Whig Party to win
the White House for the first time. Whigs supported policies that promoted commercial and industrial growth, and they nominated war hero
William Henry Harrison for president and John Tyler of Virginia for
vice president. The Campaign of 1840 was heavy on symbolism. Whigs
attacked Van Buren as an elitist because of his taste for fine wines and
exotic foods, and they appealed to "the people" by portraying Harrison
as a common man who preferred hard cider to fancy wine. A model of
a log cabin was rolled out at torchlight parades, where hard cider was
given to the voters and campaign song sheets were passed out for the
voters to salute the ticket of "Tippecanoe & Tyler Too," a reference to

Harrison's war heroism at the Battle of Tippecanoe. The campaign succeeded, and Harrison defeated Van Buren. Harrison died within a month of his inauguration, though, and Tyler became president. The Election of 1840 is considered the first modern political campaign because of its heavy use of symbols, such as the log cabin, and because it featured heavy use of slogans, songs, and modern paraphernalia like buttons and hats.

Economic and Territorial Changes

By the mid 1800s, the three regions of the United States were developing different economies.

Rapid Industrialization in the North

- The completion of the Erie Canal in 1825 allowed goods to be shipped from Albany, New York, on the Hudson River, to Buffalo, New York, located on Lake Erie. The canal provided a continuous navigable route from the Atlantic Ocean to the Great Lakes. The North's excellent ports allowed trade with Europe as well.

- The influx of large-scale immigration from Germany and Ireland in the 1840s and 1850s provided cheap labor for the textile factories.

- Technological and mechanical improvements, such as the invention of the steamboat by Robert Fulton in 1807, in New York, made it easier and cheaper to ship goods along the nation's rivers. Eli Whitney's development of interchangeable parts, first used to produce rifles, provided the basis of mass-production methods in the northern factories.

- Clay's American system, which included the tariffs of 1816 and 1825, protected American goods from competing with British imports, allowing industry to expand. The Second National Bank, approved by Congress, provided loans for businessmen and helped industry to develop.

"Cotton is King" in the South

- Southern cash crops such as rice, tobacco, and cotton were grown extensively until the late-eighteenth century. However, in 1793 Eli Whitney's invention of the automatic cotton gin revolutionized the industry, because it ended the tedious process of removing the seed from the cotton by hand. This machine reduced the amount of labor required to harvest the cotton, making it extremely profitable for Southerners to grow cotton.

- Increased production of cotton met the needs of the textile factories springing up in the North and England.

- Slaves became the dominant labor force in the region, as more slaves were needed to plant and pick cotton.

- Although the planter class, which owned a large number of slaves, was a small minority of the population, they dominated the political, economic, and social life of the region.

- As slavery, or the "peculiar institution," became more important, southern whites became almost unanimous in supporting slavery. They argued that it was justified in the Constitution and even in the Bible.

From Subsistence Farming to Commercial Farming in the West

- John Deere's steel plow reduced the time it took to till soil by half, and it was more effective than the wooden plow.

- Cyrus McCormick's mechanical reaper reduced the amount of manual labor used to produce grain, and it dramatically increased overall grain production, both in the United States and the world. It also allowed the farmers to grow a more profitable crop, wheat, rather than just corn.

- McCormick's reaper, like Whitney's cotton gin in the South, dramatically changed the West's economy.

By 1850, the economic differences among the regions caused political strains and growing conflicts. The North relied on the western foodstuffs that allowed its cities to prosper. In return, westerners became more dependent on the North for consumer products, and more economically joined together. Meanwhile, the South seemed to be increasingly left behind in the nation's growing market economy.

Review

4-1)   A major political development during the Jacksonian Era was

A) introduction of the primary system to select candidates for office

B) the caucus system replaced the selection of political candidates by party leaders

C) white male suffrage for those over twenty-one

D) the civil service system replaced the spoils system

E) the direct election of senators instead of their selection by state legislature

4-2)   John C. Calhoun's *Exposition and Protest* expressed his opposition to

A) Tariff of 1828

B) Tariff of 1832

C) President Jackson's Maysville veto

D) Specie Circular

E) *Worcester v. Georgia* Supreme Court Case

4-3)   Which of the following is closely identified with the Second Great Awakening?

A) Jonathan Edwards

B) George Whitefield

C) Charles G. Finney

D) George Ripley

E) Joseph Smith

4-4) All of the following were part of Henry Clay's American System except

A) internal improvements
B) protective tariff
C) national bank
D) uniform currency
E) limiting the role of the government in the economy

Review Chapter 5:
Manifest Destiny and
Sectional Conflicts

Territorial Expansion

Between 1845 and 1853, the United States acquired the western territories of Texas, Oregon, California, and parts of the southwest, including Arizona and New Mexico. The ideology of western expansion can be traced to the Puritan belief that America should be a "city upon a hill" with a divine mission. In 1845, a New York journalist, John O'Sullivan, boldly asserted that America had a "manifest destiny"—in other words, that it was part of a God-given right for the nation to expand and spread democracy across the continent. The ideology of manifest destiny assumed that whites would civilize the Indians and conquer anyone who stopped the progress of democracy.

During the 1820s and 1830s, American fur traders streamed into Texas, Oregon, and California. The pioneers pushing into these territories pushed America's borders westward.

Texas

After Mexico won its independence from Spain in 1821, Mexicans welcomed Americans to their sparsely settled country. By 1836, there were more Americans in Texas than Mexicans. Many of them defied the Mexican law requiring them to be Catholics, as well the prohibition of slavery. Conflict arose when the Mexican government decided to restrict immigration and vigorously enforced laws regarding slavery. In 1836, the Texans revolted and proclaimed their independence. They were led by Sam Houston. Mexico's president, Santa Anna, was determined to crush the revolt. He overwhelmed 136 Texans at the Alamo, a Spanish mission in San Antonio, with a force of three thousand men. Rallying to the cry of "Remember the Alamo," Texans later defeated the Mexicans at the battle of the San Jacinto River, capturing Santa Anna and forcing him to grant them independence. Texas would remain an independent republic, the Lone Star Republic, for a decade. The chief obstacle to admission to the Union was slavery. Northerners feared that admitting Texas would rekindle the slave state/free state conflict.

Oregon

Since the early 1800s, the United States and Great Britain had agreed to joint occupation of Oregon, but by the 1840s, "Oregon fever" gripped the country and five thousand Americans traveled the Oregon Trail, lured by the promise of free land. By the election of 1844, Americans believed it was their right to occupy all of Oregon as well as Texas, and many saw California as a logical addition to the United States

The Election of 1844

Slavery and the question of what to do with Texas and Oregon were dominant campaign issues. The Democratic nominee, James K. Polk of Tennessee, supported westward expansion. The Democratic slogan, "54/40 or fight," referred to the desired northern boundary of the Oregon territory. The annexation of Texas appealed strongly to the nation's expansionist mood. Henry Clay, the Whig candidate, straddled the issue of Texas annexation. James Birney, the Liberty Party candidate, opposed slavery.

Consequences of the Election

Polk won the electoral vote overwhelmingly, but he won the popular vote by only forty thousand votes. Nonetheless, Congress interpreted the victory as an endorsement of westward expansion, and on March 1, 1845, it approved the annexation of Texas, which was admitted into the Union as the twenty-eighth state.

As for Polk, he was more concerned with ongoing problems in Mexico than Oregon, and because the British were eager to preserve their good relations with the United States, he was able to work out a peaceful solution. The Oregon Treaty set the United States and British border at the 49th parallel, with the exception of Vancouver Island, which was retained in its entirety by the British. The treaty established the border between the United States and Canada to the Pacific and improved relations with England.

The annexation of Texas angered Mexico, and its rejection of Polk's offer to buy additional land from Mexico, including California and New Mexico, created more friction between the two countries.

The Mexican-American War

In March 1846, President Polk sent General Zachary Taylor with a force of four thousand men to defend disputed borders along the Nueces and Rio Grande rivers. In April, Mexican troops fired on American troops in the disputed area. In May, Polk asked for a declaration of war, asserting that American blood had been shed on American soil. By 1847, the military had gained control of the entire southwest, including California, where American settlers revolted against Mexico and joined forces with the United States. General Taylor seized Northern Mexico, and in 1847 General Winfield Scott gained control of Mexico City, the capital, thus ending the war.

The **Treaty of Guadalupe Hidalgo**, signed in 1848, officially ended the war. It included the following provisions:

- Mexico ceded California and New Mexico to the United States for $15 million.

- Rio Grande was established as the southern border of the United States.

- The U.S. government agreed to assume responsibility for the $3.2 million debt Mexico owed to American citizens.

As a consequence of the war, the United States had increased its territory by a third. But some Whigs in Congress, including Abraham Lincoln, saw the war as an excuse by southerners to expand slavery. The Mexican War would intensify the debate over slavery. As early as 1846, David Wilmot of Pennsylvania introduced, as a part of an appropriation bill to fund the war, an amendment to forbid slavery in any of the territories acquired from Mexico. **The Wilmot Proviso** passed in the House, but southern Democrats killed it four times in the Senate.

The Election of 1848

The Whigs and Democrats both wanted to avoid the issue of slavery:

- Lewis Cass, the Democratic candidate, advocated "popular sovereignty" on the slavery issue. It would allow each territory to choose whether it was free or slave.

- Zachary Taylor, the Whig candidate and hero of the Mexican War, took no stand on the slavery issue.

- Martin Van Buren, a Free Soil candidate, ran on a platform that opposed slavery in the territories newly acquired from Mexico.

Van Buren split the Democratic vote in the key northern states of New York and Pennsylvania, allowing Taylor to win. Taylor's election defused tension over the expansion of slavery in the new territories, but it reemerged as an issue again in 1850.

The Union Breaks Apart

Prior to the 1850s, Americans had worked out compromises on the issue of slavery. But by the mid-1850s, the debate became more intense, and compromise became impossible. The Union was disrupted by the discovery of gold in California in 1849, leading to rapid settlement of the area and a request by the inhabitants to enter the Union as a free state. Southern radicals feared that California's admittance would upset the balance between the free and slave states. Some southerners even called for secession. Assisted by Stephen Douglas, Henry Clay hammered out the **Compromise of 1850**. Its stipulations were as follows:

- California was admitted as a free state.

- Popular sovereignty would determine whether western territories were free or slave states.

- Buying and selling slaves was banned in Washington, D.C.

- Government officials in the North must return runaway slaves to their masters, as required by a more stringent fugitive slave law.

The Compromise of 1850 postponed civil war for another decade and increased the political power of the North, since there were more free states than slave states.

Stronger fugitive slave laws angered northern abolitionists and created more sectional tension. Some northern abolitionists helped organize the "underground railroad," which enabled slaves to escape. Harriet Tubman, who had escaped from slavery in 1849, became known as the "Moses" of the anti-slavery movement. She rescued more than seventy slaves.

In 1852, Harriet Beecher Stowe published *Uncle Tom's Cabin*, which was written in response to the Fugitive Slave Act. The book sold more than three hundred thousand copies within a year and convinced many northerners of the immorality of slavery.

The **Kansas–Nebraska Act of 1854**, proposed by Stephen Douglas, created the territories of Kansas and Nebraska north of the 36'30 line. Since the Missouri Compromise prohibited slavery in this territory, southerners resented it, and hoped to open the territories to slavery. Important provisions of the law were as follows:

- The Missouri Compromise was repealed.

- The issue of slavery would be decided by popular sovereignty.

Armed fighting took place between southern pro-slave settlers and northerners over whether Kansas would be free or slave. In 1856, John Brown and a band of abolitionists killed seven pro-slavery settlers in the Pottawatomie Massacre, further escalating the violence. The episode, known as **Bleeding Kansas**, foreshadowed the impending violence of the Civil War, and the physical violence fueled increasing national tensions. The Kansas-Nebraska Act destroyed the unity of the Democratic Party, since northern Democrats opposed the repeal of the Missouri Compromise. In addition, the Whig party was completely destroyed. But a new party—the Republican Party, consisting of Democrats and Whigs who opposed the Kansas-Nebraska Act—was formed. Its goals were to prevent the expansion of slavery in the Kansas and Nebraska territories.

By 1856, the Republicans were sufficiently organized to endorse John C. Fremont as their presidential candidate. James Buchanan, the Democratic candidate, won easily, because the vote was split between Fremont and the candidate of the Know-Nothing Party, Millard Fillmore. The Know-Nothings, a nativist and anti-Catholic party, formed in the 1840s in reaction to the influx of Irish and German immigrants. Buchanan won without a majority of the votes. Fremont won 33 percent of the vote and Fillmore won 21 percent, giving them 54 percent of the popular vote.

The Dred Scott Decision (1857)

Dred Scott was a slave who had lived in Missouri. His master's widow took him to live in Illinois and Wisconsin, both free states. When his owner died, Scott sued for freedom, based on the fact that he lived in a free state. The case eventually ended up before the Supreme Court.

Chief Justice Roger Taney, a southerner, ruled that Scott could not sue because he was property, not a citizen. Taney further ruled that the Missouri Compromise was unconstitutional because it excluded slavery, and Congress did not have power to pass laws depriving people of their property.

The decision intensified sectional tensions. Northerners were shocked that slavery would expand to the new territories, while southerners were glad that the Supreme Court had vindicated their views.

Lincoln/Douglas Debates (1858)

Abraham Lincoln, the Whig turned Republican who had served only one term in the House, challenged the well-known Senator Stephen Douglas in his campaign for reelection. In a series of seven debates across Illinois, the main issue was slavery and its extension to the new territories. Douglas won the Senate seat, but Lincoln's strong performance in the debate helped his political future.

John Brown's Harper Ferry Raid (1859)

John Brown, a fierce antislavery crusader, and seventeen of his followers seized control of the federal arsenal in Harper's Ferry, Virginia. He had hoped to incite a slave revolt. The plot failed. Brown was captured and hanged. Brown was hailed as a hero in the North by many abolitionists. Southerners considered him a fanatic, and many thought that they could no loner live safely in the Union. Some incorrectly thought that the Republican Party had financed Brown's raid.

The **Election of 1860** revealed how divided the nation was and set the stage for the Civil War. The Candidates were

- Abraham Lincoln, the Republican candidate, whose main platform was to prevent extension of slavery in the new territories

- Stephen A. Douglas, the northern Democratic candidate, who ran on a platform of popular sovereignty regarding slavery in the new territories

- John Breckinridge, a southern Democrat, who supported the unrestricted extension of slavery in the territories

- John Bell, the Union Party candidate, who advocated the preservation of the Union

Lincoln was elected president, winning a majority of the electoral votes but only about 39 percent of the popular vote. He failed to win the support of any southern states, where, in most cases, his name did not even appear on the ballot.

Secession Crisis (1860–1861)

Within weeks of Lincoln's election, the process of disunion began. South Carolina seceded first on December 20, 1860. It was followed by six other states from the South. By February 1861, these states met in Montgomery, Alabama, and formed the Confederate States of America, with Jefferson Davis serving as president. By March 1861, when Lincoln was inaugurated, the Union had come apart, and the North and South were two separate nations. The main question was whether President Lincoln would use force against South Carolina to bring it back into the Union.

Review

5-1)   Which was the main reason that Andrew Jackson and Martin Van Buren opposed the annexation of Texas?

A) They feared provoking a war with Mexico.

B) Britain and Spain had rival claims on the territory, which had to be arbitrated.

C) The state had not paid off its debt to foreign creditors.

D) Northerners were fearful that the admission of Texas would rekindle the slavery controversy.

E) Texas had not set aside land for public education as required by law.

5-2)   A major issue in the Election of 1848 was

A) renewal of the National Bank of the United States

B) the status of slavery in the new territories gained in the Mexican War

C) the extension of railroads in the territories gained in the Mexican War

D) whether the Missouri Compromise should be extended westward to the Pacific Ocean

E) the Indian removal policy established during the Jacksonian presidency

Courtesy of the Milwaukee County Historical Society

5-3)   Which political party would have supported the above banner in the United States during the 1840s?

A) Know-Nothing Party

B) Republicans

C) Whigs

D) Liberty Party

E) Democrats

5-4)   Which of the following is NOT an accurate statement about the Election of 1860?

A) Lincoln won with a minority of the popular vote.

B) Lincoln did not win the support of any southern states.

C) Lincoln supported a halt to the extension of slavery.

D) Lincoln was selected as the Republican nominee because he was the least controversial.

E) The Democrats were united behind the candidacy of Stephen Douglas.

Review Chapter 6:
The Civil War and
Reconstruction

After declaring independence in December, 1861, South Carolina demanded that the federal government withdraw its troops from Fort Sumter, located in Charleston Harbor. President James Buchanan claimed that he had no authority to compel the states to remain in the Union, and he did nothing. The southern states waited to see if the president-elect, Abraham Lincoln, would use force.

Meanwhile, John Crittenden of Kentucky made one last attempt to save the Union. He proposed a constitutional amendment guaranteeing the existence of slavery south of the 36'30 parallel. Lincoln and the Republicans believed it would allow slavery to spread to other territories, and they rejected it. When Lincoln was inaugurated in March 1861, the question of what to do about South Carolina's secession was still unresolved.

Lincoln refused to withdraw troops from Fort Sumter and sent a ship to supply it. On April 12, 1861, Confederate forces began shelling the fort, and the troops stationed there surrendered on April 14. The fall of Fort Sumter led to the immediate secession of Arkansas, North Carolina, Tennessee, and Virginia from the Union. Robert E. Lee resigned from the Union Army and agreed to lead the Confederate Army.

Fighting the War

Both sides believed the war would end quickly. The North had a large industrial economy, a larger population, more resources, and a stronger central government. The South, however, had superior military leaders and were fighting a defensive war. The hope of a quick war ended in July 1861, at the First Battle of Bull Run, when Northern troops retreated in chaos.

The North realized that it needed to develop a long-term strategy. General Winfield Scott proposed the Anaconda Plan. It would

- use the U.S. Navy to blockade all the Southern ports, cutting off essential supplies that the South needed

- take control of the Mississippi River, dividing the South in half

The idea was to suffocate the south as a snake suffocates its victim, but the North instead settled on a plan to attack Virginia and try to take Richmond, the Confederate capital.

Following is a list of the battles that enabled the North to win the war.

Battle of the Monitor and the Merrimac (March 1862)

In an attempt to break the naval blockade that prevented them from receiving cotton exports and European shipments of war supplies, the South developed the first ironclad ship, called the *Merrimac*. Initially, the *Merrimac* wreaked havoc on the North's wooden ships, but the North soon produced its own ironclad, the *Monitor*. In a two-day battle, the two ships fought to a draw.

The battle made wooden ships obsolete and ended the South's hope of breaking the blockade. It also enabled northern naval forces to gain control of the Mississippi River.

Battle of Antietam (September 1862)

This was the first major battle to take place on northern soil, near Sharpsburg, Maryland. Lee had hoped after the first Battle of Bull Run that another major Confederate victory would help the South gain British support. General McClellan and Union forces fought Lee's troops in a bloody battle that resulted in more than twenty-two thousand causalities.

Antietam turned back the Confederate invasion and convinced foreign powers, like England and France, not to support the Confederacy. Not long after the battle, Lincoln issued the Emancipation Proclamation, freeing the slaves in the South, adding to foreign sympathies for the North.

The Battle of Gettysburg (July 1863)

Nearly fifty thousand troops died near a Pennsylvania farm town in the bloodiest battle of the Civil War. Lee's attempt to invade the North failed, and he was forced to march his army back to Virginia

The battle is considered the turning point of the war, because it ended any possibility of another invasion of the North by the South.

Siege of Vicksburg (July 1863)

After a six-week siege, General Grant forced the South to surrender the strategic fortress city of Vicksburg, on the Mississippi River. The victory gave the North control of the full length of the Mississippi River, cutting the Confederacy in half. The three Confederate states in the West (Texas, Louisiana, and Arkansas) were divided from the rest of the Confederacy, depriving the South of its primary mode of transportation in the West.

Sherman's March to the Sea (1864)

From November to December, 1864, William T. Sherman conducted a march across Georgia. The campaign began with Sherman's troops capturing the city of Atlanta, marching toward the port of Savannah, and moving northward to the Carolinas. Along the way he destroyed both military targets and civilian property, burning homes and destroying crops, in an attempt to break the South's will to fight.

Appomattox (April 9, 1865)

The combined effects of the blockade, Sherman's march to the sea, and Grant's continued march toward the southern capital of Richmond convinced Lee that the South could not win the war. On April 9, 1865, he surrendered to Grant at Appomattox Court House. The Civil War had ended and the Union was preserved. Five days later, just a month into his second term, President Abraham Lincoln was assassinated by John Wilkes Booth.

Impact of the War

The Civil War expanded the powers of the presidency. It established that the Constitution gave him the authority, in emergency situations, to take certain actions without consulting Congress. For example, Lincoln had

- called up the military, increased its size by seventy thousand men, and spent funds on the war

- blockaded Southern ports and authorized a conscription

- suspended the writ of habeas corpus and established military tribunals to try civilians in certain areas. At the end of the war, nearly fifteen thousand individuals were imprisoned without formal trials. But the Supreme Court, in *Ex parte Milligan* (1866), ruled that Lincoln had overstepped his power. It ordered that these civilians be set free.

Lincoln's **Emancipation Proclamation** on January 1, 1863, demonstrated his executive leadership. It declared that slaves living in the Confederate states were free and liberated. But slaves living in border states (Delaware, Kentucky, Maryland, Missouri, and West Virginia), and those living in areas conquered by the North, were not free.

The Proclamation had no immediate effect on slaves in the South, but it helped make slavery the war's central issue and rekindled support for the waning war effort in the North. It also ended any hope that England would aid the South.

Effects on Women

Women provided the labor force for factories that produced war supplies, since thousands of men had gone away to fight. The need for nurses also opened up new opportunities for them. Clara Barton and other women provided medicinal help for those wounded in battle. In 1881, Clara Barton would help found the American Red Cross.

Effects on African Americans

At the beginning of the war, African Americans were not allowed to serve in the military in either the North or the South. Some were eventually allowed to serve in segregated units, but only in secondary roles like food preparation and construction. After the Emancipation Proclamation in 1863, many free blacks and ex-slaves served in the military, and by 1865, more than 180,000 African Americans joined the Union Army, serving in segregated units with white officers.

Draft Riots

Until 1863, enlistment in the Union Army was voluntary. But when Congress passed a draft law that compelled people to serve in the army, violent disturbances broke out in New York City from July 13 to July 16, 1863. The rioters were primarily working-class men, but they directed their anger at African Americans, who competed with them for jobs. Many African Americans died during the four days of rioting.

Economic Effects

Congress passed the following measurers that had a lasting influence on the United States:

- The Morrill Tariff of 1861 raised tariff rates to protect northern manufacturers.

- The Homestead Act 1862 promoted settlement of the far West.

- The Morrill Land Grant Act of 1862 stimulated the growth of higher education by giving land to the states for the building of new agricultural colleges.

Congress also created a national banking system to finance the war and authorized the building of a transcontinental railroad connecting the East and the West.

Political Effects

The Civil War established the Republicans as the dominant political party, and the North's victory established the supremacy of the federal government over the states. The perception that Republicans had won the war helped the Party dominate American politics for the next forty years.

The Reconstruction Era

By the end of 1865, a triumphant North faced the problem of how to reconstruct the South. It had to decide how to treat the former Confederate states and their leaders, as well as what to do with the slaves set free by the Thirteenth Amendment. Another issue was whether the president or Congress had the authority to deal with the defeated South. Reconstruction refers to these post-war years, from 1865 to 1877, when Northern troops occupied the defeated South and tried to reshape their state governments, so they could rejoin the Union.

Lincoln's Ten Percent Plan

Under Lincoln's plan, 10 percent of state voters had to take an oath of allegiance to the United States to be readmitted to the Union. He offered full presidential pardons to all southerners, except high-ranking Confederate military and civilian leaders, who took the loyalty oath and agreed to the abolition of slavery.

Radical Republicans in Congress rejected Lincoln's lenient policy. In 1864, they passed the Wade Davis Bill, which required that at least

50 percent of a state's white, male population take an oath of loyalty to the Union. Lincoln refused to sign it and vetoed it after Congress adjourned.

Andrew Johnson's Plan

Andrew Johnson of Tennessee became president after Lincoln's assassination. He had been selected by Lincoln as his running mate in order to encourage pro-Union Democrats to vote for the Republican Party. His plan was similar to Lincoln's.

Northern Republicans distrusted Johnson because he had been a Democrat from Tennessee, a seceding southern state. He also angered many Republicans, because he granted presidential pardons to wealthy planters. As a result, many former Confederate leaders were back in Washington by the end of 1865.

Radical Republicans' Program

The Radical Republicans, led by Charles Summer of Massachusetts in the Senate and Thaddeus Stevens of Pennsylvania in the House, wanted to punish the South for its role in the war, and they wanted to insure that blacks received the same rights as whites. To accomplish these goals, they promoted a program that included several major pieces of reform legislation.

The **Freedmen's Bureau (1865)** helped ex-slaves get employment, education, and emergency assistance in the form of clothing and food. A bill extending the bureau was vetoed by President Johnson in 1866, but Congress overrode his veto.

The **Civil Rights Act of 1866** was passed to combat the **black codes**, which were laws that imposed severe restrictions on freed slaves in the former Confederate states. They denied former slaves the right to vote or sit on juries, limited their right to testify against white men, and prohibited them from carrying weapons in public, working in certain occupations, and travelling without a permit. Southerners argued that these codes were necessary to maintain order. The Civil Rights Act granted freedmen all the rights and benefits of U.S. citizens and noted that federal troops would enforce these rights. The Civil Rights Act also helped enforce the Thirteenth Amendment, which Congress passed in December 1865. Johnson vetoed it, but Congress overrode his veto.

The **Fourteenth Amendment (1868)** guaranteed citizenship for blacks and reduced representation in Congress for states that did not give freedmen the right to vote. Riots in Memphis and New Orleans pushed Congress to send this amendment to the states for ratification.

Despite Johnson's veto, Congress divided the South into five military districts, each under the control of the Union Army. For a state to be readmitted, it had to ratify the Fourteenth Amendment and guarantee the right to vote to all adult males, regardless of race.

In 1867, Congress passed the Tenure of Office Act over the President's veto. It prohibited the president from firing or removing a federal official without the Senate's approval. In 1868, Johnson challenged the law and fired Secretary of War Edwin Stanton. The House responded by voting to impeach Johnson. The Senate fell one vote short of the necessary two-thirds majority required to remove him from office.

Johnson served out the rest of his term without incident, posing no further threat to the Radical program, and in the 1868 presidential election, the war hero Ulysses S. Grant led the Republicans to victory.

With an ally in the White House, the Radical Republicans pushed for passage of the **Fifteenth Amendment**, which stated that no American could be denied the right to vote because of "race, color, or previous conditions of servitude." In effect, it guaranteed voting rights to African Americans. These Reconstruction Amendments—the Thirteenth, Fourteenth, and Fifteenth—were passed to protect the civil rights of African Americans.

The **Civil Rights Act of 1875** was the last civil rights reform passed by Congress during the Reconstruction era. It called for full equality in public accommodations, such as hotels and railroads, for all races, and it prohibited the exclusion of African Americans from juries. Unfortunately, it was poorly enforced, as many northern whites grew tired of Reconstruction, and Democrats did not support it. The Act was declared unconstitutional by the Supreme Court in 1883. Congress would not pass another round of civil rights legislation until the 1960s.

Southern Reaction to Reconstruction

Many Southerners were embittered by the laws passed during Reconstruction. Republican control of southern state governments began to weaken in 1869. Tennessee was the first southern state to elect a postwar government dominated by conservative Democrats. Reconstruction ended when federal troops were withdrawn from Florida in 1877.

Southerners attempted to regain control of state legislatures from their hated rivals, known as "carpetbaggers," a nickname referring to the large bag many of them supposedly brought to the South, seeking their fortune, and "scalawags," southern whites who supported the Republicans.

One method they used to regain power was to organize secret societies, such as the **Ku Klux Klan** and the Knights of the White Camellia, to intimidate black voters. These organizations used violence—burning homes, beatings, and lynching to prevent blacks and sympathetic whites from voting. Congress passed the Force Acts of 1870 and 1871, which authorized Congress to stop this violence, but the influence of the Radical Republicans was declining as the recession of 1873 turned the nation's concerns to economic rather than political or social issues.

The End of Reconstruction

By 1876, federal troops had withdrawn from all the southern states but South Carolina, Florida, and Louisiana. In the **election of 1876**, Democrats chose Samuel Tilden, governor of New York, to run against Republican Rutherford B. Hayes, governor of Ohio. Tilden received 51 percent of the popular vote but only 184 Electoral College votes, one shy of the number needed to win. Hayes received 165 electoral votes. There were twenty disputed votes.

To resolve the controversy, Democrats and Republicans worked out the Compromise of 1877. It stipulated that Hayes would be the next president, and in return, he would order the last Union troops out of the South and stop enforcing Reconstruction-era laws.

The Legacy of Reconstruction

Political Alignments

Republican policies made the South virtually a one-party region. The so-called "Solid South" voted almost exclusively Democratic for the next hundred years.

Economic Changes

The plantation system was replaced by tenant farmers, who provided their own seeds, mules, and provisions. The landlord gave them a piece of land to farm, and in return he received a certain share of the tenant farmer's crop. The system kept blacks in economic bondage, though they were legally free.

Jim Crow Laws and Disenfranchisement

By the 1890s, the South passed Jim Crow laws, which established the segregation of public facilities. Through the use of the literacy test, poll tax, and grandfather clause (which exempted whites from the literacy test), southern states also made it difficult or impossible for African Americans to vote.

Plessy v. Ferguson (1896)

Homer Plessy, a black citizen from Louisiana, sued a railroad company for not allowing him to sit in a section restricted to whites. The Supreme Court ruled that the "separate but equal" facilities provided by the railroad were constitutional and did not violate the equal protection clause of the Fourteenth Amendment. The Supreme Court's decision legalized segregation for nearly sixty years.

Review

6-1)   In the Tenure of Office Act, in 1867, Congress stated that

A) the president had to submit all Reconstruction plans to a special committee for evaluation

B) southern states had to approve thirteen amendments before they were re-admitted

C) the president could not fire or remove any federal official without the Senate's approval

D) the Secretary of War had to meet with Congress before troops were ordered into the states seeking admission to the Union

E) Congress and the president had to work jointly to establish programs to ensure civil rights for freed slaves

6-2)   The Copperheads were

A) southerners who opposed the Civil War on philosophical issues

B) Republicans who opposed Lincoln's Emancipation Proclamation

C) Free-Soil Party leaders who opposed Lincoln's Emancipation Proclamation

D) northern military leaders, like General McClellan, who were critical of Lincoln's war aims

E) northern Democrats who refused to support the Civil War

6-3)   The battle that gave the Union virtual control of the Mississippi River occurred at

A) Gettysburg

B) Vicksburg

C) Shiloh

D) Antietam

E) Second Battle of Bull Run

6-4)   In the election of 1876

    A) Rutherford B. Hayes won the popular vote but lost the electoral vote

    B) Samuel Tilden received more electoral votes but fewer popular votes

    C) the Republicans swept the South

    D) the Supreme Court ultimately decided the outcome

    E) a special electoral commission was established to decide the winner

Review Chapter 7:
The Politics and Problems
of the Gilded Age

T he main characteristics of this era, from 1868 to 1892, were:

- Republicans dominated the federal government, with the support of big business and farmers. With the exception of Grover Cleveland's terms in 1884 and 1892, Republicans controlled the presidency.

- Democratic power came from white voters in the South and the big city machines, like Tammany Hall in New York.

- Politicians of both parties were conservative. Both Republicans and Democrats promoted limited government involvement in the economy. Their major disagreement was over the protective tariff. Republicans supported it while southern Democrats and some northern Democrats (and later western farmers) opposed it, because it raised the price of consumer goods.

The Presidents of the Gilded Age
"The Gilded Age" was the title of a book by Mark Twain, and it became a common descriptor of the latter half of the nineteenth century. Historians have dubbed the presidents during this era as the Forgotten

Presidents, because they were lackluster and ignored the problems created by the country's industrialization. These presidents included Rutherford B. Hayes, James Garfield, Chester A. Arthur, Grover Cleveland, and Benjamin Harrison. The most memorable of these was Grant, who presided over the end of Reconstruction. However, his administration was tainted by the Credit Mobilier Scandal, which involved the illegal manipulation of contracts in building the Union Pacific Railroad, and the Whiskey Ring Scandal of 1874, in which federal officials defrauded the government of millions of dollars in liquor taxes. While Grant was not involved in these scandals, members of his administration were implicated.

By the 1890s, Republicans and Democrats began taking actions to address problems created by the economic transformations of the post-Civil War industrial era. However, farmers and workers began to question whether they were benefitting from these changes.

The Industrialization of America, 1865–1900

The industrial economy of the United States accelerated during the Gilded Age. Growth was so extensive that some historians call it the "Second Industrial Revolution." A combination of factors—the technological improvement of the Bessemer process for steel production, an abundance of natural resources, a growing population fueled by the influx of immigrants, the establishment of large-scale factories and production centers, and the friendly attitude of the government—contributed to the rapid growth of the economy.

The Business of Railroads

The Republican majority provided land grants and federal loans for thirty years, helping spur construction of the Transcontinental Railroad. The Union Pacific began construction in Omaha, Nebraska, in 1863, and pushed westward until the railroads came together near Ogden, Utah, in 1869. Railroads were built that helped tie the country together. Federal grants and subsidies helped make the building of railroads a big business. Railroad building captured the imagination of the public, as state and local communities invested in their development. Railroad tycoons like Cornelius Vanderbilt and James E. Hill dominated the industry. Unfortunately, corruption incidents like the Credit Mobilier scandal hurt many people who had invested in them. The railroad also advanced the settlement of the West and revolutionized its economy. Settlers began to participate in a global market, and their livelihood was tied to the shipping rates established by the railroads.

Leaders of Industry

Business growth owed much to the leadership of men who helped transform the economy and became enormously wealthy. Admirers called them Captains of Industry. Critics called them Robber Barons.

Andrew Carnegie was a poor Scottish immigrant who came to dominate the steel industry by using "vertical integration," or the control of all the steps necessary to turn raw materials into finished commodities. By his retirement in 1900, when he sold his company to J.P. Morgan, he had become one of the wealthiest men in the United States.

John D. Rockefeller became synonymous with the oil industry. He organized the Standard Oil Company in 1870, and by 1890 he controlled 90 percent of all the oil refined in the United States. His method of "horizontal integration," buying out all competitors to eliminate competition, enabled him to control the oil industry. Eventually, Standard Oil became one of the most powerful corporations in America.

Capitalism at Its Zenith

The significant growth of the American economy reinforced the belief that laissez-faire capitalism was the best method of progress. The following theories reinforced faith in limited government:

Social Darwinism

It was the most influential justification for laissez-faire capitalism. The British philosopher Herbert Spencer applied Charles Darwin's idea of natural selection to the economy. Business leaders like Rockefeller and Vanderbilt used it to argue that they were successful because they were the "winners" in the process of natural selection. Social Darwinism, which was popularized by William Graham Summer in the United States, asserted that God had chosen the wealthy because they deserved it, and that the poor didn't deserve government's help.

Gospel of Wealth

Carnegie would argue that the wealthy had a responsibility to act as guardians of wealth in the United States. It was their role—not the government's—to contribute to society through philanthropic programs. By the time of his death, he gave more than $350 million to libraries, schools, and hospitals.

Horatio Alger

The books of Horatio Alger popularized the stories of poor boys who, by hard work and sacrifice, became successful. These rags-to-riches stories were exemplified by the rise of Andrew Carnegie, whose success reinforced the idea that "the American dream" could happen to anyone without help from the government.

The Struggle of Labor

After 1865, as business firms became larger and their profits grew enormously, the plight of workers tended to become worse. The increased mechanization of labor, and the influx of immigrants, depressed wages and forced workers to organize into trade unions. The most important labor unions are shown in the following chart.

UNION	GOALS AND RESULTS
Knights of Labor (1869) Led by Terence Powderly Members were skilled and unskilled workers; African Americans and women included	Sought eight-hour workday Supported worker cooperation Sought racial and gender equality Preferred arbitration to strikes Membership peaked at 700,000 in 1885, declined in wake of Haymarket Riots on 1886
American Federation of Labor (AFL) (1886) Led by Samuel Gompers Members were skilled workers; African Americans and women were excluded	Key issues included higher wages, better working conditions Became one of the more powerful unions in the twentieth century
Industrial Workers of the World (IWW) (1905) Led by Big Bill Haywood Members were skilled and unskilled workers; African Americans and women included	Violent strikes to gain control of factories and businesses as well as better wages Union destroyed during WWI when many members were jailed

Violent Clashes between Business and Labor

Haymarket Square (Chicago Riot of 1886)

Issue: Three hundred thousand workers demonstrated to protest the treatment of workers at the McCormack Reaper plant in downtown Chicago.

Result: An unknown protester threw a bomb that killed several police officers. Eight anarchists were arrested, and four were put to death. The public blamed unions for the violence, and particularly the Knights of Labor, which suffered a decline in membership.

Homestead Strike (Pennsylvania Strike of 1892)

Issue: Andrew Carnegie owned the Homestead Steel Plant, which cut wages. Workers went on strike.

Result: Carnegie called in the Pinkerton National Detectives to engage the strikers. Fierce fighting broke out between the two sides, resulting in deaths on both sides. The strike and the union were broken.

Pullman Strike (1894)

Issue: George Pullman, inventor of the Pullman sleeping car, announced a 25 percent cut in wages.

Result: Led by Eugene Debs, the American Railway Union and other workers boycotted the railroad industry in the Midwest. They destroyed cars, delayed trains, and refused to handle mail cars. President Cleveland ordered troops to break up the strike, claiming that the strikers were interfering with the delivery of the mail. Debs was arrested.

American Life in the Gilded Age

Urbanization

The increasing industrialization of the United States after the Civil War encouraged millions of people to move to cities to find work. The influx of native-born Americans from farms, immigrants from Europe and Asia, and free slaves from the South transformed American cities. By 1900, almost 40 percent of the American people lived in cities, compared with about 20 percent in the 1860s.

Prior to the Civil War, cities were small, and most people lived within walking distance of their jobs. A number of improvements in transportation sped the transformation of American cities. These included the electric trolley car, introduced in Richmond in 1887; cable cars in San Francisco; subways and elevated trains; and the building of steel suspension bridges like the Brooklyn Bridge, completed in 1883. Such innovations made it possible for people to move farther away from cities and commute from residential areas, which became known as suburbia.

As cities expanded outward, cities also soared upward. By 1900, skyscrapers became the symbol of urban America.

Immigration

The large influx of immigrants in the late nineteenth century played a vital role in the growth of cities. Immigration patterns changed dramatically during the 1880s.

Old Immigrants: Prior to the 1880s, a majority of immigrants were from northern Europe. They were primarily English, Irish, and German. Most of them spoke English.

New Immigrants: From the late 1880s until 1914, most immigrants came from southern and eastern Europe. Between 1900 and 1910, total immigration averaged close to a million people each year. Of the million who arrived in 1910, a large majority—about seven hundred thousand—came from southern and eastern Europe countries, including Italy, Greece, Poland, Croatia, Russia, and Slovakia. Most were poorer and less-educated than earlier immigrants, and they were largely Roman Catholics, Greek Orthodox, and Jewish. Most of these immigrants crowded into poor ethnic neighborhoods in New York, Chicago, and other urban centers.

In these neighborhoods, immigrants became part of the political machine. New York's Tammany Hall, for example, which had begun as a social club, served the needs of the immigrants by finding them jobs and apartments, and by providing food. In return, they asked for people's votes.

Most of the immigrants worked in low-paying, unskilled jobs in factories or meat-packing houses. Poverty forced them to live in tenements, which were poorly constructed and designed to house as many people as possible. They had one-room apartments, where there was little ventilation and a bathroom shared by many families on the floor. In these crowded tenements, diseases such as cholera and tuberculosis spread easily.

The outbreak of the Civil War had ended the American Know-Nothing Party, which formed in the 1840s in opposition to Irish and German immigrants. The service of Irish and German soldiers in the war silenced doubts about whether they were true Americans.

Re-emergence of Nativism

Americans were unhappy about the type of immigrants coming to America. On the West Coast, Americans, who had recruited over fifteen thousand Chinese to work on building the transcontinental railroad, claimed that the Chinese were threatening American jobs. In 1882, in response to this "yellow peril," as it was called, Congress passed the Chinese Exclusion Act, prohibiting any Chinese laborers from entering the country. Nativist anger was also directed at the "new immigrants," fearing that they would not assimilate and that they threatened the purity of the Anglo-Saxon race. Organizations like the American Protective Association, formed in 1887, and the Immigration Restriction League, founded in 1894 by three Harvard College graduates, lobbied for tough immigration laws to keep out undesirables. By the turn of the century, there were laws restricting the entry of criminals, paupers, and prostitutes.

Women's Movement

In the latter half of the nineteenth century, the struggle for women's rights continued. Elizabeth Cady Stanton and Susan B. Anthony founded the National Woman Suffrage Association in 1869 to promote the passage of suffrage legislation. In 1869, the western state of Wyoming became the first to grant suffrage to women. By 1900, most women were allowed to own property after marriage. Victoria Hull gained notoriety and attention by running for the presidency in 1872.

African Americans

In 1896, *Plessy v. Ferguson* upheld segregation and condemned African Americans to second-class status. Black leaders continued to press for equal rights, but they disagreed on the best way to achieve their goal.

Booker T. Washington founded the all-black Tuskegee Institute, which was dedicated to giving industrial and vocational training to African Americans. In a speech in 1895 titled "The Atlanta Compromise," he argued that blacks should focus on economic self-sufficiency before challenging whites on social issues.

W. E. B. Du Bois was a Harvard-educated black historian. In *The Souls of Black Folks*, he argued that blacks should fight for economic as well as social issues. He urged African Americans to fight for their rights and to oppose Jim Crow laws. In 1905, he founded **The Niagara Movement**, which was named for Niagara Falls, which was near their first meeting place, and for the "mighty current" of change that the group wanted to create. It was a call for opposition to racial segregation, disenfranchisement, and policies of accommodation and conciliation. In 1909, members of the movement joined with white reformers in organizing the National Association of the Advancement of Colored People (NAACP).

Settlement of the West

In addition to promoting industrial growth, the railroads promoted the growth of the West. To recruit settlers, railroad companies sent agents to European and American cities. Railroads sold government land grants to settlers at discounted prices, encouraging them to move west. The railroads also carried agricultural products like wheat and grain across the Great Plains to California, and they were crucial to the profitability of the cattle industry. Government policy also contributed to the migration of Americans westward. The Homestead Act of 1862 had provided cheap land for farmers, contributing to the settlement of unknown lands beyond Kansas and Nebraska. By 1890, the government declared that the area of open land had ended in North America.

Native Americans

The settlers who migrated westward disrupted the lives of Native American tribes, such as the Cheyenne, Nez Perce, and Sioux. Native Americans and whites clashed over western lands. In 1864, the Colorado militia slaughtered more than four hundred Cheyenne women, men, and children at the Sand Creek massacre. Months later, bands of Cheyenne, Sioux, and Arapahoes retaliated by burning civilian outposts and sometimes killing whole families. The federal government tried to resolve these conflicts by concentrating tribes on small reservations, where they became dependent on government support for survival.

The Sioux tribe and Nez Perce resisted efforts to put them on reservations. The Sioux, under Chief Sitting Bull, wiped out General George Armstrong Custer at the Battle of the Little Big Horn in 1876. But within a year, the Sioux were defeated. A band of Nez Perce under Chief Joseph tried to flee into Canada, but he was forced to surrender in 1877 and was driven to live on a reservation.

Native Americans continued their resistance through the Ghost Dance Movement, which they believed would help them remove whites from Native American lands and enable them to return to their traditional way of life. In 1890, during a campaign to suppress the movement, the United States Army killed more than two hundred Native American women, children, and men at the Massacre at Wounded Knee. This tragedy ended the Native American wars.

In 1881, in the bestselling book *A Century of Dishonor*, Henry Hunt Jackson described the injustices of the federal government towards Native Americans. Many Americans assumed that assimilation was the only way to help them achieve success. These efforts included

- the Carlisle School in Pennsylvania, where Native Americans were given a Christian education and taught skills to enable them to assimilate into white society. The athlete Jim Thorpe, who won numerous Olympic medals in 1912, attended this school.

- the Dawes-Severalty Act of 1887, according to which Native Americans could gain citizenship and receive 160 acres of land. To do so, they had to give up claims to their tribal lands and stay on the land they received from the government for twenty-five years. The policy failed because many Native Americans had little interest in farming, and the best lands had been sold to speculators of the railroads and mining companies. By the beginning of the twentieth century, virtually all Native Americans were living on reservations.

The Impact of the West on American Society

By 1890 the Indian wars had ended and there was no more free land available. In 1893, the historian Frederick Jackson Turner published an essay, "The Significance of the Frontier in American history," in which he argued that the frontier had helped shape the American character. The Turner thesis states that the spirit of individualism, mobility, egalitarianism, and democratic nationalism can be traced to the West. On the frontier, everyone had an equal chance to succeed, and the availability of cheap, free land encouraged a sense of optimism about a better future. In recent decades, historians have pointed out the weaknesses of Turner's thesis. He neglected to take account of the conflict between the settlers and Native Americans, for example, or the British influence on American democracy.

The Plight of the Farmer

For farmers, the post-Civil War era was the best of times and the worst of times. Improvements in technology—such as reapers, combines, and improved plows—made farmers more productive. But higher productivity did not always mean higher profits.

The railroad became the symbol and the focus of the farmers' discontent. Railroad rates were unregulated, and they would often be set at arbitrarily high rates, affecting the income of farmers. In addition, farmers were dependent on banks for credit to finance their purchases of machinery and supplies for planting. They became angry that even in good years, when they produced record crops, they received prices below those of previous years. Throughout the 1870s, 1880s, and 1890s, prices sank and farm debts soared.

Protest and Populism

The Granger Movement (1867)

The National Grange, or the Patrons of Husbandry, was formed as a social organization to help bring families together. Soon it began to focus on economic issues affecting farmers, like falling grain prices and rising railroad rates. By the mid-1870s, membership had risen to over 850,000 members, especially in the Midwest and the South. They used their political clout to help states pass Granger laws to regulate freight and storage rates. These laws were challenged in court. In *Munn v. Illinois* (1877), the Supreme Court ruled that a state could set maximum rates for the good of the public. But in 1886, the Court reversed itself and declared that only Congress could regulate railroad rates. Granger membership declined in the early 1880s as prices improved.

Populists

In the late 1880s, farmers began to form political alliances as crop prices began to drop. They were encouraged by some people to "raise less corn and more hell." By 1890, several statewide alliances had merged into the National Farmers Alliance, and it began to plan for political action on the national level.

On July 4, 1892, delegates from the Farmers Alliance held a convention in Omaha Nebraska. They created the People's Party, whose followers became known as Populists. Their party platform was designed to appeal to urban workers as well as the farmers. They wanted the following:

- government ownership of railroads and telephone companies

- a graduated income tax

- immigration restrictions

- an eight-hour workday, as well as the right to collective bargaining

- unlimited cheap silver money; they wanted a rate of sixteen ounces of silver to one ounce of gold

- direct election of U.S. senators

- a single-term limit for presidents

The Populists nominated James Weaver, a former Union Army general, for the presidency. He received over a million general-election votes and twenty-two electoral votes. Democrat Grover Cleveland was elected president. Although the Populists lost the presidency, they won some remarkable victories, electing six members to the U.S. Senate and forty-five to the House of Representatives. Most of their support was in the West, however, and they fared poorly in the South and the Northeast.

Populism in the 1890s

Cleveland's second term was even more difficult than the first. The Depression of 1893, which started a few months before his second term began, was the worst collapse of the American economy up to that time. Twenty percent of the workforce was unemployed. As the economy declined, Cleveland continued to champion the gold standard, despite calls by Democrats from the South and West for the unlimited coinage of silver. As the depression worsened, the threat of class warfare between conservatives and labor loomed. In 1894, Jacob S. Coxey, a businessman from Ohio led a march on Washington. Hundreds of the unemployed, joined by many Populists, petitioned the government for a public-works program and cheap money. They received nothing, and the marchers were arrested, not for disturbing the peace, but for walking on the grass.

Election of 1896

The Democrats were divided in 1896 between pro-gold Democrats, loyal to Cleveland, and pro-silver Democrats, who had no official leader. At the Democratic convention, William Jennings Bryan, the thirty-six-year-old "boy orator" from Nebraska, won the nomination with his rousing "Cross of Gold Speech," in which he condemned the gold standard and supported the Populist platform of expanding the currency by the unlimited coinage of silver. The Populists threw their support to Bryan.

The Republicans nominated William McKinley of Ohio, who ran on a pro-business platform. Under the campaign direction of Mark Hanna, a wealthy businessman from Ohio, the Republicans promised a strong industrial economy, supported by the gold standard and a high protective tariff. Hanna convinced wealthy businessmen to support McKinley, because he argued that the unlimited coinage of silver would lead to runaway inflation. Employers in the factories scared workers by asserting that there would be layoffs if Bryan were elected president. Bryan's whirlwind campaign across the United States fell short. McKinley carried all of the Northeast and the upper Midwest. Bryan carried the South and much of the West. McKinley won 51 percent of the popular vote and a decisive electoral majority, 271 to 176.

Following are results of the election of 1896:

- The Populist Party declined and soon ceased to be a national party. It would later merge with the Democratic Party.

- Bryan's campaign showed that it was impossible to win elections by appealing primarily to rural voters.

- The two major parties adopted two major parts of the Populists' platform, the graduated income tax and direct election of senators.

- The election represented the victory of the urban-middle class America, and big business, over agrarian interests.

- It guaranteed that America would continue its march into the twentieth century as an industrial nation.

Review

7-1)   The main difference dividing Republicans and Democrats between the 1870s and 1890s was their beliefs about

   A) the size of the government
   B) the role of the government in the economy
   C) currency issues
   D) civil rights for African Americans
   E) patronage

7-2) Which of the following was the major reason behind the Massacre at Wounded Knee in 1890?

A) U.S. Army retaliation for Custer's defeat at Little Big Horn

B) Indian rejection of the Dawes Severalty Act

C) Chief Joseph's Nez Perce Tribe's refusal to remain on the reservation in Wounded Knee, South Dakota

D) internal tribal disputes between Sitting Bull and Red Cloud, forcing the Army to intervene on the reservations

E) the refusal of Native Americans to abandon the Ghost Dance

7-3) The Populist leader who encouraged farmers to raise "less wheat and more hell" was

A) James Weaver

B) Mary Ellen Lease

C) William Jennings Bryan

D) Ben Pitchfork Tillman

E) Thomas Watson

7-4) The most radical of the American labor unions that began organizing workers in response to industrialization was the

A) Knights of Labor

B) American Federation of Labor (AFL)

C) International Ladies Garment Workers Union (ILGWU)

D) Industrial Workers of the World (IWW)

E) Congress of Industrial Organization (CIO)

Review Chapter 8:
Imperialism and Progressivism

B y the 1890s, many American leaders began to have a new attitude towards imperialism. They justified it with some of the following arguments and ideas:

- Alfred T. Mahan's *The Influence of Sea Power upon History* (1890) argued that U.S. security, and the nation's global status, depended on a strong navy, which was necessary to protect Asia and Latin America from its European rivals. Mahan's book had a strong influence on Theodore Roosevelt, who promoted an aggressive foreign policy.

- Josiah Strong, a Protestant minister, argued in his book *Our Country* (1885) that God selected the Anglo-Saxon race to civilize the less-developed regions of the world. Thus it was the duty of the civilized Christian world, represented by the United States, to spread "civilization" globally.

- Business leaders believed that with the closing of the frontier, the United States needed to expand beyond its borders to insure its continued industrial growth. In the 1890s, American minorities living in Hawaii had petitioned Congress for annexation, and were instrumental in overthrowing Hawaiian Queen Liliuokalani and seizing control of the government. Hawaii would eventually be annexed in 1898, during the Spanish-American War.

Spanish-American War (1898)

In 1898, Americans who were pushing for greater international involvement got their wish with the outbreak of the Spanish-American War.

- In 1895, Cuba revolted against Spain and their brutal treatment of the Cubans. The United States supported the independence movement.

- The United States had more than fifty million dollars invested in Cuban sugar plantations, and the war was hurting these financial interests.

- New York City newspaper publishers William Randolph Hearst and Joseph Pulitzer used headlines and dramatic pictures to sensationalize stories of atrocities in Cuba by the Spanish. These accounts were highly exaggerated, but they aroused sympathy and increased circulation.

- In a controversial letter published in American newspapers, the Spanish minister, De Lome, criticized President McKinley for being weak and ineffective. Although he resigned, the damage was done.

"Remember the *Maine*"

On February 15, 1898, a week after the De Lome letter was published, a massive explosion blew up the battleship *U.S.S. Maine*, anchored in Havana harbor, and killed 250 American sailors. Although there was no evidence that the Spanish were involved, the yellow press blamed them, and the slogan "Remember the *Maine*" became a popular cry. The constant barrage of the yellow press pressured Congress and McKinley to declare war.

On April 11, 1898, McKinley requested a declaration of war, which was approved by Congress. Congress also passed the Teller Amendment, which guaranteed Cuba its independence once Spain was defeated.

"Splendid Little War"

The Spanish-American War lasted only four months. The United States fought on two fronts, in the Caribbean and the Pacific.

Cuba: A troop of U.S. volunteers known as the Rough Riders led a successful charge up San Juan Hill, outside the city of Santiago. They were led by Theodore Roosevelt, the former assistant secretary of the Navy. After just a few weeks of fighting on land and sea, Cuba fell.

Philippines: Roosevelt, without McKinley's knowledge, ordered Commodore George Dewey to seize the Spanish-controlled Philippine Islands in Asia. Within two months, Dewey had captured the islands.

Results: The terms of the **Treaty of Paris,** signed in December 1898, were:

- Spain recognized Cuba's independence.

- The United States acquired Puerto Rico in the Caribbean and Guam in the Pacific.

- Spain sold the Philippines to the United States for $20 million.

The United States honored the Teller Amendment and withdrew from Cuba in 1901. However, the Cubans agreed to the Platt Amendment, which allowed the United States to maintain a permanent military base in the country and the right to intervene in order to preserve order.

The United States would intervene in Cuba in 1906, 1909, and 1917.

The Debate over the Philippines

How could the United States square its role as an imperial power with its belief in democracy and liberty?

Anti-Imperialist Arguments: The Anti-Imperialist league—formed by Mark Twain, William Jennings Bryan, and Andrew Carnegie—argued that taking possession of the Philippines violated democratic principles and would involve the United States in the affairs of Asia.

Imperialist Arguments: Americans like Theodore Roosevelt argued that the acquisition of the Philippine Islands, as well as Guam and Hawaii, was necessary to insure that the United States would become a major power. Religious leaders claimed that the United States needed to acquire the Islands because they needed to bring Christianity to the Filipinos. McKinley even claimed to have benefited from divine guidance in deciding to keep the islands. He also noted that he wanted to insure that they didn't fall into the hands of other foreign powers such as Germany or Russia. In February 1898, the Senate approved the treaty giving the United States control of the Philippines. However, Filipino rebels, led by Emilio Aguinaldo, opposed U.S. control. It took the United States three years to suppress them, resulting in the loss of more than forty-five hundred American lives and about two hundred thousand Filipino rebel deaths.

Imperialism remained a big issue in the election of 1900. The Republicans re-nominated McKinley, and the war hero Theodore Roosevelt as his vice president. The Democrats again nominated William Jennings Bryan, who ran on a platform that emphasized anti-imperialism and free silver. Riding the crest of popular support for the war, McKinley received nearly twice as many electoral votes as Bryan. The nation had signaled its approval of imperialism.

Significance of the Spanish-American War

With possessions in the Caribbean and in the Pacific, the United States had become a world power. The strategic and economic necessity of a canal connecting the Atlantic and Pacific Oceans became obvious. Construction on the Panama Canal, which made international shipping much easier and dramatically reduced the length of trips between the East and West coasts of the United States, began in 1904.

European powers began to realize that the United States was a rising power that would play a significant role in international affairs. In 1899 and 1900, Secretary of State John Hay forced European nations to accept the Open Door Policy, which guaranteed that all nations would have equal trading privileges in China. It both maintained China's territorial integrity, and protected U.S. commercial interests. The Open Door

Policy became the cornerstone of United States foreign policy toward China for many years.

Roosevelt's Big Stick Policy

Roosevelt became president in 1901, after McKinley was assassinated. He was determined that the United States would carry out an aggressive foreign policy that advanced the nation's position as a world power. His motto was "Speak softly but carry a big stick," which meant that he would act decisively in promoting America's national interests.

Building the Panama Canal

Roosevelt was determined to build a canal across the Isthmus of Panama (which was a part of Colombia), but Colombia refused to agree to terms to build the canal. In 1903, with the backing of U.S. naval forces stationed in the region to prevent Colombian troops from crossing the Isthmus, Panama revolted against Colombia. Within a few hours, the United States recognized the new government. Its first act was to sign the **Hay-Bunau-Varilla Treaty** of 1904, granting the United States the right to build a canal. Colombia protested, but to no effect. The canal was completed in 1914.

The Roosevelt Corollary

Roosevelt applied the "big stick policy" to Latin American nations in debt to European countries. Roosevelt feared that European countries would use the debt problem as an excuse to colonize Latin America. In 1904, he announced to Congress that the United States had the right to intervene in Latin American countries. The United States would collect the debts and pass the money on to the European countries. This became known as the Roosevelt Corollary to the Monroe Doctrine. It meant that the United States had become a major power in Latin America. Within the next twenty years, the policy would be used to justify sending troops to Haiti, Nicaragua, the Dominican Republic, and Honduras. This intervention would sour U.S. relations in Latin America throughout the twentieth century.

Ironically, Roosevelt would win the Nobel Peace Prize in 1904 for trying to negotiate a peace treaty between Russia and Japan at the end of the Russo-Japanese War. In this instance, Roosevelt saw the role of the United States as maintaining the balance of power in Asia among the different nations.

William Howard Taft, Roosevelt's successor, continued his policy of intervention in the form of **dollar diplomacy.** Supporting "dollars over bullets," Taft believed that the United States would gain allies and stability in Latin America by investing American dollars in the region. His policy failed, and Taft was forced to intervene in a number of Latin American countries to protect American investments.

Woodrow Wilson, the next president, was forced to intervene in Haiti and Nicaragua. By 1917 Latin America had become an American sphere of influence, and the United States had assumed a prominent place on the international stage.

Progressivism

As the role of the United States expanded in the 1890s, there was rising consensus that the conditions created by the nation's industrialization required a greater intervention by the government to make democracy effective once again. Progressivism was a movement that began in the 1890s and sought to attack the political and social inequalities of the age. Some influential books attacked the evils of industrialization:

- Henry George, *Progress and Poverty* (1879), proposed a single tax on property as a solution to poverty.

- In Edward Bellamy's novel *Looking Backward* (1888), the hero of the novel looks backward from 2000 and finds a society in which injustices have disappeared, and a cooperative spirit between workers and employers has replaced the ruthlessness of capitalism.

- Henry Lloyd's *Wealth Against Commonwealth* (1894) attacked the monopolistic practices of the Standard Oil Company and the railroads.

Unifying Themes of Progressivism

- Progressives were largely urban middle-class people who believed the government could be used to regulate big business and protect workers. They were reformers, not revolutionaries.

- Progressives believed that they could improve society by eliminating corruption in politics at the local, state, and national level. These efforts included the initiative, which would allow citizens to propose new laws; the recall, which allowed voters to remove elected officials from office before the end of their term in office; direct primaries, which allowed voters, not political bosses, to select candidates for office; and the direct election of U.S. senators by voters, not state legislatures. The latter idea was written into law by the Seventeenth Amendment to the Constitution in 1913.

- Protestant preachers in the 1880s and 1890s preached the cause of social justice, and they applied Christian principles to social problems. This "Social Gospel" inspired many middle-class reformers, or progressives, to get involved in improving society.

Intellectual and Cultural Progressive Leaders

Muckrakers were writers who exposed the abuses of society and helped spark social change and social legislation, such as in the following works:

Jacob Riis wrote *How the Other Half Lives* (1890), which discusses the poor conditions of tenement life and uses photographs to expose these conditions.

Lincoln Steffens wrote *Shame of the Cities* (1902), which describes the corruption of big-city politics.

Ida Tarbell wrote *History of the Standard Oil Company* (1904), which targets the corrupt practices of John D. Rockefeller's Standard Oil Company.

Upton Sinclair wrote *The Jungle* (1906), which describes the unsanitary and unhealthy working conditions of the meat-packing industry.

Frank Norris wrote *The Octopus* (1901), which exposes corrupt politicians who conspired with the railroads to exploit California farmers.

Local Community Leaders

These leaders sought to improve the health and welfare of the poor in urban conditions and tried to limit child labor. They are as follows:

Lillian Wald started the Henry Street Settlement in New York to help the poor.

Jane Addams began the Hull House Settlements in Chicago to help immigrants.

Florence Kelley began the National Consumer League and fought for strong anti-sweatshop laws against child labor. She helped set up the first U.S. Children's Bureau in 1912.

Municipal/State Reforms

Political leaders fought for public ownership of utilities and improved working conditions for the poor. On the state level, political leaders fought for control of the railroads and expansion of democracy. They are as follows:

Samuel Golden Rule Jones, of Toledo, Ohio (1897–1904), fought for the public ownership of utilities, built new parks, established eight-hour days and minimum wage laws for city employees.

Robert La Follette of Wisconsin (1901–1906), became a model for Progressive leaders. His ideas included direct primaries, tax reform, regulation of railroad rates, and limits on campaign expenditures.

Progressivism on the Federal Level

Republican Theodore Roosevelt's Square Deal sought to regulate big business, protect the consumer, end the worst abuses of labor, and protect and preserve the environment.

Its achievements included

- prosecuting the Northern Securities Railroad Company in 1902

- intervening in the Anthracite Coal Strike in 1902 to help miners gain higher wages

- passing the Meat Inspection Act of 1906

- passing the Pure Food & Drug Act of 1906, which provided for federal regulation of medicine and food

- passing the Hepburn Act of 1906, which gave the Interstate Commerce Commission the power to control railroad rates

- establishing a system of parks to conserve and protect the environment, under the authority of the U.S. Forest Service

Republican William Howard Taft, called the "Second Trust Buster," followed Roosevelt and served one term, from 1909 to 1913. Though not as dynamic as his predecessor, he busted even more trusts than Roosevelt and was his hand-picked successor. Still, he never gained the trust of the progressive members of the Republican Party, and he was weakened by several political conflicts:

- Taft's support for the Payne Aldrich Tariff of 1909, which raised rates on many products, angered progressives.

- Ballinger Pinchot, head of the Forest Service and friend of Roosevelt, opposed Secretary of the Interior Richard Ballinger's decision to sell public land in Alaska to private developers. Taft fired Pinchot for his opposition.

- Theodore Roosevelt grew disgruntled with Taft's performance and formed the Bull Moose Party in 1912 to run against him in the 1912 presidential election.

In the election of 1912, all the candidates—Roosevelt, Taft, and the Democrat, Woodrow Wilson—claimed to be progressive. Taft and Roosevelt split the Republican vote, allowing Wilson, who received only

42 percent of the popular vote, to win the election. Eugene Debs, the Socialist Party candidate, won nearly a million votes.

Woodrow Wilson's political program was called the **New Freedom**, and it included a lower tariff, reform of the banking system, and breaking up big businesses rather than regulating them, as Roosevelt had proposed under his New Nationalism program. Key accomplishments of the New Freedom included:

- The Underwood Tariff (1913), which lowered protective tariffs

- The Federal Reserve Act (1913), which established twelve regional Federal Reserve Banks and provided for greater government control of the economy

- The Clayton Anti-Trust Act (1914), which outlawed certain unfair business practices

- The Federal Trade Commission (1914), which regulated businesses by investigating unfair practices

- The Adams on Eight-Hour Act (1916), which established eight-hour work days with overtime pay for railroad workers

Legacy of the Progressive Movement

Women

Women played a major role in the Progressive movement. Besides being the main force behind the creation of settlement houses, they fought for child-labor laws and reforms in the workplace. Women also kept up pressure on political leaders for the right to vote, and they finally persuaded Wilson to support women's suffrage. In 1920, women's right to vote became law, guaranteed by the Nineteenth Amendment.

Immigrants

The Progressive movement was largely anti-immigrant. Although President Wilson opposed literacy tests for voters, most progressives agreed on the need to restrict immigrants from southeastern Europe.

Theodore Roosevelt opposed cultural pluralism that recognized the individual differences of immigrants from southern and eastern Europe.

African Americans

Many black leaders were disappointed with the progressives. Although Roosevelt met with Booker T. Washington at the White House, he did little to help blacks and failed to speak out against the lynchings that were common in the early twentieth century. Though a political progressive, Wilson allowed segregation to exist in federal buildings in Washington.

Review

8-1) Whether they will or no American must now look outward... Three things are needful: First protection of the chief harbors... Secondly, naval force...which alone encourages a country to extend its influence outward.

The above passages express the ideas of

A) Alfred T. Mahan
B) Josiah Strong
C) Albert J. Beveridge
D) William McKinley
E) Theodore Roosevelt

8-2) Which of the following was NOT contained in the Treaty of Paris, which ended the Spanish-American War?

A) The United States annexed Hawaii.
B) Spain gave up all rights to Cuba and recognized its independence.
C) The United States gained control of Puerto Rico.
D) Spain surrendered the island of Guam to the United States
E) The United States acquired Philippine Islands for $20 million.

8-3) The author whose book exposed conditions within the meat-packing industry was

A) Upton Sinclair

B) Frank Norris

C) Lincoln Steffens

D) Ida Tarbell

E) Henry Demarest Lloyd

8-4) In which way did the Progressive movement have the greatest effect on the women's movement?

A) establishment of better working conditions after the Triangle Shirtwaist Factory fire

B) passage of the Nineteenth Amendment

C) eight-hour workday for all women in federal positions

D) creation of state counseling centers to address domestic violence

E) federal government grants to promote more opportunities in higher education

Review Chapter 9:
World War I

On June 28, 1914, the assassination of Archduke Franz Ferdinand, the heir to the Austrian-Hungarian Empire, sparked a chain of events that led to **World War I**. Increasing nationalism, an arms race between Germany and England, widespread imperialism and a competition for colonies, and entangling alliances contributed to the outbreak of a wide-scale war that affected the entire European continent by the end of August. Europe was divided into two camps: the Allied powers (England, France, Italy, and Russia) and the Central powers (Germany, Austro-Hungary, and the Ottoman Empire).

American Neutrality

The outbreak of the war shocked many Americans, and they were glad that the Atlantic Ocean separated them from the political machinations of Europe. On August 4, 1914, President Woodrow Wilson issued a **Proclamation of Neutrality,** insisting that the country was nonpartisan in thought and in action. He hoped that the United States as a neutral country could mediate an end to the war in 1914 or 1915.

Difficulties of Neutrality

- **Economic Interest:** Although the United States was neutral and could trade with both sides, the British effectively blockaded all German ports, and thus most of the U.S. trade was with the British and the French. In fact the United States sold millions of dollars of materials to the Allies and extended over $3 million in credit to them. These loans sustained the Allied war effort and also aided the American economy.

- **Submarine Warfare:** German submarines challenged the British blockade. The Germans insisted that any ship that entered the war zone would be sunk on sight. This violated international law, which required any ship trying to sink another to offer safe passage to those on board before sinking it. On May 7, 1915, Americans were outraged when a German submarine sank the British passenger ship *Lusitania*. Of 139 U.S. citizens aboard, 128 died as a result of the attack. President Wilson vigorously protested Germany's unrestricted submarine warfare and continued to negotiate with the Germans to avoid war after a German submarine attacked the French ship *Sussex*, which resulted in injury to two Americans. In the Sussex Pledge of 1916, the German government promised to sink no more ships without prior warning. For the next year Germany kept its word. In the election of 1916, Democrats and Wilson campaigned on the slogan "He Kept Us Out of War" and won in a close election.

- **Ethnic Influences:** By 1914 close to 30 percent of the U.S. population consisted of first- and second-generation Americans. The sympathies of many of these immigrants were determined by their ethnicity. Many Irish Americans supported Germany because of their hatred of the British. Italian Americans gladly supported the Allies after Italy switched sides. German Americans strongly sympathized with their native homeland.

- **British Propaganda:** The British were very successful in controlling the information that Americans received about the war. They were successful in portraying the Germans as modern-day "Huns" who brutalized Belgians and anyone who tried to stop them.

- **German Actions:** In January 1917, the Germans announced plans to renounce the Sussex Pledge and resume unrestricted submarine warfare. Most historians believe that the United States was going to enter the war soon, and the Germans hoped that they could win the war before the United States officially declared war. Wilson was forced to break off diplomatic relations.

- **Zimmerman Telegram:** In February 1917, Arthur Zimmerman, German foreign minister to Mexico, proposed that Mexico ally with Germany, and in return Germany would help Mexico win back the territories (Texas, Arizona, New Mexico) it had lost in the 1840s. The British published the offer, which shocked the American public.

All of the actions above slowly pushed Americans to support the Allies.

America Enters the War

On April 2, 1917, Wilson asked Congress for a declaration of war against Germany and declared that the "world must be made safe for democracy." Wilson was willing to fight for the democracies of England, France, and Russia, the latter of which was more democratic after the overthrow of the autocratic government of Nicholas II. On April 6, Congress voted (82 to 6 in the Senate, and 373 to 50 in the House) for a declaration of war against Germany.

Mobilizing for War

The U.S. government was determined to take steps to organize the resources of the nation.

Finance: Americans were encouraged to fund the war by buying Liberty Bonds. Movie stars such as Douglas Fairbanks, Sr., and opera singer Enrico Caruso attended rallies that pushed Americans to buy these bonds. Liberty Bonds and an increase in personal and corporate taxes helped to pay for the war effort.

Industry: The War Industries Board, led by Wall Street broker Bernard Baruch, helped to coordinate all aspects of industrial production and distribution. The public was encouraged to save fuel by observing gasless Sundays and to walk on these days.

Lever Act (1917): Legislation was passed to regulate food production and consumption. Led by Herbert Hoover, head of the U.S. Food Administration, the goal was to increase production and decrease consumption. Hoover asked for voluntary cooperation in setting up wheatless Mondays and meatless Tuesdays. Daylight savings time was introduced to allow farmers more work hours of sunlight in order to produce more crops.

National War Labor Board (1918): This board, headed by former President William Howard Taft, was set up to arbitrate disputes between labor and management.

Public Opinion: The **Committee on Public Information** was created in 1917 to influence U.S. public opinion regarding American participation in World War I. It was headed by Progressive journalist George Creel. He enlisted the voluntary services of artists, writers, and movie stars, distributed newsreel posters, and supported lectures to depict the Germans as monsters who were destroying civilization. He also censored newspapers and encouraged them to write only positive things about the war effort. In their effort to promote patriotism, the committee also created distrust within society. Immigrants were considered un-American and German music, German language, and German names were banned. Frankfurters, for example, became known as hot dogs.

Civil Liberties: The **Espionage Act of 1917** called for fines and imprisonments of up to twenty years for anyone who tried to obstruct the draft. Also, the postmaster general was authorized to seize any material that was considered treasonable. The **Sedition Act of 1918** prohibited anyone from criticizing the war, the Constitution, or the government. Hundreds of people who spoke out against the war were arrested, including the socialist Eugene Debs, who was sentenced to ten years in prison for his antiwar rhetoric. In 1919, the Supreme Court, in *Schenck v. United States*, upheld the Espionage Act. Schenck, a socialist, had been arrested and jailed for mailing over fifteen hundred leaflets urging men not to report for the draft.

The Great Migration

The war provided job opportunities for African Americans. They filled factory jobs vacated by men who had enlisted or been drafted into the army. The influx or migration of African Americans from the South to the North, which had begun before the war, increased significantly because of these new job opportunities. In addition, cotton fields in the South were devastated by boll weevil infestations, and this also forced many sharecroppers to seek job opportunities in the North.

Women

For the first time, women entered the workforce to replace the men who went to war. Women also increased their efforts to gain the right of suffrage. World War I provided the final push for women's suffrage in America. After President Wilson announced that World War I was a war for democracy, women protested. Members of the National Woman's Party held up banners saying that the United States was not a democracy. On January 1918 the president acceded to the women who had been protesting at his public speeches and made a pro-suffrage speech. In 1919 Congress passed the **Nineteenth Amendment**, which gave women the right to vote.

Fighting the War

President Wilson appointed John J. Perishing as commander of the American Expeditionary Force (AEF). In 1917, some seventeen thousand troops were sent to assist the British and the French. By the summer of 1918, the arrival of more than one million U.S. soldiers helped break the stalemate on the western front. Exhausted and badly outnumbered, the Germans ultimately signed an armistice on November 11, 1918, at 11 a.m. The "war to end all wars" was over, but not before millions of lives were lost (including over one hundred thousand Americans) and four great empires were destroyed (Russian, German, Ottoman, and Austro-Hungarian). The economic cost was over $300 billion.

Woodrow Wilson and the Paris Conference

In a speech to Congress in January 1918, President Wilson outlined his goals for a peace settlement that came to be known as the **Fourteen Points**. Some of the main points were

- arms reduction
- an end to secret treaties
- free trade
- freedom of the seas
- self-determination for the territories of the Austro-Hungarian Empire
- adjustments of colonial claims
- creation of a general association of nations to guarantee political independence and territorial integrity

Wilson believed that a **League of Nations** would be the crux of the fourteen points, because it provided an international forum where disputes could be resolved through collective security.

The Treaty of Versailles

The "Big Four" nations (Italy, France, England, and the United States) dominated the peace conference that met at Versailles, a suburb of Paris, on January 12, 1919. Wilson was treated as a conquering hero when he arrived in Paris. The other members of the Big Four had suffered horrendous losses during the war and wanted a punitive peace treaty. They opposed a majority of Wilson's Fourteen Points.

On June 28, 1919, five years after the assassination of the Archduke Ferdinand, the Treaty of Versailles was signed. Wilson received only a portion of the terms for which he argued. Germany accepted full responsibility for the war and had to pay $33 billion in reparations. The treaty also divided the former Ottoman Empire in the Middle East between France and England. Wilson, however, left Paris encouraged, because the treaty established the League of Nations.

Controversy over the Treaty

Wilson had made a huge political mistake in appointing only Democrats to the peace conference delegation. He needed Republican support to get the Senate to ratify the treaty. He further erred by spending months in Paris when he should have been mobilizing public opinion for the terms of the treaty.

Reservationists led by Senator Henry Cabot Lodge (R-MA) opposed the League of Nations, but they would accept it if there were certain restrictions on America's membership in the league. Lodge wanted to ensure that Congress would have final authority before any action by the league. A group known as the **Irreconcilables** consisted of a dozen Republican senators who opposed any American participation in the league. They rejected Lodge's reservations and decided to fight. In September 1919, Wilson began a nationwide speaking tour to gain support for ratification, but on October 3, he suffered a stroke that paralyzed his left side, and he never fully recovered. He was in poor health for several months, which weakened his leadership ability.

Still, Wilson refused to compromise, even though other Democratic leaders warned him that he did not have the necessary two-thirds majority required to get Senate approval. Finally, in August 1921, after Wilson left office, the United States officially ended the war with Germany, but it never ratified the Treaty of Versailles nor did it join the League of Nations.

The Roaring Twenties: Boom and Bust

The Roaring Twenties refers to the period between the end of World War I and the economic collapse of 1929. The 1920s was a decade of economic prosperity, political conservatism, huge social changes, and massive cultural conflicts.

A Dramatic Increase in Productivity

The prosperity of the 1920s rested on technological innovations that made it possible to increase industrial output without expanding the workforce. American industries implemented Frederick W. Taylor's scientific management theories on a large scale, pouring millions of dollars into research that improved the methods of mass production. New machinery and implementation of assembly lines resulted in impressive gains in productivity. The increased use of electricity in place of steam power also significantly increased industrial production, and this increased productivity enabled workers to earn higher wages, which brought about a boom in consumer buying.

Stock Market Fever

In the 1920s American businessmen regained their status as folk heroes. Government at all levels supported the growth of big business. Buying stock became the American way, and that spirit fueled the bull market that led to record highs on Wall Street during the 1920s.

Warren G. Harding

Republican presidential candidate Warren G. Harding ran on a platform that promised a return to "normalcy," that is, the quieter time the country had known prior to World War I and the Progressive policies of Wilson. Harding ran on a platform of low taxes and a rejection of the League of Nations. Americans were disillusioned by the results of World War I and found comfort in Harding's simple appeal and old-fashioned virtues as a small-town newspaper editor. He won 60 percent of the vote and easily defeated his Democratic opponents, James Cox and Franklin D. Roosevelt.

Most historians rate Harding as one of the worst and least qualified men to be president; however, he appointed two exceptional men to his cabinet: Herbert Hoover as secretary of commerce and Andrew Mellon as secretary of the treasury. Mellon's tax plan of reducing taxes (especially for the wealthiest Americans) cemented Republican support from businesses. During Harding's three years in office, he supported big business, limited government involvement in the economy, and high protective tariffs.

Harding's presidency was dominated by corruption and scandals. He appointed many men to office who were part of the "Ohio Gang." They were mostly dishonest men who had no qualifications to hold office. Two examples of this are Albert Fall, secretary of the interior, and Attorney General Harry Daugherty. The latter had taken bribes from businessmen and bootleggers to not prosecute certain criminal suspects. The greatest outrage, however, was known as the Teapot Dome scandal. Albert Fall accepted a bribe of $325,000 to grant oil-drilling leases on public land near Teapot Dome, Wyoming. Before the scandals were fully investigated, Harding died of a stroke in August 1923.

Calvin Coolidge: A Puritan in Babylon

Vice President Calvin Coolidge became president in 1923 and was considered to be an honest politician who would restore virtue to Washington. In 1924 he was elected to the presidency. Coolidge, like Harding, believed in limited government. His philosophy was best expressed by the statement, "The business of America is business." Under his leadership, business flourished as he cut taxes and kept a close watch on the budget. He failed, however, to address economic and social issues. He ignored the economic problems faced by farmers. He vetoed the McNary-Haugen Bill, which would have allowed the government to purchase crops in order to maintain prewar prices.

The Election of 1928

Republicans nominated Herbert Hoover for the presidency when Coolidge decided not to seek reelection. Hoover ran on a platform of rugged individualism and epitomized the Republican success story of a self-made man. Democrats nominated the first Roman Catholic presidential candidate, Alfred E. Smith, the Irish American governor of New York. Smith's religion may have cost him the support of Southern Democrats, but this was a Republican decade, and the past eight years of peace and prosperity hurt Smith's chances more than religious prejudice. Smith won only eight states. In his inaugural address in March 1929, Hoover promised "a chicken in every pot" and continued prosperity. Within six months, the Great Depression would destroy the dreams of the Roaring Twenties.

The New Culture

The Census of 1920 showed that for the first time more than half of the population lived in urban areas. This transformation led to cultural changes that would affect American society and also lead to conflicts with the rural American lifestyle.

Mass Consumerism

The introduction of installment plans and buying on credit enabled millions to buy now and pay later for items that usually only the rich could have afforded. The introduction of electricity into homes led to a flood of appliances, such as vacuum cleaners, toasters, and refrigerators. Mass advertising convinced many women to purchase items that would have been considered luxuries just a generation before. Department store catalogs by Sears and Roebuck and Montgomery Ward enabled those who did not live in urban areas or near department stores to purchase these products. The advent of the radio also provided another avenue for the nation's advertisers.

Impact of the Automobile

Henry Ford was the chief figure in expanding the industry by developing a more efficient and cheaper means of production. Nowhere was mass consumerism more evident than in the automobile industry. Annual production during the 1920s rose from 2 million to about 5.5 million in 1929. By the late 1920s there was one automobile for every five Americans. The automobile industry also contributed to the growth of the petroleum, rubber, and steel industries. New service facilities such as gas stations, garages, and restaurants sprang up across the nation. Motels catered to the needs of motorists. Socially, the automobile created a mobile society that led to increased suburbanization and the breakdown of families, because cars allowed children to escape parental supervision. Of course, the automobile also brought traffic jams, injuries, and deaths on the roads. It also led to the decline of the railroad industry.

New Forms of Entertainment

In the 1920s, radio programs and movies revolutionized popular culture. The first commercial radio broadcast had an audience of a few thousand people. By 1923, millions of American households had radios. By 1930, about one-third of all homes had radios. For the first time people could tune in to NBC or CBS to listen to sports, news, and election results. The Democratic Convention of 1924 was the first to use the radio to transmit its sessions to the public.

The movie industry became a big business in the 1920s. The movie industry was transformed by the introduction of sound in *The Jazz Singer* and a new generation of movie stars such as Gary Cooper and Greta Garbo. These new forms of entertainment created a common culture and led to the rise of new popular heroes. Movie stars like Rudolph Valentino and sports heroes like Red Grange, Jim Thorpe, and Babe Ruth replaced politicians as celebrities. The most popular hero was Charles Lindbergh, who had thrilled the nation in 1927 with his nonstop flight from Long Island to Paris. "Lucky" Lindy was welcomed home by millions in a huge parade in New York City.

Emancipation of Women

The Nineteenth Amendment in 1920 enabled women to vote in every state, but many women wanted more than the right to vote. Alice Paul of the Woman's Party lobbied for equal rights and social justice. Divisions within the women's movement led to the defeat of the Equal Rights Amendment that had been proposed in 1923.

The flapper look became the symbol of the new woman. Young girls with short hair, hemlines above the knee, dangling jewelry, one-piece bathing suits, public smoking and drinking, and dancing to the beat of popular music shocked the American public. The number of actual flappers in America was small, but they frightened many people, especially in rural America, which frowned on urban America.

Culture Clash

In the 1920s, the ideals represented by urban and rural America clashed in many ways.

Prohibition

The Eighteenth Amendment, which was adopted in 1919, outlawed the sale of alcoholic beverages in the United States. The **Volstead Act** implemented the amendment. Prohibition was the result of many decades of work by the temperance movement. The campaign had been launched by Protestant fundamentalists like Carrie Nation (advocates were known as "dries") and was based on the assumption that liquor caused poverty, abuse, and broken families. In urban areas, people defied the law by going to speakeasies, where they danced, smoked, and drank liquor illegally supplied by bootleggers. Rural Americans viewed these "wets" as immoral and their lifestyle as a threat to the traditional values of American society. In large cities like New York and Chicago, bootleggers organized criminal gangs in order to evade the law. Gangsters like Al Capone used their income to expand other illegal activities and bribe police.

The experiment of prohibition divided the Democratic Party between Southern Dry fundamentalists and Wet Northern politicians. Enforcement of the law was a losing battle, and the economic downfall during the Great Depression convinced Congress to pass the Twenty-First Amendment to repeal the law.

The Scopes Trial

In 1925 John Scopes, a biology teacher in Tennessee, was arrested for violating a state law that outlawed the teaching of evolution. The American Civil Liberties Union defended him. The case focused the debate between the ideals of urban modernism and the religious fundamentalism of rural America. The case provided Christian fundamentalists with an opportunity to challenge those who questioned the teachings of the Bible about Creation. Three-time Democratic presidential candidate William Jennings Bryan was the prosecutor, and Clarence Darrow represented Scopes and poked fun at Christian fundamentalism. The Scopes Trial became the first trial in U.S. History to be broadcast to the nation. The jury found Scopes guilty, but the verdict was later overturned. The role of religion in education is still an unresolved issue in public schools today.

Nativism

The success of the Bolshevik Revolution in Russia in 1917 led to the First Red Scare (1919–20). Many Americans believed that communism would spread to the United States. When a U.S. post office found bombs addressed to prominent politicians and a bomb exploded outside the home of U.S. Attorney General A. Mitchell Palmer, there was concern that communists were trying to overthrow the government. Paranoia swept the nation and became known as the Red Scare. Palmer conducted a series of raids in November 1919, and thousands of anarchists and communists were arrested and detained. The government deported many socialists and anarchists, including several members of the New York state legislature. Palmer continued his raids despite lacking evidence of a communist plot. The Red Scare came to an end by 1921, when the public realized that there was no communist plot to overthrow the government.

The Sacco-Vanzetti Case

This case reflected the political and ethnic tensions of the 1920s. Nicola Sacco and Bartolomeo Vanzetti were two Italian immigrants who were tried and convicted of robbery and murder in Massachusetts in 1920 and sentenced to die. Many contemporaries argued that they were innocent. They felt that being poor Italian immigrant anarchists before a biased judge contributed to a guilty verdict. In 1927, after six years of international protest over the fairness of the trial, the two men were executed.

Ku Klux Klan

Unlike the original Klan that had terrorized the nation after the Civil War, the new Klan, founded in 1915 near Stone Mountain, Georgia, was as strong in the small towns of the Midwest as it was in the South. The revived Klan tried to intimidate not only African Americans but also Jews, eastern European immigrants, Catholics, radicals, and union members. By 1924 organization membership peaked at five million as it expanded into some Northern states. In its heyday, the Klan became an important force in the politics of many states. In Indiana and Oregon, both governors owed their election to the Klan's support. By 1925 the Klan began to decline in membership as the press began to reveal incidents of corruption among its top leaders.

Immigration Restrictions

Due to anxiety about the threats of foreigners to American society and the rising influx of immigrants after the war, Congress passed laws that further restricted immigration. In 1921, the Emergency Quota Act limited the number of immigrants to 3 percent of the population living in the United States based on the 1910 census. This cut the number of immigrants to about 375,000. The real blow was the **National Origins**

Act of 1924, which shifted the census date to 1890 (before the arrival of immigrants from eastern and southern Europe) and restricted immigrants to 2 percent of the foreign population in that year. By 1929 immigration was restricted to 150,000 per year, and any immigration from Asia was banned. These laws had closed the golden door of unrestricted immigration to the United States.

The Culture of Alienation

World War I not only destroyed political empires but also caused many to question the values of Western society and its emphasis on materialism and business-oriented society. Many poets and writers moved to Paris or Greenwich Village in New York. They became known as the "Lost Generation," a term coined by Gertrude Stein. Ernest Hemingway in the book *The Sun Also Rises* and F. Scott Fitzgerald in the book *The Great Gatsby* expressed dissatisfaction with American values and society. They rejected the political values and culture of the 1920s.

The Harlem Renaissance

Between 1910 and 1930 the number of African Americans in the North went from 1 million to 2.5 million. Almost 20 percent of the African American population lived in the North. Even though many African Americans improved their earnings and standard of living, many continued to endure discrimination in housing, employment, and education. By 1920, the Harlem neighborhood in New York City hosted a large African American community and became the center of African American cultural and intellectual life. Black writers and poets like Langston Hughes, James Weldon Johnson, Countee Cullen, and Zora Neale Hurston wrote about the diversity of their rich culture as well as the joy, hope, and frustration of being African American.

In a white-dominated society, jazz became the musical expression of the cultural and intellectual movement of the Harlem Renaissance. Jazz originated among African Americans in New Orleans, who then brought the music with them as they migrated to the North. The vibrant beat and self-expression of its music reflected the freedom of the 1920s as whites patronized jazz clubs in Harlem to hear the music of entertainers such as Louis Armstrong and Duke Ellington in the famous Cotton Club. Despite the popularity of jazz, African American artists continued to face discrimination and were not accepted into mainstream society.

Marcus Garvey

Marcus Garvey strongly objected to the second-class status of African Americans. Garvey was born in Jamaica and came to Harlem in 1916. He advocated that African Americans should take pride in their African heritage and experiences. In 1916 he organized the United Negro Improvement Association, which sponsored a "Back to Africa Movement," black self-sufficiency, and separatism. He argued that white Americans would never accept African Americans into society. Garvey's movement attracted about five hundred thousand members. In 1925 he was convicted of mail fraud and later deported to Jamaica in 1927, which effectively ended his influence within the African American community. Garvey's ideas, however, would reemerge in the 1960s with the rise of black pride and nationalism.

Review

9-1)   The National War Labor Board was created in 1918 to

   A) discourage union membership but encourage employers to improve working conditions

   B) establish price and wage freezes to avoid inflation

   C) encourage businesses to provide better benefits for wives of veterans

   D) prevent strikes by arbitrating disputes between labor and management

   E) encourage unions to contribute a portion of their dues to Liberty Bonds

9-2)   Frederick W. Taylor is best identified with

A) the scientific management of industry

B) Warren G. Harding's Ohio Gang

C) Franklin D. Roosevelt's Brain Trust

D) Andrew Mellon's Tax Plan

E) Herbert Hoover's Reconstruction Finance Corporation

9-3)   Which of the following candidates' campaign slogans was "a chicken in every pot and a car in every garage"?

A) Calvin Coolidge

B) Herbert Hoover

C) Warren G. Harding

D) Franklin D. Roosevelt

E) Harry Truman

9-4)   The Harlem Renaissance refers to

A) the migration of the rural African American population to large cities after World War I

B) efforts of African Americans to improve educational opportunities in the Harlem community

C) African American writers who rejected U.S. society and saw their future in Africa

D) a cultural movement of the 1920s and 1930s among African American writers and poets who expressed pride in their heritage

E) jazz musicians who supported the United Negro Improvement Association

Review Chapter 10:
The Great Depression
and the New Deal

During his campaign and inaugural address in March 1929, Herbert Hoover asserted that he saw the day when poverty would no longer exist in the United States. The stock market had continued to rise, and the prospects for the future seemed bright. On September 3, the market average reached an all-time high, but the hopes of the Roaring Twenties would come to a crashing halt within seven weeks. By the middle of October, people began to pull money out of the market. On Tuesday, October 29, 1929, the stock market collapsed. On that Black Tuesday, millions of investors panicked and sold 16.5 million shares, shattering the market. The stock market continued to decline, and by the end of December, Wall Street stocks had lost one-third of their value. The great crash would destroy the savings of millions of people who had bought stocks and would bankrupt many who had gone into debt to buy stocks.

Causes of the Great Depression

The stock market crash did not cause the Great Depression, but it triggered the economic chaos that contributed to the Great Depression which lasted from 1929 to 1940:

- **Unequal Distribution of Income:** In 1929 the top 5 percent of the population controlled 30 percent of the nation's wealth. The bottom 40 percent controlled 12 percent of the income. Despite increases in productivity, the wages of the working class had risen very little. This affected the purchasing power of millions of Americans.

- **Factory Overproduction:** Increased productivity enabled factories to produce more consumer goods. But workers whose wages were stagnant throughout the decade were unable to purchase these goods. Prices of these goods declined significantly when factories continued to produce more goods than people demanded.

- **Bad Banking Practices:** Banks had made numerous bad loans to corporations and individuals. There was no federal government regulation of banks, and many banks bought stocks on margin with their customers' savings. When the market crashed, customers lost their money because there was no federal guarantee for these deposits.

- **Agricultural Problems:** During the 1920s, farmers suffered from overproduction, low prices, and high debts. Farmers did not benefit from the prosperity of the 1920s. They borrowed from the banks to get machines to harvest more crops, but more production depressed prices and forced them to plant more next year, which continued to depress prices and drive them further into debt. Banks foreclosed on their loans to farmers, thus adding to the economic turmoil in the country.

- **Buying on Margin/Stock Market Speculation:** Throughout the 1920s, people purchased stock using borrowed funds. Investors speculated that they could use the earnings of their stocks to make a quick profit so they could repay the loans. "Buying on margin" contributed to the stock market fever. When the market crashed, these investors had no money to pay off these loans.

- **Installment Buying:** Many Americans purchased items like cars and vacuum cleaners that they could not afford. They believed that the economic boom would last forever, and advertisers convinced them that they needed the new consumer goods. When many people could no longer afford these goods, the factories began to lay off workers.

- **War Debts:** The Treaty of Versailles had stipulated that Germany would pay millions in reparations to England and France. At the same time, France and England owed millions in war loans to the United States. The United States insisted that all wartime loans be paid in full, which was difficult for England and France, because the high U.S. protective tariff reduced the sale of European goods in America. Starting in Germany, a wave of depression spread through Europe, as each country was unable to pay off its debts.

Economic Effects of the Depression

- The gross national product (total net value of goods and services) dropped from $104 billion in 1929 to $56 billion in 1933, and the national income declined more than 50 percent.

- More than 25 percent of the population was unemployed. In 1931 married women were prohibited from holding jobs as teachers.

- Bank failures increased from 550 per year in 1928 and 1929 to nearly 5,000 by 1933, with the life's savings of millions of people gone forever.

Social Effects

- Poverty and homelessness increased. Throughout the nation, homeless families lived in makeshift shacks made of scrap metal, usually on the outskirts of the cities. These villages were called Hoovervilles.

- Marriages and children were postponed until conditions improved.

- Jobless men and women sold produce on street corners in every large city.

- In the Dust Bowl (Oklahoma, Missouri, Arkansas, and Texas) farmers had to abandon their farms because of drought or dust storms. Thousands of farmers were forced to migrate to the West, especially to California, where they picked grapes to survive. John Steinbeck's novel *Grapes of Wrath* (1939) vividly depicts the struggle of these farmers.

- Attitudes of people were changed for generations. Those who lived through the Depression would insist on paying for everything on time, and they would always save for a rainy day.

Herbert Hoover and the Depression

President Hoover and most government officials believed that the depression was a normal economic down cycle and that the economy would rebound by itself. He was opposed to government intervention. He supported volunteerism by charitable organizations that would help people through the difficult times with their basic needs. Hoover insisted that the needs of the unemployed and the poor were the responsibility of local and state governments, not the federal government. He met with business leaders to plead with them not to lay off workers or reduce their wages. When these steps failed, he was forced to take more concrete actions:

- **Reconstruction Finance Corporation:** Federal funds were provided to struggling banks, railroads, and insurance companies to prevent their going into bankruptcy. Individuals were not eligible for loans. Many Americans believed that this bill only helped the wealthy at the expense of average Americans. Hoover insisted that if the government stabilized business, benefits would trickle down to everyone and bring about recovery.

- **Hawley-Smoot Tariff:** In June 1930, Hoover signed the highest import tax in U.S. History. The result was disastrous. In retaliation, Europe enacted higher tariffs against U.S. goods. The volume of trade between the United States and Europe dropped to half of its peak level. This tariff did little to help the American economy, but it contributed to further economic difficulties in Europe.

- **Federal Farm Board:** This board had been set up prior to the crash to help farmers stabilize prices. The board had the power to store surplus wheat and cotton. Unfortunately there was not enough money allocated to keep the program afloat.

As the Depression worsened there was growing anger and disenchantment about Hoover's policies. In the summer of 1932, the **Bonus Army** of seventeen thousand unemployed veterans of World War I marched into Washington, D.C. to demand the government immediately pay the bonuses due to them at a later time (1945). The veterans set up makeshift shacks on the grounds of the Capitol. Hoover ordered them to leave. When they refused, federal troops under Douglas MacArthur moved in with tanks and tear gas to break up the encampment.

The Election of 1932

The harsh treatment of the veterans and Hoover's inability to convey a sense of warmth to the people convinced Americans that he could not solve the economic crisis because he did not understand their plight. Still, the Republicans nominated Hoover for a second term. The Democrats nominated New York governor Franklin D. Roosevelt for president and John Nance Garner, Speaker of the House, for vice president. In a dramatic speech before the convention, Roosevelt promised a "new deal" for the American people, a repeal of Prohibition, aid to the unemployed, and a cut in government spending. Roosevelt won 60 percent of the votes and forty-two states compared to six states for Hoover.

Franklin D. Roosevelt and the New Deal

Between November and Inauguration Day in March 1933, the nation and the entire banking system appeared to be on the verge of collapse. Some in Congress discussed the possibility of giving Roosevelt dictatorial powers to fix the economic mess. Roosevelt's inauguration speech, in which he boldly asserted that the "only thing we have to fear is fear itself," demonstrated a sense of optimism that his New Deal could solve the problems of the Depression.

Roosevelt's New Deal program was designed to provide relief for the unemployed and recovery for businesses and the economy, as well as reform the American economic system. He surrounded himself with a group of advisors that became known as the **Brain Trust**. These advisors were mostly university professors from Columbia University, including Raymond Moley and Rexford Tugwell. Roosevelt believed in experimentation and trying new ideas to solve the problems of the Depression. Roosevelt rejected the trickle-down theory of the Republicans of rescuing the economy by primarily aiding business. Some of his advisors promoted the ideas of the economist John Maynard Keynes that the government should "prime the pump" during difficult times to create jobs and encourage investment. Keynes believed in deficit spending rather than balanced budgets. Roosevelt was always apprehensive about government spending, but he believed that the government had to play an active role in the economy.

Roosevelt effectively used the new media of the radio to promote his programs. In a series of **Fireside Chats** (radio talks to the nation), he explained to the American people his solutions for the problems. These talks were designed to instill hope in the people and faith in the government. In his first fireside chat, Roosevelt declared a bank holiday that would temporarily close the banks; the government would reopen them when they were safe. This step was aimed to instill confidence in the banks. The public responded by depositing rather than withdrawing money from the banks.

The First One Hundred Days

On March 4, 1933, Roosevelt called Congress into special session. During the following one hundred days (March 9 to June 16, 1933), Democrats controlled Congress and passed into law every request from the president that was designed to alleviate the effects of the Great Depression. These are some of the key legislation of these one hundred days:

LEGISLATION	PURPOSE
Emergency Banking Act March 1933	Reform of banking: established Federal Deposit Insurance Corporation (FDIC), insuring bank deposits and government-provided loans to banks.
Civilian Conservation Corps (CCC) March 31, 1933	Relief for the unemployed: provided young people with jobs in conservation (flood control, soil conservation).
Federal Emergency Relief Act May 12, 1933	Relief for the unemployed: under the leadership of Harry Hopkins, the government provided funds to states to aid in unemployment relief and to subsidize public works.
Agricultural Adjustment Administration (AAA) May 12, 1933	Recovery of agriculture: Government paid farmers to destroy crops as a means of limiting production and raising farm prices.
Public Works Administration (PWA) June 16, 1933	Recovery and relief: Use of federal funds to put people to work on buildings, bridges, dams, and highways.
National Industrial Recovery Act (NIRA) June 16, 1933	Recovery of business: encouraged industry to establish voluntary codes to regulate prices and production guidelines. It also recognized the right of unions to organize.

The Second New Deal

Democratic victories in the midterm election of 1934 convinced Roosevelt that he had received a mandate for more change. The First New Deal (1933 to the summer of 1935) was designed to promote relief, recovery, and reform. The Second New Deal lasted from the summer of 1935 to summer of 1938. The goal of the Second New Deal was to establish more permanent reforms in the American economy and to provide relief for the 20 percent of Americans who were still unemployed. The Second New Deal relied heavily on deficit spending to stimulate the economy. By 1935, Roosevelt reluctantly came to the conclusion that only massive government spending could help the needy. Below are some key legislation of the Second New Deal:

LEGISLATION	PURPOSE
Emergency Relief Appropriations Act (Includes Works Progress Administration) 1935	Relief for the unemployed: provided large-scale public works programs for the jobless. It employed millions who had received assistance from state and local governments.
National Labor Relations Act (NLRA/Wagner Act) 1935	Reform for labor: birth certificate of labor—confirmed the right of labor to organize collectively and join unions.
Social Security Act 1935	Reform of federal old-age pensions and unemployment insurance for those who were temporarily unemployed, funds for the disabled. One of the most lasting reforms of the New Deal.
Resettlement Administration 1935	Provided assistance to the agrarian sector of the economy, especially small farmers.
National Housing Act 1937	Federal funding for public housing and slum clearance.
Fair Labor Standards Act 1938	Federal minimum wage, forty-hour workweeks in some sectors of the economy, and outlawing of child labor.

Opposition to the New Deal

Roosevelt faced opposition from conservatives who believed that he was destroying capitalism with creeping socialism. Critics on the Left said that he did not go far enough in changing the capitalist system.

Conservative Critics: Former Democratic presidential candidate Al Smith and wealthy Republicans led the American Liberty League. They were particularly incensed by the Revenue Act of 1935, which they called a "soak the rich" tax because of the increased tax rate for those making over $50,000.

Other Critics: Dr. Francis Townsend was a retired California physician. He proposed the Old Age Revolving Pension Plan that gained popularity with a monthly stipend of two hundred dollars a month to citizens over the age of sixty. However, the people who received the money had to spend it within a month's time so as to stimulate the economy. This was the forerunner of Social Security.

Father Charles Coughlin was a Roman Catholic priest who initially supported Roosevelt but later opposed the New Deal. In his weekly radio programs, he blamed the Great Depression on the Jews who controlled the banks throughout the world. He accused Roosevelt of being a liar and under the influence of the Jewish bankers. It was estimated that he had forty million listeners at the peak of his popularity. The Catholic Church took him off the air as his remarks became increasingly anti-Semitic and for his praise of Benito Mussolini and Adolf Hitler.

As governor and senator from Louisiana, **Huey Long** represented the most serious challenge to Roosevelt's leadership. By 1934 he believed that Roosevelt was not doing enough to fight the Depression. The Kingfish, as Long was called, organized the Share Our Wealth program, which called for the federal government to provide each family a home and an annual income of two thousand dollars. There was talk of Long's running for national office in 1936, but that ended with his assassination in 1935.

The Election of 1936

The election of 1936 was referendum on the New Deal. The economy was weak, but conditions were improving. The New Deal policies of Social Security and unemployment benefits were popular with the people. Democrats renominated the Roosevelt–John Nance Garner ticket overwhelmingly. Republicans nominated Governor Al Landon, a political moderate from Kansas, who ran on an anti–New Deal platform.

Results: Political pundits predicted a close race. Roosevelt won in a lopsided victory of 61 percent of the popular vote. He also won 523 electoral votes and carried every state except Vermont and Maine.

Significance: Roosevelt's victory created a new political coalition. Democrats had always counted on the support of the Solid South.

Now, the Democratic coalition added African Americans who lived in Northern cities but until 1936 had voted Republican. In addition, the coalition included white ethnics, Midwest farmers, and workers in labor unions. Their votes would enable the Democratic Party to become the dominant party in American politics until the 1960s.

The Supreme Court and the New Deal

During Roosevelt's first term the Republican-dominated Supreme Court struck down two important pieces of New Deal legislation:

- **National Industrial Relations Act (1935):** In the "sick chicken case," the Schechter Poultry Corporation argued that industry codes established under this law gave legislative powers to the president. The Supreme Court declared the NIRA unconstitutional because it gave the president too much power, and the federal government did not have the right to control intrastate commerce.

- **Agricultural Adjustment Act (1936):** The Court ruled that Congress could not create a special tax that would benefit one sector of the economy in order to pay for the enforcement of the law. The Court also declared that AAA violated the Constitution because states, not the federal government, are responsible for agriculture.

The Court Packing Scheme

Roosevelt's landslide victory convinced him that it was time to change the Supreme Court. Without consulting the Democratic members of Congress, he proposed the Justice Reorganization Act. In 1937, critics called it the Court Packing Bill. Roosevelt proposed that he be given the power to appoint additional justices to the Court for every justice over seventy years of age. Since six of the justices were over seventy, Roosevelt would have the power to appoint six judges, which would increase the size of the Court from nine to fifteen. Roosevelt claimed that this plan would reduce the workload of the older justices.

Reaction: Roosevelt's closest supporters were shocked by this proposal. Republicans and Democrats denounced the bill as an attempt to rewrite the checks and balances system. Newspaper editorials compared Roosevelt to the dictators Hitler and Mussolini. Conservative Southern Democrats for the first time joined with Republicans to defeat a major piece of legislation in Roosevelt's presidency. Congress eventually passed a compromise bill that did not alter the size of the Supreme Court but made minor changes on the lower court level. But the political damage had been done. Roosevelt had alienated many conservative Democrats who now began to turn away from the New Deal.

Sit-Down Strikes

The Wagner Act of 1935 spurred the growth of union membership. Union membership soared from 3.4 million in 1932 to over 10 million by the beginning of 1940. During the 1930s, however, a bitter dispute broke out within the ranks of labor. Should labor focus its efforts on unionizing skilled workers according to their craft or should labor unionize all workers by industry? In 1935 **John L. Lewis** founded the Congress of Industrial Organization (CIO) to organize unskilled workers in America's mass production industry: auto, glass, rubber, and steel. In 1937, the CIO broke away from the American Federation of Labor (AFL) and became its chief rival.

The CIO organized sit-down strikes in which striking workers would simply occupy a factory and refuse to leave until their demands were met. Conservative Democrats led by Vice President Garner demanded that Roosevelt take action against the union. The president refused and asserted that it was the responsibility of the local authorities. Conservative Southern Democrats were critical of Roosevelt's hands-off approach.

Recession of 1937–38

By 1937 the economy, despite continued high unemployment, had returned to its 1929 levels. However, by the winter of 1937, the economy took a sharp downturn that lasted over a year. The decline was dubbed the Roosevelt Recession because it was partly due to government policies. Roosevelt's advisors urged spending cuts to balance the budget, which curtailed expenditures for relief and public works. In addition the newly enacted Social Security Act reduced the disposable income that workers had to spend on goods and services. The American public blamed the Democrats for the economic decline.

The Midterm Elections of 1938

The failure to address the sit-down strikes, combined with the recession, led to a reduction in the Democrats' majority in Congress in the midterm elections of 1938. By 1938 the political base of the New Deal had been weakened. A coalition of Southern Democrats and Republicans would block further New Deal reforms.

Women and the New Deal

The Great Depression put added pressure on women and family life. More and more women were forced to enter the workforce to supplement income and to feed their children. Many women received lower wages than men, and they were often accused of taking jobs away from men. In some cases they were barred from certain jobs so they would not compete with men. Women did benefit from some New Deal agencies. Roosevelt employed women in his administration, and he appointed Frances Perkins as secretary of labor, the first woman to hold a cabinet post.

African Americans and the New Deal

African Americans suffered the full impact of the Depression. They were the last to be hired and usually the first to be fired. New Deal agencies segregated blacks, and some, like the National Recovery Administration (NRA), were discriminatory. Under the industrial codes of the NRA, white workers were allowed higher wages than African Americans. Nevertheless, the New Deal did provide some opportunities, because African Americans were able to get low-paying jobs in the Public Works Administration (PWA) and the Works Progress Administration (WPA).

Roosevelt himself addressed racial abuses. He created a Black Cabinet consisting of distinguished African Americans like Robert C. Weaver and Mary Jane McLeod Bethune to informally advise him on issues affecting their community. In addition, African Americans sat as delegates for the first time at the 1936 Democratic national convention. Nevertheless, Roosevelt showed occasional indifference to the plight of African Americans. He refused to support an anti-lynching bill for fear of alienating Southern Democrats.

First Lady Eleanor Roosevelt was probably the greatest advocate for increased rights for African Americans and raised funds for the National Association for the Advancement of Colored People (NAACP).

The Roosevelts won a reputation for promoting racial justice, even though African Americans made few gains. However, their efforts convinced blacks to continue their support of the Democratic Party over the Republicans.

Native Americans and the New Deal

The New Deal provided assistance for Native Americans. In 1934, Congress passed the Indian Reorganization Act (IRA), which stipulated that instead of owning individual plots of land, tribes should stress tribal ownership and tribal authority. The IRA reversed the 1887 Dawes Severalty Act, which encouraged Native Americans to be independent farmers. New Deal programs like the CCC, PWA, and WPA did provide some relief for Native Americans, but despite these efforts and reforms, Native Americans suffered greatly during the Great Depression.

The Legacy of the New Deal

The New Deal did not end the Depression, but it provided Americans with economic security. The legacies of the New Deal include unemployment insurance, old-age pensions, and bank deposit insurance. The Wagner Act allowed workers to organize and became an integral part of the middle class. The New Deal created a shift in government philosophy. Americans accepted the idea that the federal government should play an indispensable part in solving the problems of industrial society.

As the New Deal permanently shifted attitudes toward the role of government in society, war clouds were developing in Europe during the 1930s that would drastically alter the world role of the United States.

Review

10-1) Which of the following legislation was NOT part of Roosevelt's first hundred days?

A) National Recovery Act

B) Civilian Conservation Corps

C) Public Works Administration

D) Federal Deposit Insurance Corporation

E) National Labor Relations Act

10-2) The purpose of the Reconstruction Finance Corporation was to

A) provide emergency loans for individual businesses

B) set up funds for public works programs for the unemployed

C) offer emergency loans to struggling banks, railroads, and insurance companies to prevent them from going bankrupt

D) set up farm boards that would help farmers stabilize their prices for goods and commodities

E) provide additional bonuses for veterans of World War I to stimulate the economy

10-3) The economic philosophy of John Maynard Keynes that influenced the New Deal is associated with

A) the trickle-down theory

B) balancing the budget

C) priming the pump

D) deregulating the economy

E) bloc grants to help states spur employment

10-4) One result of the Indian Reorganization Act of 1934 was

A) Native Americans became citizens

B) it restored tribal ownership of lands and recognized tribal constitutions

C) it promoted assimilation of Native Americans into society

D) technical and agricultural colleges were set up on reservations to educate Native Americans

E) it instituted religious programs for Native Americans on the reservations

Review Chapter 11:
World War II

Foreign policy in the U.S. during the 1920s was torn between isolationism and international cooperation. The United States did not retreat into isolationism but sought to cooperate with the international community to promote peace through disarmament. Various international agreements were made to limit the size of the military and resolve political disputes. The United States was particularly alarmed by the rapid growth of the Japanese navy. In 1921, President Harding convened the Washington Naval Conference in which the attendees agreed to the following treaties:

- **Five Power Naval Treaties:** The five nations with the largest number of battleships agreed to limit the size of their navy by the following ratios: United States (5), Britain (5), Japan (3), France (1.67), and Italy (1.67). The Japanese were upset because they wanted parity with their Western rivals.

- **Four Power Treaty:** The United States, Britain, Japan, and France agreed to respect each other's territorial possessions in the Pacific.

- **Nine Power Treaty:** The nine attendees (United States, Britain, Japan, France, Italy, China, Belgium, the Netherlands, and Portugal) agreed to respect the territorial integrity of China as well as the Open Door Policy.

The United States also took part in movements to outlaw future wars. In 1928, the United States signed the Kellogg-Briand Pact that outlawed war as an instrument of foreign policy. However, there was no provision for enforcement if any country violated the agreement.

U.S. Foreign Policy in the 1930s

During the Great Depression, the United States was more concerned with its problems at home than foreign problems. Many Americans became convinced that they should avoid war at all cost. **The America First Committee**, an isolationist group, had close to eight hundred thousand members by 1940. Charles Lindbergh was a supporter of the group and traveled the country to warn about the dangers of getting involved in another European war.

During the first years of the Depression, Roosevelt was unable to devote much attention to foreign policy. He was an internationalist who realized that Nazism was a threat to peace, but he understood that public opinion would not allow him to pursue a more active foreign policy. Congress, which was dominated by isolationist senators from both parties, passed a series of neutrality laws from 1935 to 1937 to keep the country out of war:

- No arms should be shipped to nations at war.

- No U.S. citizens should travel on ships belonging to belligerent nations.

- No loans or credit should be extended to belligerents.

The Outbreak of War

At the 1938 Munich Conference, England and France allowed Hitler to take the Sudetenland in Czechoslovakia, where a large number of German-speaking people lived.

By March 1939, Hitler took over all of Czechoslovakia. On September 1, 1939, German forces invaded Poland, and two days later France and England declared war on Germany. World War II had begun in Europe.

Changing U.S. Neutrality Policy

After the invasion of Poland, Roosevelt persuaded Congress to revise the neutrality laws, because he understood that it was in the nation's interest to aid England. By 1940 most Americans also realized they had to build up the country's military defenses to prepare for war. Most Americans who wanted to avoid involvement in any European war still did not want to give direct aid to Great Britain.

The **Neutrality Act of 1939** allowed the United States to ship arms and munitions to countries at war, as long as they used their own ships to carry the arms and paid cash. The law helped the United States sell military equipment to England and France because the British navy still controlled the seas. The bill passed along party lines.

The **Selective Service Act of 1940** provided for the first peacetime draft in U.S. History and the training of over one million troops. All men between the ages of twenty-one and thirty-five had to register for the draft for at least one year. Isolationists strongly opposed the bill, but public opinion was moving away from the restrictive policies of neutrality.

The **Destroyers for Bases Agreement of 1940** helped Britain defend against the crippling attacks of the German submarines. Roosevelt secretly circumvented the cash-and-carry principle. He agreed to give fifty vintage destroyers to Great Britain in exchange for the right to build military bases on British islands in the Caribbean. By 1940 the United States was neutral in name only.

The Election of 1940

Throughout 1940 there was speculation over whether Roosevelt would break the two-term tradition and run for a third term. Just before the Democratic Convention met in Chicago, he indicated that he would accept the nomination if it were offered during these critical times. Roosevelt was easily nominated.

Republicans nominated Wendell Willkie, who criticized the president for breaking the two-term tradition and for leading the country into war. Roosevelt countered by asserting to the public, "Your boys are not going to be sent into any foreign wars." Roosevelt won reelection by a smaller margin than in the previous two presidential elections. Many voted for him because the economy was recovering based on defense spending and the feeling that the country needed an experienced leader to deal with the war in Europe.

The Arsenal of Democracy

Roosevelt interpreted his electoral victory as a mandate to continue preparing for America's entry into war. He explained that the United States had to become the "Arsenal of Democracy."

The Lend-Lease Act (1941)

In March, after three months of debate and bitter criticism by the America First Committee, Congress passed the Lend-Lease Act. The president was authorized to lend or lease arms to any country he deemed vital to the defense of the United States. Britain immediately received more than seven billion dollars in aid. Later the Soviet Union would receive help when Germany invaded the country in the summer of 1941. The Lend-Lease Act was considered an economic declaration of war against Germany because the United States committed its resources to help Great Britain fight off German assaults.

The Atlantic Charter (1941)

On August 1, Roosevelt and Prime Minister Winston Churchill met at Newfoundland. The two leaders signed a document that became known as the Atlantic Charter, which formulated a statement of common war aims that were similar in some respects to Woodrow Wilson's Fourteen Points:

- self-determination for all people
- free trade
- freedom of the seas
- a world organization to replace the League of Nations
- destruction of Nazi tyranny

By the fall of 1941, Hitler clearly understood that the United States was not a neutral country. He ordered German vessels to fire on American ships. In response, Roosevelt ordered the arming of all merchant ships and later ordered American ships to shoot on sight German submarines. In effect, the United States was fighting an undeclared war against Germany.

Pearl Harbor and the Declaration of War

Throughout the 1930s Japanese aggression in China had alarmed the United States. When Japan joined the Axis Powers (Germany and Italy) in 1940, Roosevelt prohibited the sale of steel and scrap iron to Japan. In July 1941, Roosevelt froze all Japanese assets in the United States, cut off the sale of oil to Japan, and closed the Panama Canal to all Japanese ships.

Roosevelt refused to lift the embargo until Japan withdrew from China and French Indochina. Japan refused. Despite continued negotiations with the U.S. to resolve their differences, Japanese military leaders decided that a surprise attack on the American naval fleet in the Pacific might cripple U.S. forces in the Pacific long enough for Japan to achieve dominance in the region. The United States knew of the imminent attack but was uncertain of the target: the Philippines, Malaysia, or the Dutch East Indies.

On December 7, 1941, the Japanese attacked the American naval base at Pearl Harbor, Hawaii. In the attack, 2,402 Americans were killed, 21 ships were sunk or damaged, and 188 aircraft were destroyed. On December 8, Roosevelt asked for a declaration of war against Japan and asserted that December 7 was a "day that would live in infamy." Congress voted overwhelmingly for war: 470 to 1. On December 11, because of the Tripartite Pact of 1940, Germany and Italy declared war on the United States. The attack on Pearl Harbor united the American people, who put aside their differences and rallied around the war effort.

War on the Home Front

The Economy

America's success in World War II depended heavily on mobilizing the home front. The government established the War Production Board to manage the conversion of private industry to war production. In 1942 Congress authorized the Office of Price Administration (OPA) to regulate prices, and rents and ration consumer items such as gas, oil, and auto tires.

To finance the war the government had to increase spending from $9 billion in 1940 to $98 billion in 1944. To pay for this, the government increased taxes on the wealthy, and by 1944 Americans for the first time had income tax automatically deducted from their paychecks. The government also sold war bonds to raise money.

Women

World War II, like World War I, changed the lives of women. Over two hundred thousand women served in the armed forces, but not in combat units. As men were called into uniform, the popular poster of "Rosie the Riveter" was used to recruit women to enter the labor market. About six million women entered the labor force during the war. Women participated in every aspect of the war industries, from making military clothing to building fighter aircraft.

African Americans

The war generally improved the economic position of African Americans. The northern migration of African Americans from the agricultural South continued as the availability of good-paying jobs in the defense industry increased, but they still faced discrimination. In 1941, A. Philip Randolph, head of the Brotherhood of Sleeping Car Porters, announced a March on Washington to protest against contractors who discriminated against African Americans in hiring and kept a segregated labor force. To avoid a racial confrontation, Roosevelt created the Fair Employment

Practices Commission, which banned discrimination in hiring. The War Labor Board outlawed unequal pay to whites and nonwhites. While discrimination was not eliminated in the workforce, twice as many African Americans held skilled jobs at the end of the war than at the beginning.

The large-scale migration of African Americans and other minorities from rural to urban areas created tensions in working-class ethnic neighborhoods. Many of these residents were reluctant to compete with African Americans and other minorities for jobs and housing. There were race riots in New York, Detroit, and several other cities across the country that resulted in the loss of lives. In Los Angeles, the so-called Zoot Suit Riots in the summer of 1943 led to conflicts between whites and Mexican Americans.

Civil rights organizations like the NAACP organized the Double V campaign, which stood for victory over fascism and victory for equality at home. Membership in the NAACP increased during the war, and the Congress of Racial Equality (CORE) was formed in 1942 to promote equality at home.

African American soldiers likewise faced prejudice. Roosevelt led the stand against segregation in the armed forces. Over one million African Americans served in the armed forces, but a majority of them were relegated to inferior jobs. Some, like the Tuskegee Airmen, served in combat and became decorated heroes.

Japanese Internment

After the attack on Pearl Harbor, hysteria swept the West Coast against people of Japanese descent. In February 1942 Roosevelt signed **Executive Order 9066**, which directed the relocation and internment of American citizens in areas the military deemed sensitive. The government rounded up 130,000 people of Japanese descent living in California and forced them to sell all their possessions and live in barbed-wire compounds, called internment camps or relocation centers. Japanese Americans living in other parts of the United States, including Hawaii, did not fall under this order. Most of the

Japanese were released before the war ended, but those suspected of disloyalty were kept in these centers until the end of the war. In 1944, the Supreme Court decided in *Korematsu v. U.S.* that the internment camps were legal because of the military necessity of the war. In 1988, the U.S. government issued a formal apology for these actions.

During the first year of war, thousands of Italian Americans along the West Coast were forced to relocate. These restrictions on Italians ended when Italy switched sides in 1943. The Italian population in the Northeast, especially the munitions producing centers in Bridgeport and New Haven, Connecticut, faced no restrictions.

Propaganda War

The government used every means at its disposal to ensure that people sacrificed and supported the war effort. Communities were encouraged to plant victory gardens in order to grow their own food. Others were encouraged to collect scrap metal, old tires, and newspapers for recycling that would help the war effort. Entertainers promoted patriotism, such as Kate Smith's rendition of "God Bless America." The Office of War Information controlled the information that the public received about the war. Everyone was encouraged to do their part to defeat the enemy.

Election of 1944

It was expected that Roosevelt would run for a fourth term. The only question was the vice presidential slot on the ticket. Roosevelt, under pressure from Democratic leaders, dropped Henry Wallace of Iowa because they thought he was too radical and picked Harry S. Truman of Missouri. Truman had gained a national reputation for his investigation of fraud in the defense industry. Although Roosevelt denied any medical problems, historians believe that the party leaders picked Truman because they were fearful that Roosevelt would not survive another term and believed Truman was better qualified for the presidency.

Republicans nominated Thomas Dewey of New York, who had gained a reputation for prosecuting corruption and racketeering. Roosevelt won the election, but he died less than four months after his inauguration.

War in Europe

Although the Japanese had attacked the United States at Pearl Harbor, Winston Churchill convinced Roosevelt that the focus of the war should be to defeat Germany first and then concentrate on Japan. One of the major turning points of the war in Europe was Hitler's decision in June 1941 to break his nonaggression pact with the Soviet Union and launch an invasion of the Soviet Union. Hitler's failure to conquer the Soviet Union drained Germany's resources and meant that Germany, as it had in World War I, had to fight a two-front war. Hitler now faced three formidable enemies: the United States, Great Britain, and the Soviet Union.

Turnings Points of the War in Europe

- **The Battle of Stalingrad:** After a six-month siege of Stalingrad, from August 1942 to February 1943, the German army surrendered. Stalingrad was a turning point in the war because the Soviets struck a crushing blow to Hitler's war machine and seized large quantities of German military equipment as well as men.

- **Invasion of North Africa and Sicily:** In November 1942, Americans under General Dwight D. Eisenhower were involved in the fighting in North Africa. They joined forces with the British to force the surrender of the German Afrika Corps. From this North African base, British and American troops invaded Sicily in July 1943 and then the Italian mainland. After eighteen months of bitter fighting, Rome was liberated in June 1944.

- **Invasion of Normandy:** On June 6, 1944 (D-Day), Eisenhower directed the Allied forces of Great Britain, Canada, and the United States in the liberation of France. The D-Day invasion was the largest amphibious (sea to land) assault in history. By crossing the English Channel, the Allies achieved the objective of securing several beachheads on the Normandy coast in northern France. Paris was liberated in August. Allied troops then pushed eastward toward Germany.

- **Battle of the Bulge:** In December 1944 the Germans launched a desperate counterattack in Belgium. Nearly nineteen thousand Americans were killed, but the Allies regrouped and continued to push into Germany.

- **Germany Surrenders:** In the spring of 1945 Allied troops advanced through central Germany. Soviet forces began the battle of Berlin on April 20, and on April 25 American troops linked with advancing Soviet troops at the Elbe River. On April 30, Hitler committed suicide rather than be captured by Soviet troops. Germany officially surrendered on May 8, 1945 (V-E Day). The war in Europe had ended.

The Holocaust

As the Allies advanced across Germany, they encountered remnants of concentration camps that were part of **Hitler's Final Solution** of the "Jewish Problem," the murder of every Jew in Europe. Allied troops were horrified and outraged at what they saw in these camps and the extent of the Nazi genocide program. The world was shocked to learn that the Nazis had either systematically murdered or worked to death over six million Jews. The Nazi's genocide policy also claimed the lives of millions of other ethnic groups, invalids, homosexuals, and political and religious opponents.

The War in the Pacific

The war in the Pacific was fought primarily by U.S. naval and ground forces. By 1942 the Japanese had extended their power over much of East and Southeast Asia.

Turning Points of the War in the Pacific

• **Battle of the Coral Sea (May 7–8, 1942):** U.S. aircraft carriers thwarted the Japanese invasion of Australia.

• **Battle of Midway (June 4–7, 1942):** A U.S. carrier fleet destroyed four Japanese carriers and three hundred planes and prevented an invasion of Hawaii. The battles of the Coral Sea and Midway established American naval superiority in the Pacific.

• **Battle of Guadalcanal (August 1942–February 1943):** Under the leadership of General Douglas MacArthur, U.S. marines defeated the Japanese after seven months of vicious combat across the island. This was the first campaign in the strategy of island hopping. The goal was to capture strategic Japanese-held islands and bypass others. These islands would serve as a springboard for an invasion of Japan and enable American aircraft to attack Japanese cities. By late 1944 American bombers were able to reach Japan's major cities.

• **Battle of Leyte Gulf (October 1944):** The Japanese navy was virtually destroyed during this battle. In desperation, the Japanese unleashed for the first time kamikaze pilots to make suicide attacks on U.S. ships.

• **Battle of Okinawa (April–June 1945):** American forces defeated the Japanese but suffered fifty thousand casualties. After this battle, U.S. forces had a clear path to invade Japan.

The Atomic Bomb

Fearful that Germany was developing an atomic weapon, Roosevelt had secretly directed the United States to develop its own nuclear weapon. In 1942, Robert Oppenheimer was named director of the Manhattan Project to develop an atomic bomb. More than one hundred thousand people worked on the project for two and a half years. On July 16, 1945, the atomic bomb was successfully tested at Alamogordo, New Mexico. President Harry Truman, who succeeded Roosevelt after his death, issued an ultimatum to the Japanese that if they did not surrender unconditionally by August 3 they would face utter destruction. When Japan refused to surrender, Truman ordered the military deployment of the bomb. On August 6, 1945, a U.S. bomber dropped an atomic bomb on Hiroshima, and on August 9 an atomic bomb was dropped on Nagasaki. These bombings resulted in the deaths of more than 250,000 people. On August 15 Japan announced its surrender. On September 2, 1945 (V-J Day), the Japanese officially surrendered.

Wartime Conferences (1943–45)

From 1943 to 1945 the Big Three (the United States, Great Britain, and the Soviet Union) met to discuss military strategies and how to prepare for the postwar world:

Casablanca Conference (1943)

Leaders: Churchill, Roosevelt

Results: They agreed (1) to launch an invasion of Italy and (2) to accept nothing less than the unconditional surrender of Germany.

Teheran Conference (December 1943)

Leaders: Stalin, Churchill, Roosevelt (first time the three leaders met together)

Results: (1) The United States and Great Britain agreed to open a second front to liberate France in 1944, (2) all three agreed to the creation of international peace organizations, and (3) Stalin agreed to enter the war against Japan after Germany was defeated.

Yalta Conference (February 1945)

Leaders: Roosevelt, Stalin, Churchill

Results: Leaders (1) agreed that Germany would be divided into four zones of occupation after the war, (2) free elections would be held in the liberated countries of Eastern Europe which were then occupied by Soviet troops, (3) the Soviets would declare war against Japan ninety days after the defeat of Germany which they did on August 8, 1945, just a few weeks before Japan surrendered, and (4) the Soviet Union would receive territories they had lost to Japan in the 1904–5 Russo-Japanese War.

The Yalta Conference would be a major source of controversy because many believed that Stalin took advantage of a gravely ill Roosevelt, who handed over the countries of Eastern Europe to Stalin, who had no intention of holding free elections.

Potsdam Conference (July–August 1945)

Leaders: Clement Attlee, Stalin, and Truman

Results: Leaders (1) agreed to issue a warning to Japan to surrender, (2) hold war crimes trials for Nazi leaders, and (3) Truman demanded that Stalin allow free elections in Eastern Europe. Stalin refused Truman's demand, which created postwar tensions between the two countries.

Impact of the War

- Human losses were staggering. U.S. losses included 416,800 killed in action and more than 800,000 wounded.

- The war cost the United States over $296 billion.

- The United States endorsed the plan for the establishment of the United Nations. Unlike the debate over the ratification of the League of Nations after World War I, the Senate ratified the charter of the United Nations in July 1945, and the United States became a charter member of the organization.

- The United States and the Soviet Union emerged as the world's two superpowers.

- Conflicting ideologies between democracy and communism and mutual distrust between the two nations laid the foundation for the

Cold War. The Cold War would influence the world for the next forty-five years.

Review

11-1) The goal of the Manhattan Project was to

A) devise war strategies that would open up a second front against Germany in Europe

B) establish the foundation for the United Nations

C) develop an atomic bomb

D) plan for the invasion of Japan in 1945

E) work with the International Court of Justice to ensure that Nazi war criminals were brought to trial

11-2) Which of the following statements describes the Double V campaign during World War II?

A) a legal assistance program to provide aid to children of Japanese Americans in internment camps

B) a program established by the State Department to help Jewish refugees from Eastern Europe

C) the U.S. Defense Department's promise to ban discrimination in hiring

D) a government program to ensure that people sacrificed and supported the war effort

E) a program organized by civil rights organizations

11-3) At which wartime meeting did the Big Three agree to open a second front against Germany?

A) Casablanca

B) Teheran

C) Yalta

D) Dumbarton Oaks

E) Potsdam

11-4) The agreement signed by the United States that prohibited the use of war as "an instrument of national policy" was known as the

A) Kellogg-Briand Pact

B) Four Power Treaty

C) Nine Power Treaty

D) Washington Disarmament Conference

E) Four Freedoms

Review Chapter 12:
From Truman's Fair Deal to
Johnson's Great Society

Postwar America

The first major task after World War II was the demobilization of the armed forces. Between 1945 and 1947, over ten million U.S. troops returned to civilian life and looked for jobs. Many Americans were fearful that there would be no jobs for these men. However, pent-up consumer demands for automobiles and housing, combined with government spending, contributed to a period of prosperity and economic growth.

GI Bill

To help American soldiers (or GIs, the nickname for U.S. troops in World War II), Congress passed the Servicemen's Readjustment Act, which was known as the GI Bill of Rights. Under this bill, veterans were entitled to free hospital care, educational loans to attend college, and low-interest loans to buy homes, farms, or start a business. The GI Bill of Rights impacted veterans as well as higher education. About eight million veterans took advantage of the opportunity to continue their education at the government's expense. The government's focus on education and housing was a major contributor to the postwar economic boom of the 1950s.

Baby Boom

Returning GIs married and started families, resulting in a substantial increase in births following World War II. Americans who were born between 1945 and 1960 and came of age in the midst of the Cold War became known as baby boomers. There were about sixty-two million babies added to the U.S. population during these years, representing an almost 20 percent increase, the largest since the height of immigration at the turn of the century. This population explosion had a profound effect on the social, economic, and political life of the country for the next forty years.

Suburbanization

Veterans' benefits, including government loans, enabled Americans to find suitable housing in tracts of land on the outskirts of the cities. A postwar suburban housing boom began in planned communities such as towns named Levittown in New York, Pennsylvania, and New Jersey. These mass-produced homes, which were offered at low interest rates and modest prices, made the move from the city to the suburbs affordable for middle-class Americans. By the beginning of the 1960s, this massive movement from the inner cities to the suburbs had a major impact on the economies of urban areas. The "white flight" also made the inner cities poorer and racially segregated.

Inflation and Strikes

Congress rejected President Truman's request that wartime price controls continue in order to hold down inflation. Consumers were in a buying mood, and prices increased by almost 15 percent in just one year. Labor unions went on numerous strikes to get higher wages to keep up with inflation. By 1946, nearly two million workers went on strike. Truman, who was usually supportive of labor, ordered soldiers to operate the coal mines when the United Mine Workers refused to work.

Conflict with the Republican Congress

Unhappy with inflation and numerous strikes, Americans elected Republican majorities to Congress in 1946. The Eightieth Congress battled with the Democratic president. In 1947, over the veto of President Truman, Congress enacted the Taft-Hartley Act to limit the powers of labor unions. The bill limited labor practices such as boycotts, sympathy strikes, and closed shops. The bill also gave the president the right to call for a cooling-off period for workers in industries that involved national security. Union leaders were also required to swear that they were not communists.

Results: The Taft-Hartley Act ended the pro-labor legislation of the New Deal. For years, unions fought unsuccessfully to repeal the law. It became a major issue between Democrats and Republicans in the 1950s and 1960s.

The Election of 1948

The Republicans were sure that they would win the White House after a sixteen-year hiatus and nominated Thomas Dewey of New York, who was expected to win easily. Truman's popularity was at its lowest. His civil rights policy had alienated the Southern wing of the Democratic Party. Despite their opposition, he desegregated the federal government and the armed forces and appointed black judges. He also asked Congress to create the Fair Employment Practices Commission, which would prevent employers from discriminating against hiring African Americans. Congress refused to enact this legislation.

Southern Democrats left the party and supported **Strom Thurmond** of the States' Rights Party, better known as the **Dixiecrats**. The liberal wing of the Democratic Party believed that Truman took a tough stance on foreign policy toward the Soviets. They joined the Progressive Party and nominated **Henry A. Wallace**, Roosevelt's vice president in 1940.

Results: Dewey ran a very cautious and lackluster campaign because he expected to win easily. Truman campaigned vigorously against the "do-nothing" Republican Congress, and his "give 'em hell" speeches resonated with the public. In a stunning upset victory, Truman received more than one hundred more electoral votes than Dewey (303–189) and a two million majority of the popular vote.

The Fair Deal

In his 1949 inaugural address, Truman asked for a "fair deal" for the American people. He urged Congress to pass laws for federal aid to education, national health insurance, civil rights for African Americans, and funds for public housing. Congress rejected most of the Fair Deal's proposals except for an increase in the minimum wage from 40 to 75 cents an hour and an extension of Social Security benefits to cover ten million more people. The opposition of conservative Democrats and Republicans and the deepening problems created by the Cold War contributed to the defeat of Truman's major efforts at reform.

The Cold War Begins

The grand alliance of Great Britain, the Soviet Union, and the United States began to unravel before the end of the war. At the Yalta and Potsdam conferences, the Soviet Union disagreed over the status of the liberated countries in eastern and central Europe. Roosevelt had naively hoped that he could use personal diplomacy to work with Stalin. Truman took a harder stand toward the Soviets, and this approach led to tension between the two countries. Thus by 1947 the United States found itself in a Cold War with the Soviet Union. The rivalry between these two superpowers was based on conflicting ideologies and mutual distrust. The United States was a democratic capitalist country and the Soviet Union was a totalitarian communist state.

The Iron Curtain

Stalin had promised to hold free elections in the postwar countries of eastern Europe. Between 1946 and 1948, all of these countries—including Poland, Romania, Bulgaria, Hungary, Albania, and Czechoslovakia—fell under communist control. These countries became satellites of the Soviet Union. The United States became fearful of the spread of communism. In 1946, Winston Churchill, with Truman on the dais at Fulton, Missouri, declared that an iron curtain had descended across the European continent as the Soviets attempted to spread their power. The iron curtain became a symbol of the fear of communist power and helped to convince many Americans that the United States needed to get involved to prevent the further spread of communism.

Containment

By 1946, Truman was determined to follow a get-tough policy with the Soviets. In July 1947, George Kennan, an American diplomat and specialist in Soviet affairs, stated in an anonymous article in *Foreign Affairs* that the Soviet Union needed to expand because it felt threatened by the United States. Kennan recommended that the United States adopt a policy of containment to stop the spread of communism. This policy would allow the United States to defeat the Soviet Union without directly confronting it on the battlefield. This policy became the basis of American foreign policy for the next forty years. Truman implemented containment in the following instances:

- The **Truman Doctrine (1947)** was the opening shot in the Cold War. The United States pledged to assist all free peoples who were fighting communists or armed revolutionaries. Greece and Turkey received $400 million in aid. The United States wanted to prevent these countries from becoming victims of communism. The Truman Doctrine gained bipartisan support in Congress, and these countries did not become communist.

- The **Marshall Plan (1947):** World War II left Europe in ruins, and the United States believed that these countries could fall under the influence of communism. Secretary of State George C. Marshall offered over $13 billion in aid to Western countries and lessened the dangers of communism. The hope was also that Europe would spend much of its money to achieve recovery and also help the American economy by buying American goods.

• The **Berlin Airlift (1948–1949)** was the first major crisis of the Cold War. At the end of World War II, Germany was divided into four zones of occupation. In June 1948, the Soviet Union cut off Western access to Berlin. Truman rejected any use of force as well as any plans to withdraw from Berlin. He ordered U.S. planes to fly supplies of food, clothing, and other goods into West Berlin. The Berlin Airlift lasted for almost a year, and in 1949 the Soviet Union lifted the blockade.

• The **North Atlantic Treaty Organization (NATO) (1949):** Buoyed by the success of the Berlin Airlift and fearful of the threat of the Soviet Union to the security of Western Europe, the United States, Canada, and ten Western nations formed the North Atlantic Treaty Organization, a defensive alliance. An attack on one country would be considered an attack on all the member countries. NATO put the United States squarely in the center of Europe for the foreseeable future. When Germany became a member of NATO in 1955, the Soviet Union formed its own military alliance, the Warsaw Pact, consisting of seven satellite nations in Eastern Europe.

Cold War in Asia

China: Since 1945, the United States had provided economic and military aid to the Nationalists forces of Chiang Kai-Shek. In 1949, Mao Tse-tung defeated the Nationalist forces and captured Peking (Beijing). He established the People's Republic of China, and Chiang was forced to flee to Formosa (Taiwan), an island off the Chinese coast. There were now two Chinas, and Chiang claimed that his was the only legitimate Chinese government. The United States refused to recognize Mao's communist government until 1979. However, the United States provided financial aid to the Nationalists throughout these years.

The Cold War escalated in 1949. The Soviets tested their first atomic bomb, which ended the U.S. nuclear monopoly, and the world's largest population embraced communism. Republicans accused the Truman administration of losing China because he had not given an ally enough aid and because the Democrats were "soft on communism."

The Korean War

At the end World War II, Korea was divided at the thirty-eighth parallel between the Soviet-backed government in the north and the U.S.-backed government of Syngman Rhee in the south.

On June 25, 1950, North Korea invaded South Korea. Truman took immediate action, applying the doctrine of containment to Asia. He ordered troops from occupied Japan to help the South Korean troops. He was able to get the support of the United Nations for his decision because the Soviet Union was boycotting the UN Security Council over the Taiwan Chinese membership of the council rather than the People's Republic of China. The majority of the UN forces were made up of U.S. troops under the leadership of General Douglas MacArthur. The initial stages of the war went badly, as the North Koreans pushed the combined South Korean and American forces to the tip of the peninsula.

Counterattack: In September, MacArthur devised a surprise amphibious attack at Inchon, behind the North Korean lines. This maneuver pushed the North Koreans back toward the Chinese border. MacArthur ignored the warning that the Chinese would intervene if their security were threatened. In November, a half million Chinese troops crossed the border into North Korea and overwhelmed UN forces and drove them back across the thirty-eighth parallel.

The Firing of MacArthur: During the heavy fighting, MacArthur was insistent that China should be directly attacked, but Truman refused to give permission in favor of a political solution. MacArthur was outraged and began to convey his ideas to congressional leaders and to publicly campaign for bombing the Chinese mainland. He criticized Truman for not using nuclear weapons in Korea or China. Truman cautioned MacArthur not to make public statements that were critical of official U.S. policy. The general disobeyed his orders, and Truman fired him.

MacArthur returned to the United States as a hero. Despite MacArthur's popularity, most Americans supported Truman's policy of avoiding a full-scale war with China.

Stalemate: By the summer of 1951, the war became stalemated at the thirty-eighth parallel. Negotiations began that summer and dragged on until 1953. Dwight D. Eisenhower fulfilled his campaign pledge of ending the war in Korea if he were elected president. The armistice signed in 1953 established the thirty-eighth parallel as the line between the opposing forces, which was the same boundary that had existed before the war.

Aftermath: Truman achieved his goal of containing communism in Korea. He was able to limit aggression without involving the Soviet Union and China in a full-scale war. Unfortunately, fifty-four thousand American lives were lost. Politically, the stalemate enabled Republicans to reinforce the image that the Democrats were soft on communism.

The Cold War at Home: The Second Red Scare

The loss of China in 1949, the iron curtain in Eastern Europe, and the stalemate in Korea convinced Americans that the Soviet Union was winning the Cold War. Some people suspected that communist spies within the United States had infiltrated American institutions from the government to the entertainment industry and were helping the Soviet Union. The fear of communism created the **Second Red Scare**. Political leaders, President Truman, and later President Eisenhower would use the fear of communism as a political tool to rid the United States of perceived threats to national security. The following cases contributed to the fear of the growing communist influence in the country:

- The espionage trial of **Julius and Ethel Rosenberg** in 1951: After a controversial trial, the Rosenbergs were convicted of passing atomic secrets to the Soviet Union. They were executed in 1953 despite worldwide appeals on their behalf from the pope to Albert Einstein.

- The **Alger Hiss** case: Hiss was a prominent State Department official who had assisted Roosevelt at the Yalta Conference. In 1948 Hiss denied charges that he was a communist and had given secrets to them. He was convicted of perjury and sent to prison. This reinforced the belief among many Americans that the communists had spies at the highest level of government.

Government Action and the Red Scare

- **Loyalty Oaths:** When Republicans began to criticize the Truman administration of being soft on communism and reports appeared in newspapers about Canadian government workers who had been given secrets about the atomic bomb, the president ordered the creation of a Loyalty Review Board. The board's job was to investigate the background of federal employees and to remove any worker who had connections to any communist organizations. Between 1947 and 1951 over three million government workers were investigated, and about two hundred lost their jobs for security reasons.

- **House Un-American Activities:** During the 1940s a special committee of the House of Representatives, the House Un-American Activities Committee, began to investigate communists in the government and in the entertainment industry. The committee investigated State Department officials like Alger Hiss as well as communist influence in such organizations as the Boy Scouts and in Hollywood films.

- **McCarran Internal Security Act (1950):** This law required all communists or communist front organizations to register with the attorney general and prohibited the employment of communists in defense organizations.

- **McCarran Walters Act (1952):** This law limited immigrants from eastern and southern Europe and empowered the attorney general to deport any aliens considered to be subversive. Congress passed both bills over President Truman's veto.

McCarthyism

Republican Senator Joseph McCarthy of Wisconsin was the most effective politician to use the fear of subversion and communist influence to help him gain reelection and national prominence. On February 9, 1950, at Wheeling, West Virginia, McCarthy gave a speech in which he claimed that 205 known communists worked for the State Department. McCarthy skillfully played on the anticommunist fears and suspicions of Americans. He held public hearings between 1950 and 1954 in which public officials, scholars, and military officers were charged with being communists. McCarthyism refers to making ruthless accusations of people's disloyalty or treason without any real proof. Republicans were skeptical of many of McCarthy's charges and disliked his tactics, but they realized that he was primarily hurting Democrats and that he was helping Republicans gain political support as the patriotic party that was fighting communism.

Reaction: By 1954, McCarthy had crossed the lines of acceptability. He accused the U.S. Army of containing communists. In a series of televised hearings between April and June 1954, over twenty million people saw McCarthy for the first time. He was exposed as a bully who made reckless and unsubstantiated charges to intimidate people. Public opinion turned against him. In December 1954, Senate Democrats and Republicans voted to censure McCarthy.

The Eisenhower Years, 1953–1961

President Dwight David Eisenhower dominated the political landscape of the 1950s. Eisenhower was a national hero of World War II, president of Columbia University, and commander of NATO. In 1952 he ran as a Republican and easily defeated Adlai Stevenson of Illinois. His campaign slogan "Time for a Change" was popular with the people who were tired of two decades of Democratic leadership. Millions of middle-class Americans trusted and admired the former military leader popularly known as Ike. After four years of peace and prosperity, he would defeat Stevenson again by an even larger margin in 1956. Ike's victory, however, was more of a personal triumph, since both houses of Congress remained Democratic.

Domestic Agenda

Eisenhower was a fiscal conservative whose priority was balancing the budget while retaining many New Deal programs. His policies, known as moderate Republicanism, included

- raising the minimum wage from 75 cents an hour to one dollar

- increasing Social Security benefits for retired people to include state and local government employees and farmers

- funding a public works program that included the interstate highway system

- Creating a new cabinet-level department: the Department of Health, Education and Welfare. He chose a woman, Oveta Culp Hobby, to head the new department.

- Approving the National Defense Education Act (1958), which appropriated $1 billion in education in response to the Soviets' success in placing the first satellite into orbit. The act also provided financial aid to college students and matching funds for states to improve instruction in science, math, and language arts.

The Civil Rights Movement

The economic prosperity of the 1950s did not have a major impact on many African Americans. "Jim Crow" laws that denied them equal rights still existed in the South. African Americans in the 1950s were still prevented from voting by literacy tests and poll taxes, and most of them were poorly educated. President Eisenhower expressed little interest in civil rights. In 1954, the landmark decision of *Brown v. Board of Education*, which integrated public schools, was a turning point for African Americans.

The origins of the civil rights movement can be traced to the following:

- World II veterans who had fought in Europe and Asia for freedom were angry that their civil rights were still ignored at home. In the context of the Cold War, how could the United States stand as the bastion for freedom in Asia and Africa when they denied civil rights to African Americans?

- Breakthroughs in higher education: African American enrollment in colleges began to increase after World II. This led to an increased growth of an African American middle class that provided support for the civil rights movement.

- Breakthroughs in sports: In 1947 Jackie Robinson broke the color line in baseball and became the first African American to play in the Major Leagues. Truman's decision to integrate the armed forces was another indication that race relations were slowly changing in postwar America.

Brown v. Board of Education: The NAACP had for decades tried to overturn *Plessy v. Ferguson*, which allowed "separate but equal facilities." Aided by a team of NAACP lawyers led by Thurgood Marshall, Oliver Brown from Topeka, Kansas, sued the Topeka school district because his daughter Linda could not attend an all-white school close to his home and had to take a bus to an all-black school across town.

In May 1954, the Supreme Court under the leadership of Chief Justice Earl Warren unanimously overturned the *Plessy v. Ferguson* decision. The Court ruled that "separate but equal" was unconstitutional and that segregation in schools should end with "all deliberate speed."

Resistance in the South: Many Southern whites, especially in the Deep South, opposed the Supreme Court decision and even temporarily closed schools. In 1957, Arkansas governor Orville Faubus posted the National Guard outside Little Rock Central High School to keep a group of nine African American students from entering the school. President Eisenhower sent U.S. soldiers to protect the safety of the "Little Rock

Nine." Although Eisenhower did not support the *Brown* decision, he realized that it was his constitutional responsibility to uphold federal authority. His decision demonstrated that the federal government would support desegregation.

Protests in the South: Besides schools, African Americans began to challenge other municipal laws that promoted segregation.

Montgomery Bus Boycott: In December 1955, Rosa Parks, an African American resident of Montgomery, Alabama, refused to give up her seat on a bus to a white person and sit in the back, which was reserved for African Americans. She was arrested. Parks's arrest sparked a massive boycott by the African American community against riding the bus. Dr. Martin Luther King, Jr., who was a Baptist minister where the boycott took place, successfully rallied the religious community behind a nonviolent boycott of the Montgomery bus system. Montgomery city officials agreed to desegregate the bus system in 1956, after the Supreme Court ruled that segregated bus laws were unconstitutional. The boycott and King's nonviolent leadership helped the civil rights movement gain national support.

Civil Rights Legislation: The Civil Rights Act of 1957 provided for a permanent Civil Rights Commission to investigate any illegal activities that prevented African Americans from voting. The Civil Rights Act of 1960 made these abuses a federal crime. These two civil rights acts signed by President Eisenhower were the first civil rights laws passed since Reconstruction. The laws, however, were weak and failed to provide real protection for African American voters. Still, they prepared the way for the stronger civil rights legislation of the 1960s.

Eisenhower and the Cold War: Massive Retaliation

During the 1952 campaign, Eisenhower advocated a more aggressive foreign policy. He selected John Foster Dulles as his secretary of state. Dulles had been critical of Truman's policy of containment. He believed that communism was a moral evil that needed to be rolled back and that Eastern Europe should be liberated. His diplomatic strategy was based on brinkmanship and massive retaliation. He believed that the Soviet Union would back down if brought to the brink of war and that it would be best for the United States to build up a strong nuclear arsenal to deter the Soviets from ever challenging the United States.

Unrest in the Third World

Covert Actions: Eisenhower's New Look foreign policy also relied on covert operations by the Central Intelligence Agency (CIA) to prevent communists from taking power in strategic countries. In 1953 the CIA helped to overthrow an elected government that allowed the return of the Shah (king) to Iran. He returned the favor by providing cheap oil to the West. In 1954 in Guatemala the CIA helped topple a democratically elected government and replaced it with a pro-U.S. military regime. This added to the frustration of South Americans toward the United States. In late 1960, after Fidel Castro came to power in Cuba, the United States planned an invasion of the island.

Vietnam

At the end of World War II, the French tried unsuccessfully to hold on to their empire in Southeast Asia. In 1954, Ho Chi Minh, the pro-communist leader of Vietnam, defeated the French at Dien Bien Phu and declared independence from France. Eisenhower had provided aid to the French, but he refused to commit U.S. troops to an Asian conflict. The Geneva Convention of 1954 divided the country into North Vietnam (controlled by Ho Chi Minh) and South Vietnam (which was anti-communist). From 1955 to 1961 the United States provided millions in economic and military aid to South Vietnam to build a stable government. Eisenhower supported the Domino Theory because he thought that if South Vietnam fell under communism, all of Southeast Asia would also fall. Vietnam would be a persistent problem for the United States during the 1960s.

The Middle East

At the end of World War II, the United Nations voted to divide Palestine into the Jewish state of Israel and a new Palestinian state for Arabs, and in 1948 the United States and the Soviet Union recognized the independence of these two nations. The Arab nations of the Middle East, however, refused to recognize the right of the State of Israel to exist and fought unsuccessfully to prevent the formation of the State of Israel. Ever since then, U.S. policy in the Middle East has walked a tightrope between support for Israel and friendly ties with the oil-rich Arab states.

The Suez Crisis

In 1956, Egyptian president Gamal Abdel Nasser decided to nationalize the mostly French- and British-owned Suez Canal, and use the revenue to build the Aswan Dam on the Nile River.

Seeking to regain control of the canal, which controlled the flow of oil to Western Europe, Great Britain, France, and Israel carried out a joint attack against Egypt without U.S. approval.

Eisenhower condemned the attack and was fearful that the Soviet Union would enter the war to support Egypt. As a result of U.S. pressure, the invading forces withdrew and UN forces moved in to keep the peace. The United States became the leading Western influence in the area. In 1957 Eisenhower defined the Eisenhower Doctrine, which promised U.S. military assistance to any Middle Eastern nation that requested aid to fight communism. In 1958 the United States would send troops to help Lebanon deal with a communist threat.

U.S.–Soviet Relations

The Spirit of Geneva: After Stalin's death in 1953, there was a sense that both the Soviet Union and the United States would reduce tensions. In 1955, in a desire to improve relations, Eisenhower met with the Soviets at Geneva and called for "open skies" over each other's territories in order to eliminate the fear of a surprise attack. The Soviets rejected this proposal, but the spirit of Geneva did reduce tension between the two countries. In 1956, the new Soviet leader, Nikita Khrushchev, attacked Stalin's cult of personality and called for peaceful coexistence between the two countries. He initiated a "thaw" in the Cold War. In 1959 the Soviet premier visited the United States and appeared on American television. Tensions seemed to be diminishing.

Uprising in Poland and Hungary: The anti-Stalin campaign led to revolts in Poland and Hungary. In 1956, the Soviets managed to calm the situation in Poland, but in October 1956, a poplar uprising in Hungary led to the overthrow of the government and the demand that Soviet troops leave the country. Khrushchev sent tanks into the country, and the Hungarian revolt was crushed. Eisenhower sympathized with the Hungarian freedom fighters, but he wanted to avoid a European war. He did not want to interfere in the Soviet "sphere of influence" in Eastern Europe. Eisenhower's decision ended Dulles's hope of liberating the countries behind the iron curtain.

Sputnik and the Space Race: In 1957 the Soviet Union launched an artificial satellite into orbit around the earth. It was a shock to the American people and the U.S. government. The United States feared it was losing its technological superiority over the Soviets. There was a fear that these Sputnik satellites might be used to carry nuclear weapons that could attack the United States. Soon the United States began to commit millions of dollars to compete with the Soviets in the race for space. They also began to train human astronauts for orbital missions around the earth. The goal was to beat the Soviets in space.

The U-2 Incident: The hope that Cold War tensions were diminishing ended quickly in June 1960. Prior to the Paris Summit Conference, the Soviet Union shot down a U.S. U-2 spy plane inside Soviet territory. Soviet leader Khrushchev charged that the plane was spying on his country. At first Eisenhower denied this was true, and then later accepted responsibility for the flights, but refused to apology. As a result, Khrushchev cancelled the summit, and the Cold War tensions increased.

American Society in the 1950s

The postwar economic boom gave rise to a consumer culture that encouraged social conformity. The middle class move to the suburbs and the growing influence of television contributed to a homogeneous society.

Role of Television: Television was the new consumer item of the 1950s that profoundly influenced society. By 1953 television had become the center of American life. Almost one-half of American households had a television in their home. The majority of the shows were westerns, situation comedies, quiz shows, or professional sports. Most of America watched the same shows, like *Father Knows Best, The Adventures of Ozzie and Harriet*, and *I Love Lucy*, which reinforced the social mores of the decade.

Advertising: Television advertising also influenced the tastes and habits of the public. Because of aggressive advertising, the people who watched similar shows also bought the same name-brand products in appliances and consumer goods. Advertising promoted the need for common wants, which contributed to the consumer culture. The introduction of suburban shopping malls and credit cards reflected the need to satisfy all a person's wants.

Social Critics: The conformity of American life in the suburbs was carried over into corporate America. By the 1950s more Americans had white-collar jobs than industrial or blue-collar jobs. Most of these new jobs were in industries such as advertising, finance, food processing, and insurance. Large corporations promoted conformity in dress (white shirt and tie) and behavior and encouraged teamwork as the way to achieve success.

In 1956 William Whyte wrote *The Organization Man*, which criticized American business for its lack of innovation. He argued that the corporate culture's stress on conformity was stifling the country's enterprising spirit.

Emergence of a Youth Counterculture: During the 1950s most young people accepted the traditional values of society and became known as the Silent Generation. The birth of rock and roll music gave these teenagers a separate identity but also frightened older Americans. They were critical of its fast tempo and loud music. Teen idol Elvis Presley was condemned as immoral for his music and behavior. Teenagers also adored movie stars like James Dean and Marlon Brando, who portrayed rebellious youths who rejected the core values of American society of the decade.

Rebellious writers, known as Beats (short for Beatnick), attacked the materialism of American society. Some major works of the Beat writings were Allen Ginsberg's poem *Howl* (1956) and Jack Kerouac's book *On the Road* (1957). These writers encouraged spontaneity, experimentation with drugs, and rebellion against the traditional norms of society. The Beat Generation would influence the youth movement in the 1960s.

The Kennedy Presidency

In 1960 the Republicans nominated Richard M. Nixon, Eisenhower's vice president, and Democrats chose Senator John F. Kennedy of Massachusetts. Many thought that Nixon's experience and tough campaign style would defeat Kennedy, who lacked national exposure and experience. The medium of television directly influenced the outcome of this election. A series of four televised debates, the first such debates in campaign history, convinced many Americans that Kennedy appeared more self-assured and confident than the "tired and pale Nixon." As the first Roman Catholic to run for president since 1928, religion became important in the campaign. Kennedy addressed the issue before a group of Protestant ministers, but undoubtedly Kennedy's religion benefited him in the large cities and helped Nixon in Protestant rural America.

The election of 1960 was one of the closest in U.S. History. Kennedy defeated Nixon by only 112,000 votes out of 34 million that were cast.

The New Frontier

Kennedy's election was greeted with excitement and enthusiasm. At the age of forty-three, he was the youngest man to be elected president. He projected a vigorous image, and his attractive and glamorous wife, Jacqueline, only added to that image. The media dubbed the new administration the new Camelot. His inaugural address contained the memorable phrase, "Ask not what your country can do for you; ask what you can do for your country," which appealed to the idealism of America's youth.

Kennedy's New Frontier domestic program included proposals for federal aid to education, greater Social Security benefits, and protection of African American civil rights. His program languished in Congress because conservative Southern Democrats and Republicans joined together to defeat most of his program. One of his successes, however, was a bill that increased the minimum wage to $1.25 an hour.

Foreign Affairs

Kennedy sought to change foreign policy by combining realism with idealism. He moved away from Eisenhower's policy of massive retaliation and adopted the doctrine of "flexible response," which was developed by Defense Secretary Robert McNamara. The focus was to spend more on conventional non-nuclear forces and special forces like the Green Berets to fight insurgents in Southeast Asia and Africa. In his tilt toward idealism in 1961, Kennedy set up the Peace Corps, which recruited young volunteers to go to third-world countries to provide technical aid.

He also proposed the Alliance for Progress. Under this program the United States gave more than $20 billion in aid and promoted land reforms in Latin American countries, except Cuba, as a way to contain communism in the hemisphere. Some foreign problems Kennedy faced follow:

- **The Bay of Pigs Invasion (1961):** When Kennedy became president in 1961, he continued to support the CIA-planned invasion of Cuba to overthrow Fidel Castro's communist government. In April 1961, fifteen hundred Cuban exiles launched an invasion on the southern coast of Cuba at the Bay of Pigs. The forces were easily defeated because Castro's forces were waiting for them and Kennedy rejected using American air power to rescue the exiled forces. The Bay of Pigs was a great embarrassment for the newly elected president.

- **The Berlin Crisis (1961):** In 1961 Soviet premier Khrushchev, who had warned Kennedy at a meeting in Vienna to get U.S. troops out of West Berlin, supported the construction of a wall between West and East Berlin. The Berlin Wall blocked East Germans from fleeing into West Germany. Kennedy called up reserve troops but made no effort to tear down the wall. The Berlin Wall quickly became a symbol of the Cold War until East Germans tore it down in 1989.

- **The Cuban Missile Crisis (1962):** In October, U.S. spy planes detected the presence of ballistic missiles in Cuba. Kennedy ordered a blockade of Cuba to intercept Soviet ships that might be carrying additional missiles to Cuba. In a message to Khrushchev, Kennedy indicated that he would use force if the Soviets decided to challenge the blockade. The world was on the verge of war. Finally, Khrushchev ordered the ships to turn around and later removed the missiles from Cuba in exchange for Kennedy's promise not to invade Cuba. The thirteen days in October (October 14–27) were the greatest challenge to peace in the Cold War, and the missile crisis is considered the greatest success of Kennedy's presidency. One of the aftereffects of this crisis was the establishment of a hotline so that superpower leaders could speak directly to each other during a crisis. In addition, the two countries agreed to the first arms control agreement when they signed the Nuclear Test Ban Treaty, which limited the testing of nuclear weapons.

The Assassination

On November 22, 1963, in Dallas, Texas, America's "Camelot" came to a tragic end. Lee Harvey Oswald assassinated Kennedy. The reports of the president's death stunned Americans and sent the nation into mourning. The nation and many countries in the world were glued to their televisions and even saw Jack Ruby, a Dallas nightclub owner, kill the alleged assassin as Oswald was being transported from police headquarters to the county jail.

The assassination of Oswald fueled the belief that the president's murder involved a conspiracy. An investigation headed by Chief Justice Earl Warren concluded that Oswald was the lone assassin. Many believe, however, that the Warren Commission left a number of questions unanswered. Movies, books, and individual researchers have continued to foster the idea that there was a conspiracy to assassinate the president and more than one person was involved in the assassination.

The Great Society of Lyndon Johnson

Lyndon Johnson took over the presidency at a traumatic time in the nation's history. Johnson was a great admirer of Franklin D. Roosevelt's New Deal and had spent over thirty years in Washington and was familiar with how Congress operated. His folksy Southern style differed sharply from the sophisticated Harvard-educated Kennedy. However, he was committed to pushing Kennedy's social programs through Congress. Johnson was determined to extend the reforms of the New Deal to improve the equality of lives for millions in America.

Great Society: In 1962, Michael Harrington's book *The Other America* exposed most Americans for the first time to the number of poor and homeless living in the nation. In January 1964, in his State of the Union address, Johnson pledged that he wanted to build a great society by waging a war on poverty. Johnson claimed that a country as prosperous as the United States should be able to eliminate poverty. Congress gave the president everything that he wanted to set up the Great Society.

The Economic Opportunity Act (1964): This act provided $1 billion for the war on poverty. The Job Corps was created to provide vocational training and educational programs for underprivileged youth. It also set up Head Start, a program for disadvantaged preschoolers.

The Election of 1964: Johnson and his running mate, Senator Hubert Humphrey of Minnesota, ran on a liberal platform against the conservative Republican Barry Goldwater of Arizona. Goldwater denounced the Great Society and the welfare state and was depicted in television ads as a dangerous militarist who would use nuclear weapons to solve international problems, especially in Vietnam. Johnson won by a landslide. He received over 61 percent of the popular vote, even more than Roosevelt had ever polled. In addition, the Democrats increased their majorities in Congress. Johnson interpreted this victory as a mandate to implement laws that would fulfill the dreams of the Great Society.

Great Society Reforms

During 1965 and 1966, Johnson persuaded Congress to pass a series of laws and programs that would have a lasting impact on all areas of American life.

- The **Elementary and Secondary Education Act** provided extensive aid to public and parochial schools, especially to poor school districts.

- **Medicare** provided health insurance for the elderly.

- **Medicaid** offered federally funded health insurance for the poor.

- The **Immigration Act of 1965** eliminated the national quota system established in 1920. This change greatly increased the number of immigrants from Asia and Latin America.

- Two cabinet-level agencies were created: the **Department of Housing and Urban Development** (HUD), which was led by Robert Weaver, the nation's first black cabinet secretary, and the **Department of Transportation** (DOT), which was led by Alan Stephenson Boyd.

- The **Appalachian Development Act** set aside $1 billion for aid to the poverty-stricken Appalachian mountain region.

Significance of the Great Society

The Great Society provided needed assistance to many Americans who had been left out of the economic prosperity of the 1950, especially the poor, disabled, and elderly. Unfortunately, America was frustrated when the War on Poverty had only limited success in ending the plight of the needy. Yet the number of people living in poverty fell by 35 percent due to Great Society programs. By 1965, however, the Vietnam War would divert money from the War on Poverty and would contribute to the end of Johnson's Great Society.

The Growth of the Civil Rights Movement

By the beginning of the 1960s, the civil rights movement was already a force for change. A majority of the groups sought to end segregation in American life. The more radical groups stressed Black Pride or Black Power.

Moderate Civil Rights Groups

NAME	GOALS
Student Nonviolent Coordinating Committee (SNCC)	Included young Black students and Northern college students Organized sit-ins and other peaceful demonstrations Wanted the immediate end of the Jim Crow laws in restaurants in the early 1960s
Congress of Racial Equality (CORE)	Under the leadership of James Farmer began protests known as Freedom Rides Sought to integrate interstate traveling facilities, such as bus stations and waiting rooms Many activists experienced violence as they rode through the South
National Association for the Advancement of Colored People (NAACP)	Oldest civil rights organization Focused on winning racial justice by arguing cases in court New groups like SNCC and CORE thought the NAACP was too conservative
Southern Christian Leadership Conference (SCLC)	Founded by Dr. Martin Luther King, Jr., in 1957 Coordinated anti-desegregation efforts of African Americans in the South Used nonviolent methods such as boycotts and sit-ins and marches to achieve social justice King would dominate the civil rights movement

Radical Groups

In the mid-1960s, the civil rights movement split as some leaders claimed that a nonviolent approach was not effective in promoting change for African Americans.

Nation of Islam: Malcolm X became the most famous spokesman for the group. The goal of the Nation of Islam was the separation of the races and a separate state for African Americans in the United States. Malcolm X had a large following in Northern cities. He was assassinated in Harlem in 1965.

Black Power: The idea of black nationalism appealed to young African Americans. Stokely Carmichael, a SNCC leader, began to preach about black power, which was similar to many of the ideas supported by Malcolm X. Carmichael advocated that African Americans seek their independence from corrupt white society.

Black Panthers: Organized in 1966 in San Francisco by Huey Newton and Bobby Seale, they advocated the use of force to achieve black power and pride and claimed "violence was as American as apple pie." They encouraged schools to teach African American History and culture. Their violent reputation damaged their image and organization, however.

Kennedy and Civil Rights

The election of Kennedy in 1960 created hope in the African American community that he would help in the struggle to end segregation. The closeness of the election results and the fear that he would antagonize white voters made him reluctant to aggressively press the issue of civil rights. However, civil rights groups like CORE and SNCC forced Kennedy to deal with the sit-ins and Freedom Rides in 1961. The president ordered his brother, Attorney General Robert F. Kennedy, to end segregation on all interstate bus travel.

In 1962 Kennedy was forced to send in federal troops to quell the violence when **James Meredith** tried to attend the University of Mississippi as its first African American student. Two people were killed in the violence and 188 were injured, including 28 marshals. Under the protection of the federal government, Meredith attended classes.

In 1963, Martin Luther King led nonviolent protests against the segregation laws of **Birmingham, Alabama**. City officials attacked marchers with dogs and turned fire hoses on the crowd. King and his supporters were arrested and jailed. Television brought the confrontation to a national audience. Kennedy for the first time publicly raised the issue of civil rights to a moral issue, and it moved him to support a strong civil rights bill.

In August 1963, King and other civil rights organizations led a **March on Washington** of close to two hundred thousand people in support of the civil rights bill. The highlight of the rally was King's powerful and inspiring "I have a dream" speech.

Civil Rights and the Great Society

After Kennedy's assassination, Johnson persuaded the majority of both Republicans and Democrats to pass the most important civil rights legislation since Reconstruction.

Civil Rights Act of 1964: This act outlawed discriminatory voter registration requirements and racial segregation in schools, at workplaces, and in facilities that served the public, such as restaurants, hotels, and schools. The **Equal Opportunity Employment Act** monitored racial and gender discrimination in the workplace. The federal government promised to withhold funds from states that did not enforce the laws.

Voting Rights Act of 1965: In March 1965, Martin Luther King organized a protest march from Selma, Alabama, to the state capital, Montgomery, to publicize voting discrimination against African Americans. The brutality of the police attacks against the marchers enabled Johnson to aggressively push for passage of the Voting Rights Act of 1965. This act forbade literacy tests and provided federal registrars to assist African Americans in registering to vote. Only one year after the law was passed, the number of Southern blacks registered to vote increased by 50 percent.

Riots

Many unemployed African Americans living in poverty in northern cities did not see how the civil rights acts were improving their lives. They felt that social changes were too slow. Pent-up anger and frustration resulted in violent outbursts in cities across the country. The first riot broke out in Watts, Los Angeles, in 1965. Riots occurred again in 1966 and during the summer of 1967. More than 167 cities were affected by these riots. The worst took place in Detroit, Newark, and Washington, D.C. The rioters had no specific goals other than expressing their anger over continued inequalities in American society. President Johnson appointed the Kerner Commission to investigate the causes of the rioting. The commission concluded that the United States was becoming two separate but unequal societies, one black and one white.

In 1968 the assassination of Martin Luther King, Jr., by James Earl Ray in Memphis, Tennessee, shocked the nation. News of King's death touched off riots in many cities. The violence did not reflect King's ideals—he had received the Nobel Peace Prize in 1964—but revealed the continuing discontent in the African American community.

Social Revolutions

The civil rights movement provided the spark for women and other minorities who suffered discrimination to organize to gain equal rights.

Rise of Feminism: Women in the 1960s who participated in the civil rights movement contributed to a renewal of the women's movement. Women protested that they were still relegated to domestic duties like serving coffee rather than being considered for leadership roles. Betty Friedan's book *The Feminine Mystique* (1963) contributed to the growing spirit of feminism.

Her book expressed the frustration of many middle-class suburban women who were beginning to question the traditional role of women in society. She challenged women to pursue professional careers rather than be homemakers.

In 1966 Friedan and other feminist leaders formed the **National Organization of Women (NOW)**. The organization was predominantly middle class, and its goals included equal pay for women at work and the passage of antidiscrimination laws. Women adopted the tactics of the civil rights movement to gain their objectives. The Civil Rights Act of 1964 made it illegal for employers to discriminate on the basis of gender. Their greatest victory was in 1972 when Congress passed the Equal Rights Amendment, which stated that "equality of rights under the law shall not be denied or abridged by the United States or by any state on account of sex." In 1973 the Supreme Court decision *Roe v. Wade*, which legalized abortion with some restrictions, sparked controversy that continues today. The Equal Rights Amendment was also controversial, and despite the efforts of NOW and other groups, they were not able to get the required thirty-eight states to ratify the amendment.

Native Americans: Inspired by the women's movement and the civil rights movement, Native Americans began to protest for equal rights. The National Congress of American Indians complained bitterly that the Bureau of Indian Affairs was failing to improve their economic conditions, and the organization pursued legal action to obtain their ancestors' lands, which they insisted were illegally taken away from them. In 1973, a more radical group, the **American Indian Movement (AIM)** took up arms and gained control of Wounded Knee, South Dakota, on the Sioux reservation and demanded that their old treaty rights be recognized. After a three-month standoff, the Indians gained no concessions. However, court decisions in the 1970s granted Native Americans more autonomy and returned many of their lands that were illegally taken.

Mexican Americans: Like the previous groups, Mexican Americans began to protest for equal rights. Mexicans had for generations migrated to the Southwest to work as migrant farmers for low pay and long hours. **Cesar Chavez** organized the United Farm Workers to improve the conditions of the migrant farm workers who harvested grapes in California. From 1965 to 1970, Chavez' "La Causa," the goal of winning better working conditions, led to strikes against the California grape owners and called for boycotts against buying nonunion grapes. In 1970 the larger grape owners agreed to recognize the unions.

The Environment: There was also an increased awareness during the 1960s of the need to protect the environment. Rachel Carson's *Silent Spring* (1962) exposed the dangers of pesticides and led to the passage of laws to control pollution and protect the environment. First Lady Claudia Alta "Lady Bird" Johnson's efforts to beautify America also contributed to a greater awareness of the need to be responsible in dealing with the environment.

Escalating the War in Vietnam

When Kennedy became president in 1960, he continued Eisenhower's policy of providing military aid to South Vietnam. He increased the number of military advisors, known as the Green Berets, to help fight the Vietcong, a communist guerrilla force in South Vietnam. Kennedy hoped that American support would help the Ngo Dinh Diem government prevent the country from being overtaken by the communists. Diem, who was a Roman Catholic, brutally crushed Buddhist opposition to his government. Diem's tactics alienated the people, and with assurances from the United States, South Vietnam military generals assassinated Diem and a new government was established.

Johnson and Vietnam

Johnson promised that he would keep Kennedy's commitment to Vietnam, but American troops would not be sent to fight an Asian war. By 1964, Johnson had lost faith in the South Vietnamese government. He did not want to be known as the president who lost Vietnam, like Truman who was associated with the loss of Nationalist China. In 1964, an incident occurred that gave Johnson a reason to send American troops to Vietnam. In a televised speech in August, Johnson announced that North Vietnamese gunboats had attacked two U.S. destroyers in the Gulf of Tonkin. In an almost-unanimous vote, Congress passed the **Gulf** of **Tonkin Resolution**, which gave the president the power to do whatever was necessary to protect American forces from attack.

Expanding U.S. Involvement

Between 1965 and 1968, the United States increased troop strength from about 180,000 to almost a half million men. Johnson hoped that his policy of escalation would prevent the fall of South Vietnam. By 1965 U.S. aircraft began to attack North Vietnam in the hope of preventing supplies from being shipped to the Vietcong in the South. Johnson and his military advisors assured the American people that U.S. and South Vietnamese forces would eventually win the war.

By 1967 the Vietnam War seriously divided American society. College students who had been active in the civil rights movement protested against the war. Some were opposed to the draft and others questioned why the United States was involved in a civil war in Vietnam. Students staged sit-ins, marches, teach-ins, and other forms of civil disobedience, occupied college buildings, and burned draft cards in acts of defiance against the war. In New York City an antiwar protest attracted five hundred thousand people. As the situation in Vietnam deteriorated, students continued to protest and even shut down universities. Many of these protesters embraced violence and vandalism in their attacks on American institutions. They became known as the New Left. Despite these protests, many Americans continued to support the war. Americans who supported the war were known as hawks, while the opponents of the war were known as doves.

1968: A Troubled and Defining Year

Tet Offensive

In January 1968 the communists launched the Tet Offensive (because it began on the first day of the lunar new year) in every major city in Vietnam and even breached the grounds of the American Embassy in Saigon. The attackers were repelled, but the American public believed it showed the continuing strength of the Vietcong. Johnson and his military advisors had assured the nation that the United States was winning the war, but television, which brought the war into American living rooms, presented a different image. Americans had been uneasy about the search-and-destroy missions of U.S. troops and the use of Agent Orange and napalm to clear villages. Television images of the Tet Offensive convinced Americans that the end was not in sight and that it was time to withdraw. Massive demonstrations and protests continued against the war. Johnson's popularity declined even further among the American people. In March, in a televised address to the nation, the president called a halt to the bombing of North Vietnam in the hope of beginning peace talks. He also announced that he would not run for reelection.

Hippies and Counterculture

Many of the political protesters of the New Left who opposed Johnson's Vietnam policy promoted a rebellious lifestyle that glorified a drug culture and communal living. They preached love and nonviolence. Their style of dress—long hair, beards, and jeans—offended the older generation of Americans. These flower children, or hippies, became part of a counterculture that promoted sexual freedom, rock and folk music, and a distrust of authority. Their mantra was "You can't trust anyone over thirty." The counterculture reached its apex at the Woodstock, New York, festival in 1969. The gathering of thousands of hippies was a visible demonstration to the nation of the glorification of drugs, peace, and love. By the early 1970s the movement ended.

Assassinations

In April 1968, Dr. Martin Luther King, Jr., was assassinated. This tragedy combined with the shock of the Tet Offensive, the national conflict over race, and the generational divide between the young and the old threatened the social fabric of American society. Then on June 5, 1968, Robert Kennedy—the younger brother of John F. Kennedy, who was running for president on a platform of opposition to the Vietnam

War and support of civil rights—was assassinated by an Arab nationalist shortly after winning the California primary. Kennedy's death created even more tension in the country.

Review

12-1) The provision that allowed the attorney general to deport immigrants or naturalized citizens engaged in subversive activities and also allowed the barring of subversives from entering the United States was part of

A. loyalty oaths during the Truman administration

B. the McCarran Internal Security Act

C. the Espionage Act

D. the McCarran-Walters Act

E. the Refugee Act of 1948

12-2) Which of the following was NOT a part of President Dwight Eisenhower's New Look foreign policy?

A. massive retaliation

B. brinksmanship

C. covert operations

D. a roll back of communism

E. use of special forces in response to guerrilla warfare

12-3) Which of the following may have been most helpful in contributing to John F. Kennedy's election in 1960?

A. Nixon's Checkers speech

B. Kennedy's widespread support among ethnic urban voters

C. Kennedy's televised debates with Richard Nixon

D. Kennedy's Democratic Party leaders' strong support of Kennedy's nomination

E. the selection of Lyndon Johnson of Texas as vice president, which strengthened his support in the South

12-4) What was one major result of the Tet Offensive?

    A. It vindicated the U.S. "search and destroy" policy in Vietnam.

    B. It strengthened the public's belief that the South Vietnamese had an effective military army.

    C. President Johnson's approval ratings among the American people increased.

    D. A majority of Americans began to question and reject Johnson's Vietnam policy.

    E. The Vietcong took possession of large amounts of territory in South Vietnam.

Review Chapter 13: From Nixon to Obama

The Election of 1968

The Democrats held their nominating convention in Chicago. Hubert Humphrey, Johnson's vice president, had enough support to win the nomination. Humphrey had loyally supported Johnson's domestic and foreign policy. His refusal to denounce the president's Vietnam policy divided the party. There were antiwar demonstrations led by Abbie Hoffman and others to protest Humphrey's nomination. Chicago Mayor Richard Daley ordered the police to deal harshly with the protesters. The split television images of the police battling protesters in the street and Humphrey speaking before the convention did not help the party. The Republicans nominated Richard Nixon on a platform of returning law and order to America. Alabama Governor George Wallace represented the American Independent Party, who appealed primarily to Southern voters who opposed forced busing. Wallace's goal was to win enough votes to throw the election into the House of Representatives.

Results: Nixon won a close election. Although he gained an electoral majority of 301 to 191, he had only 43 percent of the popular vote and a plurality of 512,000 votes, or less than 1 percent more votes than Humphrey. However, Nixon's and Wallace's combined popular votes represented 57 percent of the American people. The election is significant because it demonstrated that Americans were turning away from the liberal reforms of the New Deal and the Great Society. Nixon's election would help to reestablish Republican dominance of the presidency.

The Nixon Years, 1969–1974

Foreign Policy

When Nixon became president, he promised to end domestic strife and to reduce American involvement in Vietnam. He adopted the policy of Vietnamization—a slow withdrawal of five hundred thousand troops from Vietnam while training South Vietnamese troops to carry on the war by themselves. Nixon also announced the Nixon Doctrine, by which he promised to continue to provide aid to Asian allies, but without the extensive use of American ground forces.

Continued Opposition

Vietnamization at first reduced the number of antiwar protests. In April 1970, however, Nixon ordered the invasion of neutral Cambodia to cut off supply lines in the country that were being used by the North Vietnamese. This action resulted in nationwide protests across college campuses. At Kent State University in Ohio, four college students were killed by National Guard troops, and two African American students were killed at Jackson State University in Mississippi. Colleges and secondary schools temporarily closed to show their support of the students who had been killed.

Other scandals also shocked the American public and sparked protests. In 1970 Americans learned of the 1968 massacre of Vietnamese men, women, and children by U.S. troops at My Lai. The publication of top-secret Pentagon papers on the front pages of the *New York Times* added to the antiwar sentiment among the people. The Pentagon Papers revealed that Kennedy and Johnson had systematically lied about the Vietnam War.

Ending the War

By 1972 American troop strength had been reduced to fewer than 130,000. Meanwhile Henry Kissinger, Nixon's National Security Advisor, was involved in peace talks with the North Vietnamese in Paris. These talks had been going on since the end of Johnson's presidency. When the talks broke down in December, Nixon ordered a two-week massive bombing of Hanoi, the capital of North Vietnam. He hoped this would end the war. In January 1973, Kissinger and the North Vietnamese announced a ceasefire. The United States agreed to withdraw its troops from Vietnam within sixty days, and the North Vietnamese agreed to return all American prisoners of war. The North Vietnamese were allowed to keep their forces in South Vietnam. By March 1973 all American forces left Vietnam. Unfortunately, more than fifty-eight thousand Americans lost their lives, and the civil war continued for the next two years.

Consequences of the Vietnam War

- Vietnam syndrome: Americans for the next decade would be reluctant to get involved in another conflict.

- The War Powers Act (1973) was passed over President Nixon's veto. The law required the president to inform Congress within forty-eight hours of sending troops into combat. The president needed congressional approval for any military action that lasted more than sixty days.

Détente

Nixon and Kissinger believed that the best way to promote peace was to improve relations with the Soviet Union and China. Nixon would play the China card to pressure the Soviet Union to reduce production of nuclear weapons. One of the principal goals of détente was to reduce nuclear proliferation. In 1972 Nixon visited the Soviet Union, and in his talks with Soviet premier Leonid Brezhnev, they agreed to set a limit on the buildup of nuclear weapons. In the first rounds of the Strategic

Arms Limitation Talks (SALT), both countries agreed to set limits on the number of ballistic missiles it produced and reduce the number of intercontinental missiles on each side. In the spirit of détente, Nixon also agreed to sell the Soviet Union over $750 million worth of U.S. wheat to help the Soviets through a bad food shortage.

Nixon's Journey to China

Nixon and Kissinger believed in realpolitik, or basing policies on practical rather than idealistic considerations. They realized that there was a great deal of suspicion between the Soviet Union and China. Nixon, who had been a fierce anticommunist throughout the 1950s and '60s, decided to normalize relations with Communist China. Nixon realized that a friendly China could be used to pressure the Soviet Union to make more concessions in the ongoing disarmament negotiations. After a series of secret meetings between Kissinger and Red Chinese officials, Nixon stunned the world by announcing that he would visit the country to meet with Mao Tse-tung in February 1972. This trip was a major shift in U.S. foreign policy because it stressed the importance of Mainland China in the world and ultimately led to U.S. recognition of Communist China in 1979. Most critics of Nixon's presidency applauded his foreign policy, which helped to reduce tensions and enhance world peace.

Nixon's Domestic Policy

Although Nixon concentrated mostly on foreign affairs, he was determined to shift the focus of domestic policy. He wanted to slow down Johnson's Great Society's programs. He proposed a program called the **New Federalism**, which was designed to shift the responsibility for social programs from the federal to the state level. Nixon wanted the federal government to share its revenue with local governments and allow them to use these grants as they saw fit. The hope was that this would cut down the size of the federal government, which had been expanding since the New Deal.

Economic Policies: In his first term Nixon was faced with inflation, increased unemployment, and a decline in the gross national product.

The combination of slow growth and inflated prices is referred to as **stagflation**. In an effort to slow inflation, Nixon cut government spending while reducing personal income tax. When this policy was not successful, he announced in August 1971 a ninety-day wage and price freeze. Even this was not successful. Finally, the fiscally conservative Nixon adopted deficit spending. He also took the U.S. dollar off the gold standard, which helped address the large trade deficit by making American products more affordable. By 1972 the economy was improving. However, the economy would worsen again in 1973 mainly due to the Organization of Petroleum Exporting Countries (OPEC) embargo to punish the United States for its support of Israel during the 1967 Six-Day War.

Election of 1972

Nixon's foreign policy successes in the Soviet Union and China, the winding down of the war in Vietnam, and the moon landings in 1969 boosted the country's morale, and the improving economy enhanced his chances for reelection. Nixon had further improved his chances for success by formulating a Southern strategy that would appeal to disaffected voters, whom he referred to as the "Silent Majority." This group opposed the antiwar protests, the tactics of black militants, the youth culture, and forced busing. Many of these voters were white Southern Democrats, Catholics, and ethnic and blue-collar workers who had been supporters of the New Deal but were now discontent with Democratic domestic and foreign policies. Nixon sought to win over the support of Southern whites by nominating two conservative Southern judges to the Supreme Court. The Senate did not confirm either man, and the courts rejected his efforts to delay integration. Yet this action gained him support among white voters.

Nixon and Vice President Spiro Agnew, who used to attack liberals and antiwar protesters, proved successful in 1972. Nixon had won only 43 percent of the popular vote in 1968, but this time he easily defeated the Democrat George McGovern. In a landside victory, he won 60 percent of the popular vote and carried every state but Massachusetts.

Significance: The election shows that Nixon's Southern strategy was successful. Although the Democrats still held majorities in Congress, Nixon had changed the voting patterns in the country that had started in 1968, and in 1972 the growing power of the Sunbelt, combined with suburban votes and Southern whites, helped to form a growing Republican majority in the country.

Watergate

Nixon's electoral mandate was destroyed by the Watergate scandal. In June 1972 five men broke into Democratic Party headquarters in the Watergate complex in Washington. The break-in was an attempt to bug the headquarters. The men were arrested and found to be part of a group that was connected to the **Committee to Re-Elect the President (CREEP).** At first this was considered a second-rate burglary, and there was no known connection with the White House. Two *Washington Post* reporters, however, investigated the affair and began to expose criminal activities at the highest level of government. Nixon and his aides attempted to cover up these activities. Throughout 1973, the president vigorously asserted that he had no knowledge of the break-in or the cover-up and forced some of his closest aides to submit their resignations. Meanwhile, a Senate investigating committee in the summer of 1973 discovered that Nixon had recorded all of his Oval Office conversations. The committee and the Justice Department demanded the release of the tapes. Nixon refused and claimed "executive privilege." He insisted that he would be violating the separation of powers if he turned over the tapes.

Nixon's Resignation: In July 1974 the Supreme Court decided that the president had to turn over the tapes. The tapes revealed that Nixon was involved in the cover-up from the very beginning. The House Judiciary Committee, which had begun impeachment hearings in April, voted to impeach the president on the grounds of his abuse of power and obstruction of justice. Faced with an impeachment trial, Nixon resigned on August 9, 1974. It was the first time in the nation's history that a living president left office before completing his term of office.

The Ford Administration

When Nixon resigned, Vice President Gerald Ford became president. He was not elected to the office but was appointed to the vice presidency in 1973. In October 1973 the elected vice president, Spiro Agnew, had resigned the office after it was revealed that he had taken bribes while serving as governor of Maryland. Ford is the only vice president to become chief executive under the Twenty-Fifth Amendment and the only president in U.S. history who was never elected.

Highlights of the Ford Presidency

Nixon's Pardon: One month into office, Ford pardoned Nixon for any crimes committed during the Watergate affair. This was the most controversial decision of his presidency. The American people were angry and annoyed that the whole truth of Watergate would never be known. Ford insisted that he wanted to end the "national nightmare." However, historians believe it was the cloud over Ford's administration that would never go away.

Fall of Saigon: By 1975 Ford pulled out the last remaining American troops from Vietnam. In April 1975 a combined force of Vietcong and North Vietnamese troops took control of Saigon and the rest of Vietnam. The United States was able to evacuate 150,000 Vietnamese from the country. In 1975, Cambodia and Laos also fell to the communists. This defeat was a damaging blow to America's prestige in the world.

Economic Crisis: Ford's biggest problem was inflation. He believed in voluntary measures to get business and the American people behind his policy. He distributed WIN (Whip Inflation Now) buttons to get the public behind his economic policies. Inflation, however, was not whipped. Unemployment rose to 9 percent, and the economy sank deeper into recession.

The Carter Administration

The cloud of Watergate hung over the Republican Party as well as internal bickering between the moderate and conservative wings of the party. Ford faced a tough challenge from former governor of California and actor Ronald Reagan. Ford won the nomination, but conservatives were not enthusiastic about supporting him.

More than one dozen Democrats sought the nomination. Jimmy Carter, a former governor of Georgia, eventually won. Few people had heard of Carter, but running as an outsider from Washington and his promise to bring honesty to government made him a likable and attractive candidate. Although Ford was able to cut into Carter's huge lead at the very end of the campaign, Carter won the close election. Carter won because he carried most of the South. He was the first U.S. president elected from the South since 1848.

Key Events in the Carter Presidency

Carter was a hardworking president, and many found his folksy style—such as buying his inauguration suit off the rack in a department store—refreshing. However, as an outsider, he did not establish enough contact with the Democratic leadership in Washington to get his programs through Congress. He was a detail-oriented man who sometimes did not see the big picture, which frustrated Democratic lawmakers and confused the American public. His most notable achievements were in foreign policy:

- **Human Rights:** In an attempt to improve the U.S. image in the third world, Carter insisted that human rights would be the cornerstone of his foreign policy. He was the first president to condemn South Africa for Apartheid. He also cut off aid to countries in Latin America that violated human rights.

- **Panama Canal Treaty:** After much controversy, Carter was able to get the Senate to approve the treaty that turned over the Canal Zone to Panama in 2000. Conservatives were angry and accused Carter of giving the canal away.

- **Camp David Accords:** Some say this was Carter's greatest accomplishment. In September 1978 he invited Egyptian president Anwar-Sadat and Israeli prime minister Menachem Begin to the presidential retreat at Camp David, Maryland. While acting as mediator, he negotiated a peace treaty that ended decades of war between Egypt and Israel. Egypt became the first country to recognize Israel, and in return, Israel withdrew from the Sinai Peninsula. The treaty did not bring peace to the Middle East, but it was a ray of hope for the region.

- **Relations with the Soviet Union:** Carter continued the policy of détente. He signed the SALT II agreement with the Soviets in 1979 and recognized the People's Republic of China. Conservatives applauded his actions after the Soviet invasion of Afghanistan when he boycotted the 1980 Moscow Olympics and placed an embargo on grain exports to the Soviet Union. He also supplied Afghan guerrillas with weapons and supplies. Although he had campaigned for arms reductions, he was forced to increase defense spending.

- **The Iran Hostage Crisis:** The United States had supported the Shah of Iran's repressive regime since 1953. In 1979, Islamic fundamentalists led by the Ayatollah Ruhollah Khomeini overthrew the Shah, who went into exile. In October, Carter allowed the Shah, who was suffering from cancer, to enter the United States to seek medical treatment. In November, outraged Iranians seized the American Embassy and took fifty-two hostages. They demanded the return of the Shah, but Carter refused and insisted that the hostages be released. The hostage crisis dragged on for 444 days. Carter made various attempts to obtain their release, from negotiation to a failed assault in April 1980. The Iranian crisis was the biggest failure of Carter's presidency and was a major reason for his electoral defeat in 1980. The hostages were released as soon as Carter left office on January 20, 1981.

- **Domestic Policy:** Inflation and unemployment remained the biggest issue. Like Ford, Carter asked for voluntary controls. He urged businessmen not to raise prices and urged workers not to demand higher wages. He also asked the American people to limit excessive energy use in order to bring down inflation. He also cut federal spending to reduce the budget. This angered liberal Democrats. Carter also asked the Federal Reserve to raise interest rates, which would tighten the money supply and stem inflation. Interest rates shot up as high as 20 percent. None of these policies worked. Nothing seemed to work. Unemployment reached 8 percent, and inflation fell to 12 percent. The public lost confidence in the president's ability to solve the country's problems.

The Reagan Administration

Carter won the presidential nomination despite a serious challenge from Senator Edward "Ted" Kennedy of Massachusetts. The primary challenge divided the party and weakened Carter's candidacy.

The Republicans selected Ronald Reagan as their nominee. Reagan was aided by the Iranian hostage crisis and the worsening economy. He attacked the Democrats for poor leadership. In one famous line in their presidential debate, Reagan pointedly asked, "Are you better off than you were four years ago?" The voters elected Reagan in a landslide. Reagan won forty-four states and 50 percent of the popular vote. Reagan had been successful in attacking big government, which he said was destroying the American spirit. He promised to cut taxes and return the government to the people and often said that the government is the problem in America, not the solution. He also promised to end affirmative action and other social welfare programs of the New Deal.

Significance: Reagan's election destroyed the New Deal coalition of blue-collar workers who traditionally supported the Democratic Party but now agreed with Reagan's conservative philosophy. The election also marked the emergence of the Religious Right and the Moral Majority as a potent force in American politics. The Moral Majority was composed primarily of Protestant ministers, such as Jerry Falwell, who opposed abortion and homosexuality. The group supported Republicans in subsequent elections and organized their constituents to defeat liberal Democrats. Southern whites that had supported Carter in 1976 turned to Reagan and the Republicans, because they had more in common with their principles. The combination of the Religious Right, blue-collar ethnic workers, and Southerners enabled Republicans to increase their numbers in the House and to gain control of the Senate for the first time in twenty-eight years. Reagan's election has been termed the **Reagan Revolution** because it led to a political realignment that made the Republicans the majority party for the next twenty years.

The Reagan Revolution reflected the conservative mood of the American people in the 1980s. The following are examples of this conservative trend:

- Both Democrats and Republicans wanted to avoid labels such as liberals or big spenders. The focus was on trimming the budget.

- The Supreme Court's decisions reflected conservative ideas.

- The antiestablishment look of the hippies was replaced by the yuppies: young urban professionals who dressed for success.

- The dominant idea that "greed is good" was portrayed in the movie *Wall Street*.

The Republican presidents of the 1980s reflected this trend toward conservatism.

Domestic Policy

Reaganomics is also known as supply-side economics or the trickle-down theory. The idea is that the economy benefits if the government cuts taxes for the wealthy so they can invest in the economy and create more jobs. Government also would make major cuts in welfare programs:

- In 1981 and 1982 Reagan cut taxes by about 25 percent across the board.

- With the help of Southern Democrats (known as Boll Weevils), Republicans cut more than $40 billion from domestic programs. Reagan did not cut out benefits for Medicare and Social Security, but Social Security was reformed by raising the retirement age and taxes on the benefits to the upper class.

- Deregulation of the banking, airline, and trucking industries that had begun in the Carter administration were continued. In addition, restrictions on savings and loan institutions and mergers by large corporations were made easier. Unfortunately, bad loans and poor management led to a rush of savings and loan bankruptcies, which forced the public to pay for a $200 billion bailout of the savings and loan industry.

Recession of 1982

In 1982, the nation suffered the worst recession since the Great Depression. The failure of the banks, the decline of the stock market, and rising unemployment contributed to the severe economic times. However, the tight monetary policies of the Federal Reserve and a decline in oil prices due to the recession helped the economy to rebound. Not all Americans benefited from the return of prosperity, however. The middle class and the poor did not make any substantial economic gains. The wages of union workers in particular suffered, since memberships continued to decline. Reagan was perceived as an anti-union president for his tough stand in firing striking air traffic controllers and destroying their union.

Conservatism in the Court

Reagan fulfilled his pledge to change the direction of the Supreme Court. He appointed Sandra Day O'Connor, the first woman, as well as Antonin Scalia, the first Italian American, and Anthony Kennedy. These conservative judges did not overturn longstanding decisions on controversial issues, like *Roe v. Wade*, but they maintained the status quo.

Reagan's Second Term

The return of prosperity and Reagan's slogan "Morning in America" created a renewed sense of confidence in the country. Reagan was renominated in 1984. For the Democrats, the African American civil rights leader Jesse Jackson made an unsuccessful run for the presidency under the guise of the Rainbow Coalition of minorities, women, and workers. Democrats selected Walter Mondale, Carter's vice president, and Geraldine Ferraro of New York, the first woman to run for vice president. Reagan easily defeated Mondale.

Effects of Reaganomics

Budget and Trade Deficit: Critics of Reagan's policies argued that his tax cuts and spending increases created huge deficits. In his eight years in office Reagan added nearly $2 trillion to the national debt. Democrats and Republicans in the 1980s and 1990s who were faced with these huge deficits were confronted with the problem of how to cut programs rather than expand them in order to bring the deficit under control. Reaganomics had changed the debate from "what can the government do to help" to "what cuts can be made in government and by how much to bring costs under control."

Foreign Policy

Reagan believed that Carter's foreign policy of focusing on human rights had weakened the image of the United States. He was determined to restore its image by building up America's military power. Under Reagan, the Pentagon's annual budget expanded from $317 billion in 1981 to $426 billion in 1986. In 1983, the president proposed the Strategic Defensive Initiative (SDI), popularly called "Stars Wars," a space-based missile defensive system that would destroy enemy missiles before they could reach U.S. territory. Reagan saw the Soviet Union as the "evil empire" and viewed communism, not poverty, as the motivating force behind instabilities in the third world. The **Reagan Doctrine** was designed to oppose the global influence of the Soviet Union. The United

States would provide overt and covert aid to any group that would fight communist insurgency.

Reagan did not hesitate to intervene anywhere in the world. In 1983, the president sent troops to Grenada in the Caribbean to oust a Cuban-backed dictatorship. In El Salvador, he spent millions to support the Salvadoran government in a civil war with leftist guerrillas. After ten years and more than $600 million in U.S. aid, the civil war was not resolved, and both sides in 1991 agreed to a cease-fire.

The Iran-Contra Affair

In Nicaragua, the Reagan administration provided military aid to anticommunist forces known as the Contras against the Marxist Sandinistas, who had come to power in 1979. In 1982 and again in 1984, Democrats who opposed Reagan's Nicaraguan policies passed the Boland Amendments, which specifically forbade providing aid to the Contras with either troops or money. In 1988, the media reported that the White House was ignoring the law: the Reagan administration was supplying weapons to Iran—a sworn enemy of the United States—with the hope of securing the release of hostages held in Lebanon by a radical Arab group. The administration then decided to take the millions of dollars from these weapons sales and route them to the right-wing Contras in Nicaragua. Congress launched televised investigations into these activities, and several White House officials were convicted on criminal charges. It was never proven that either Reagan or Vice President George H. W. Bush were directly involved.

Failure in Lebanon

Reagan's policies were unsuccessful in the Middle East. In 1983, when a civil war broke out in Lebanon, the United States sent marines in to restore order. The mission ended abruptly in 1984 after a truck packed with explosives blew up the American barracks and killed 241 servicemen.

Changes in the Soviet Union

In 1985, Mikhail Gorbachev became the leader of the Soviet Union and attempted to bring about changes in his country. His policies of **perestroika** (economic changes) and **glasnost** (introduction of democracy) into Soviet life and politics helped bring the Cold War to an end. Gorbachev realized that the Soviet Union could no longer compete in the arms race with the United States. In a series of summit meetings, Gorbachev and Reagan signed the Intermediate Nuclear Force Treaty (INF) and promised to remove all nuclear weapons and dismantle all nuclear weapons in Europe. By the end of Reagan's second term, many believed that the Cold War would soon end.

Reagan's Legacy

Ronald Reagan's popularity with the American people remained high at the end of his second term. Despite the stock market crash of October 1987 (average prices fell 20 percent), drastic increases in the deficit, and claims that the president delegated too much authority to others (as demonstrated in the Iran-Contra affair), many Americans believed that Reagan had restored America's image in the world. He would be an icon of the Republican Party for decades.

The George H. W. Bush Administration

The election of 1988 was seen as a referendum on the Reagan presidency. George H. W. Bush, his vice president, was closely identified with Reagan's policies. Bush easily won the Republican nomination and selected Dan Quayle as his vice president. Bush had considerable experience in foreign affairs as a former director of the Central Intelligence Agency and former U.S. ambassador to the United Nations.

Bush easily defeated Democratic candidate Massachusetts Governor Michael Dukakis. The campaign was noted for negative commercials linking Dukakis to the release of a convicted murderer who later committed more crimes. Bush appealed to voters by promising to continue to build a strong military defense with no new taxes. Bush won by seven million votes, but the Democrats retained control of Congress.

Foreign Problems

The Collapse of Communism: The first year of the Bush presidency was dominated by major changes in the communist world.

In 1989 communist governments fell throughout Eastern Europe in Poland, Hungary, Bulgaria, Czechoslovakia, and Romania. In November 1989, protesters from East Germany tore down the Berlin Wall, a symbol of the Cold War. In October 1990, Germany, which had been divided since 1945, was united.

By 1991 most of the republics of the Soviet Union had declared their independence. In December 1991, Boris Yeltsin, who had replaced Gorbachev as president, announced the end of the Soviet Union and the formation of the Commonwealth of Independent States. Bush referred to these changes as the beginning of a **New World Order** that was free from the stalemate of the Cold War and celebrated a respect for human rights.

In the spring of 1989, the wind of democracy spread to China. Students demonstrated in Tiananmen Square in Beijing for more freedom. The Chinese communists brutally crushed these demonstrations, and the West was unable to do anything.

In Latin America, Bush (like Reagan) did not hesitate to intervene. In 1989, he sent twelve thousand troops to overthrow Panamanian dictator Manuel Noriega, whom the United States claimed was involved in drug trafficking.

Operation Desert Storm: The biggest crisis of the Bush presidency came in August 1990 when Iraq invaded the oil-rich nation of Kuwait. The United Nations condemned the aggression. President Bush announced, "We have drawn a line in the sand," and sent four hundred thousand troops to the region by the end of 1990. A UN-supported coalition of thirty-two nations—including troops from Europe as well as Saudi Arabia, Syria, Turkey, and Egypt—joined the U.S. forces. When

Iraq did not meet the UN deadline for its withdrawal from Kuwait by January 15, 1991, Bush ordered a massive invasion of Kuwait by international forces led by the United States. The campaign, known as Operation Desert Storm, consisted of five weeks of air strikes and a ground invasion that began on February 24 and lasted one hundred hours. Iraq surrendered and was forced to withdraw from Kuwait. American forces, however, did not move into Iraq to oust Saddam Hussein.

Domestic Problems

Bush was not as successful in domestic policy. He ran on a campaign of not raising taxes by famously saying, "Read my lips: no new taxes." In 1985, Congress had passed the Gramm-Rudman-Hollings Act, which required Congress to take measures to balance the federal budget by 1990.

In 1990, Bush went back on his pledge. The growing deficit and a weak economy persuaded him to sign a bill that increased taxes. Conservatives and liberals criticized the president. Conservatives would never forgive him for breaking his no-new-taxes pledge and would be reluctant to support him in the future. Liberals were critical because they thought Bush should have placed a heavier tax burden on the wealthy. The divided government between a Republican president and a Democratic Congress created a gridlock in Washington, which meant that very little domestic legislation was passed during Bush's presidency.

The Election of 1992

In 1991, Bush's popularity was at record high, and he was expected to win reelection easily. However, at the beginning of 1992, the economy went into recession and experienced the worst decline since the Great Depression. The Republicans renominated Bush and Quayle. They pointed to the success of Operation Desert Storm and the end of the Cold War, and blamed the poor economy on the Democrats in Congress.

The Democratic nominees were William Jefferson Clinton, former governor of Arkansas, and Albert Gore, senator from Tennessee. They ran a campaign known as "New Democrats" that focused on economic issues like jobs, health care, and education. They claimed not to be typical big-government and big-spending liberals. They tried to move the Democratic Party to the center. Clinton's mantra was, "It's the economy, stupid!" Clinton and Gore had to attract more voters by supporting a strong national defense as well as closer ties with the business community.

Third-Party Candidate: Texas multibillionaire Ross Perot was an independent candidate for president who spent millions on television ads to present his program directly to the public. He promised to end the deficit and revive the economy.

Results: Clinton won 370 electoral votes but only 43 percent of the popular vote. Bush won 38 percent of the vote, and Perot claimed 19 percent of the vote. This was the best showing for a third-party candidate since Theodore Roosevelt in 1912. Perot's strong performance hurt Bush more than Clinton.

The Clinton Administration

Bill Clinton was the first baby boomer president, and his election represented a shift away from the ideas of Reagan and Bush. He appointed minorities and women to his cabinet. In 1993 he selected Janet Reno as attorney general and appointed Ruth Bader Ginsberg to the Supreme Court. Later in 1997, he selected Madeleine Albright as the first woman secretary of state.

Clinton's First Term

During his first term, Clinton achieved some successes. Working with a Democratic-majority Congress, the Family and Medical Leave Act was passed, requiring employers to give twelve weeks of unpaid leave to care for newborn infants and handle family emergencies. Clinton was also successful in securing passage of the Brady Bill, which mandated a five-day waiting period before one could purchase a handgun. He also signed an Anti-Crime Bill, which provided $30 billion in federal funds to hire more police.

Despite these successes, Clinton's initiative on ending the ban on gays in the military created difficulties with the armed forces as well as civilian sectors. His proposal to create a national health care system created even more controversy. The opposition of the American Medical Association and the effective television advertising of the insurance industry managed to thwart any Democratic efforts to reform health care.

"Contract with America"

By 1994, many Americans were dissatisfied with the Clinton administration. Some thought the president was too liberal on social issues, and liberals attacked him because of his failure to pass a healthcare reform bill. In 1994, the Republicans gained control of Congress for the first time in forty years. Led by Speaker Newt Gingrich, Republicans supported the "Contract with America." They pledged that within one hundred days they would pass legislation that would cut the federal bureaucracy, balance the budget, and promote welfare reform. Under pressure from Republicans, Clinton signed a Welfare Reform Bill that made sharp cuts in the amount of money the federal government spent for welfare and food stamp programs and required welfare recipients to work. Many liberals were critical of Clinton for supporting such a harsh measure. Others pointed out that this demonstrated that Clinton was a New Democrat who was pushing the party toward the political center.

Clinton and the Republicans fought over balancing the budget. They disagreed over the extent of cuts to social programs in Medicare and education. The inability to resolve the differences led to a shutdown of the federal government in 1995 and 1996. In both instances, Clinton was able to depict the Republicans as extremists and himself as taking the more responsible position. Clinton undercut the Republican Party by adopting many of their positions. He endorsed a balanced budget and declared in his 1996 State of the Union Address that the "era of big government is over."

Foreign Policy

Clinton was successful in getting Congress to pass the North American Free Trade Agreement (NAFTA) in 1994, which eliminated all tariffs and trade barriers between Canada, Mexico, and the United States. Labor unions were critical of the agreement, but Clinton promoted globalization. He thought that the lowering of the tariff would expand the world economy and benefit the American economy in the long run.

In a major diplomatic breakthrough in the Middle East, he arranged for a historic "land for peace" agreement in Washington, D.C., between Israeli prime minister Yitzhak Rabin and Palestinian Liberation Organization (PLO) leader Yasir Arafat. The agreement resulted in self-rule for the Gaza Strip. Throughout his presidency, Clinton tried to mediate peace in the Middle East.

The Election of 1996

The rebounding economy, the dramatic rise in the stock market, and the drop in unemployment were among Clinton's greatest achievements. Americans were optimistic about the economy and approved of Clinton's moderate stance on social issues. Clinton easily defeated the Republican nominee, Senator Robert Dole of Kansas. Republicans, however, retained control of Congress.

Clinton's Second Term

Scandals and impeachment became the dominant issues of Clinton's second term. From the early days of the Clinton administration, Congress investigated some of the president and first lady's financial dealings. The Republican Congress appointed Kenneth Starr, an independent counsel, to look into real estate dealings known as the Whitewater Affair. The Clintons were exonerated. However, in 1998, Starr investigated an alleged presidential affair with a White House intern, Monica Lewinsky, and found that Clinton had perjured himself while testifying before the prosecutor's committee. Starr's report, which also included his investigation of sexual harassment by the president while he was governor of Arkansas, led to a vote supporting impeachment by the House of Representatives on December 19, 1998. Members of both parties condemned the president's reckless behavior. The Senate's vote of impeachment fell short of the two-thirds majority necessary to convict the president on charges of perjury and obstruction of justice.

Although Clinton's reputation was tarnished, he still remained popular with the American people. The U.S. economy was booming and enjoying the longest peacetime expansion in its history, with annual growth over 4 percent. Technological developments such as the Internet and desktop computers increased productivity and contributed to an improved business climate. The booming economy produced a projected surplus. Clinton, with the help of the Republican-controlled Congress, balanced the budget for the first time in thirty years.

The Balkans, however, became a troubled area for Clinton in his second term. In 1999, he supported a NATO air raid and provided U.S. troops for a multinational force to stop Serbian president Slobodan Milosevic's policy of ethnic cleansing against Muslims in Kosovo. Serbian troops burned villages and raped and murdered many Muslims. After seventy-two days of consecutive bombings, Serbian troops withdrew from Kosovo. On June 3, 1999, Milosevic signed a peace agreement to withdraw from Kosovo.

Despite the impeachment trial and his sexual indiscretions, Clinton left office with the highest approval rating of any president since the end of World War II.

Election of 2000

The campaign of 2000 lacked drama at first. Vice President Al Gore captured the Democratic nomination with little opposition and selected Joseph Lieberman of Connecticut as his running mate, the first Jewish American vice presidential candidate. Republicans nominated former Texas Governor George W. Bush, son of the former President Bush, and Dick Cheney as vice president. Ralph Nader ran as the Green Party candidate. On election day, after more than one hundred million voters cast their ballots, Gore received five hundred thousand more popular votes than Bush, but victory hinged on who won Florida's twenty-five electoral votes. Bush led by less than six hundred votes in Florida, and Gore's supporters demanded a recount. The recount lasted for five weeks. The conflict was resolved in December 2000, when the Supreme Court, by a five-to-four decision, ordered the recounting to stop because the hand count violated the equal protection clause of the Fourteenth Amendment. Bush was declared the winner by an electoral vote of 271 to 266.

Presidency of George W. Bush, 2001–2009

Bush called himself a compassionate conservative, a philosophy based on limited government, personal responsibility, strong families, and local control.

Bush's domestic agenda included the following:

- **Education Reform:** A bipartisan measure entitled No Child Left Behind raised standards in schools and insisted on accountability in return for federal dollars.

- **Tax Cuts:** Faced with a recession, Bush proposed a $1.35 trillion tax cut. The president gave taxpayers an immediate $300 to $600 rebate and reduced taxes for every federal taxpayer. Democrats insisted that lower taxes favored the wealthy rather than the middle class.

- **Medicare:** Bush added a prescription drug benefit for seniors.

- **Abortion:** The president signed a partial-birth abortion ban that prohibited late-term abortions.

Bush and Terrorism

The defining moment of Bush's first term was the terrorist attack on September 11, 2001. Members of al Qaeda, a Muslim extremist terrorist group headed by Osama Bin Laden, hijacked four passenger planes. Two planes crashed into the twin towers of the World Trade Center in

New York, a symbol of American economic might. One plane crashed into the Pentagon, a symbol of America's military strength. And one plane crashed in Pennsylvania, brought down by passengers who overwhelmed the terrorists. Nearly three thousand people died in these attacks. America was stunned and shocked. President Bush declared the attacks an act of war and vowed to hunt down those responsible.

Operation Enduring Freedom

In October 2001, the United States and its allies invaded Afghanistan. Bush claimed that the Taliban regime in Afghanistan had provided refuge for al Qaeda and Bin Laden before and after the attacks. Within two months, the Taliban regime collapsed. However, Bin Laden escaped into the mountains between Afghanistan and Pakistan.

Homeland Security

To combat terrorism at home, Congress passed the Patriot Act by a nearly unanimous vote. The goal was to enhance the ability of law-enforcement agencies to fight terrorists at home and abroad. The act enabled law-enforcement agencies to obtain warrants to investigate a citizen's medical records, e-mails, and library and book records. Wiretaps could be authorized more easily for use against suspected terrorists. Suspected terrorists could be tried in military tribunals. President Bush created a new agency, the Office of Homeland Security, which, along with the Department of Transportation, would be responsible for airline security.

Bush Doctrine

In September 2002, President Bush outlined a national security policy to guide the U.S. military in addressing terrorism. The president stated that the United States reserved the option to wage a preventive war and had the power to depose foreign regimes that represented a threat to the security of the United States. The spreading of democracy, especially in the Middle East, was also a goal of the Bush Doctrine.

Operation Iraqi Freedom

The Bush administration, which saw the war on terrorism as a global concern, shifted its focus to Iraq in 2002. The relationship between Iraq and the United States had been less than friendly since the 1991 Gulf War. Since 1991, Saddam Hussein had ignored numerous UN mandates and resolutions regarding nuclear weapons. During the Clinton administration, Saddam refused to cooperate with UN inspectors who were searching for weapons of mass destruction (WMD).

Despite massive air attacks on Iraq ordered by President Clinton, Saddam Hussein had remained in power. In 2003, President Bush was determined to end the dictator's regime. Under the Bush Doctrine, he claimed that the United States would be justified in preemptive attacks on the Iraq dictator before Hussein could use those destructive weapons on the United States or pass them on to terrorists.

Despite the fact that UN inspectors failed to find weapons of mass destruction, and without the support of the Security Council, the United States launched Operation Iraqi Freedom on March 19, 2003. Bush declared that the government of Iraq had violated numerous UN resolutions and that there were WMD in Iraq. A combination of U.S. and British forces overran Iraq within four weeks. Hussein was overthrown, and coalition troops occupied most of the country. Eventually Hussein was captured, tried, and hanged in 2003.

The military aspect of the conflict was just beginning. It was difficult to create a coalition government because of the fundamental differences between Shiite and Sunni Muslims and the Kurdish minorities in the north. Eventually, in 2005, a democratically elected government was established for the first time in Iraq. Nevertheless, Iraqi insurgents who resented the American presence in their country continued to complicate rebuilding efforts in the country, from the basic necessities of water and electricity to the building of schools. Violence was a daily occurrence throughout 2003 and 2004. Car bombings and ambushes resulted in the loss of numerous American lives. By the end of Bush's second administration more than thirty-five hundred Americans would be killed. The failure to find WMD and the problems created by the Iraq insurgency and the monetary impact on the federal budget convinced many Americans that it was time to end their involvement in Iraq.

The Election of 2004

America was uneasy about the Iraq War and concerned about the economy and the growing deficit. There were also social divisions between conservative so-called Red States and liberal so-called Blue States over gay marriage, abortion, and prayer in the public schools. Bush's popularity was around 50 percent, and the Democrats thought they had a good chance to regain the White House. Republicans renominated the Bush-Cheney ticket, and the campaign depicted Bush as a strong wartime leader who made the tough decision to fight terrorism. Democrats selected Senator John Kerry of Massachusetts, a decorated Vietnam veteran. Kerry was accused of changing positions on the War in Iraq, and some groups even questioned his actions in Vietnam. Bush won 51 percent of the popular vote. Unlike the election of 2000, Bush clearly won the popular vote.

Bush's Second Term

Bush's efforts to privatize Social Security and reform the immigration system were unsuccessful as other issues became more important. The continuing debate over Iraq and the inadequate response of the government to the devastation of Hurricane Katrina, which resulted in the death of two thousand Americans and left thousands homeless, led the public to question what was wrong with the country. In 2006, the Democrats regained control of Congress.

The Election of 2008

Democrats: In the Democratic primaries, Senator Hillary Clinton of New York and Senator Barack Obama of Illinois traded victories and struggled to the end of the primary season. At their national convention, the Democrats chose Obama, making him the first African American nominee for president of a major party. Obama picked Senator Joseph Biden of Delaware as his running mate.

Republicans: Senator John McCain of Arizona emerged as the winner of the Republican primaries, but many conservatives felt he was too moderate to represent them. He selected Governor Sarah Palin of Alaska as his running mate in an effort to satisfy the conservative wing of the party. Palin brought enthusiasm to the campaign, but many questioned her readiness to be vice president.

The Campaign: The Iraq War and the economy were the two dominant issues. McCain supported Bush's surge in sending more troops to Iraq, but Obama opposed it. Dramatic increases in oil prices during the summer and an increase in the unemployment rate created doubts among the voters about the vitality of the economy. The collapse of the subprime mortgage industry, which led to failures throughout the financial sector and a credit crunch, created even more anxieties in the country. Obama insisted that Republican policies of deregulation contributed to the economic decline. McCain accused Obama of supporting a policy that would lead the country into socialism. In September 2008, the financial system appeared to be on the verge of collapse. Congress was forced to pass a major bailout package to rescue many financial institutions from bankruptcy. The crisis may have influenced the outcome of the election. Obama appeared to be calm, secure, and to have a stronger understanding of the crisis than McCain.

Results: Obama won 53 percent of the vote, a clear majority of electoral votes, and Democrats increased their control of Congress. Obama's hopeful campaign and promises to move beyond partisanship convinced the American public to vote for him. Between November and the president's inauguration in January, the economy continued to worsen and some feared the country was headed into another economic depression. Obama faced the challenge of restoring economic vitality while also promoting a liberal agenda of health care and other social reforms.

Review

13-1) Which was one of the major results of the War Powers Act of 1973?

A. The president was allowed to immediately use his powers as commander in chief in an emergency.

B. The military draft ended and a lottery system was instituted.

C. The president was required to meet immediately with Congress before committing troops to a foreign country.

D. The president was prohibited from engaging in military actions for more than ninety days unless Congress voted its approval.

E. The president was required to present a program to end the war in Vietnam within a year.

13-2) The event that seriously damaged the effectiveness of Jimmy Carter's administration was

A. the Iranian hostage crisis

B. his "National malaise" speech

C. the Soviet invasion of Afghanistan

D. the granting of amnesty for draft evaders

E. the OPEC oil embargo

13-3) Which of the following presidents is closely identified with Strategic Defense Initiatives?

A. Bill Clinton

B. Ronald Reagan

C. George H. W. Bush

D. Richard Nixon

E. Gerald Ford

13-4) In the election of 1992 between George H. W. Bush and Bill
       Clinton, the most important issue for the American voters was the

   A. unrest in Europe created by the collapse of communism
   B. ethnic cleansing in the former Yugoslavia republics
   C. rising deficit and criticism of the government's taxation policy
   D. recession and continued economic difficulties in the country
   E. unrest in Iraq after Operation Desert Storm

Answers to Review Questions

Chapter 1

1-1) A. Between 1720 and 1775 there was a reduction of the dominant group of the English Welsh from 80 percent to a slight majority. The largest increase was in the African population, which doubled in size. The need for cheap labor on the plantations in the South necessitated the need for the import of African slaves in colonial America. There was also a heavy influx of Scots and Germans between 1700 and 1775 from less than zero to about 14 percent. Economic and political conditions in these countries contributed to their sudden influx into colonial America. By the end of the eighteenth century and early nineteenth century, these two immigrant groups would continue to grow in population. The Dutch population in colonial America would decline throughout the nineteenth century.

1-2) E. Roger Williams founded Rhode Island in 1636 because he disagreed with the Puritans in the Massachusetts Bay colony on the question of Church and State. Rhode Island was the only New England colony to practice religious tolerance. Pennsylvania founded by William Penn as a haven for Quakers in 1681 granted religious tolerance to other religious groups. Maryland founded as a refuge for Catholics in 1634 did not allow religious tolerance until 1649. None of the other colonies allowed for tolerance and freedom for other religious groups in their colonies.

1-3) A. The First Great Awakening was a religious revitalization movement that swept across the American colonies in the 1730s and 1740s. The purpose of the Great Awakening was to rekindle the spirit of Puritanism and to bring colonists, especially in New England, back to a more spiritual life. In the New England colonies, and later in others, many Americans complained that organized religion had lost its vitality. They believed that the Winthrop generation of the Massachusetts Bay Colony had possessed greater piety than the present colonists. The leader of the Great Awakening wanted to focus on renewing the spiritual component of American life in the eighteenth century. The Great Awakening was not a political movement for self-government, an economic struggle against Great Britain, or an ecumenical movement to work with Quakers as a vehicle against Catholicism.

1-4) C. The New England Town Meetings and the House of Burgesses represent the beginning of representative government in the United States even though voting was restricted to white males who were property owners. The House of Burgesses and the New England town meetings allowed individuals to meet and discuss their problems. Neither of these developments addressed the issues of unity, British taxation, ending attacks by Native Americans, or the policy of Salutary Neglect.

Chapter 2

2-1) D. Since the national government could not tax, the Congress of the Articles of Confederation began to print large amounts of paper money to pay off its war debt. However, as the value of the Continentals (paper money) began to drop due to rampant inflation, Congress had to print more of them and as more money flooded the countryside, the continentals dropped in value. The term "not worth a Continental" reflected how worthless the money had become. None of the other choices are related to the meaning of Continental.

2-2) C. The Albany Plan of Union was proposed by Benjamin Franklin at the Albany congress in 1754 in Albany, New York. It was an early attempt at forming a union of the colonists during the French and Indian War. Seven of the thirteen colonies attended and it did not take effect because colonial assemblies and the British Government did not support it. The Albany Plan had nothing to do with mercantilism.

2-3) D. The Continental Congress was adopted in the Olive Branch Petition of July 1775 in which they professed their loyalty to the crown and begged King George III to prevent further hostilities after the Battle of Bunker Hill in June. The king rejected the petition. The Continental Congress did not discuss the issue of the Intolerable Acts or the Quartering Act. The French were not involved in expanding their influence in the Northwest Territory.

2-4) B. The Battle of Saratoga in October 1777 was one of the most decisive battles in U.S. History. It provided the urgently needed aid from France, which in turn helped to ensure American independence. Without French military aid George Washington would not have been able to defeat the British at the Battle of Yorktown in 1781 that effectively ended fighting in the colonies. The Battle of Saratoga revived the faltering colonial cause and renewed their hope of victory but France's military aid made Saratoga the turning point of the war. Saratoga did not encourage Loyalists to switch sides or reinforce British determination to end the war unless they defeated the colonists.

Chapter 3

3-1) B. On July 14, 1798, Congress passed the Sedition Act during the administration of John Adams, who followed George Washington in 1796 as President. The United States was involved in an undeclared war with France and John Adams and the Federalist Party were trying to end dissent because they viewed the Democratic-Republican Party of Thomas Jefferson and James Madison as a threat to liberty. The Sedition Act expired on March 3, 1801, the day before Adams's presidential term came to an end.

3-2) E. The Treaty of Ghent was signed on December 24, 1814, in Brussels. The treaty said nothing about impressment or war damages. The blockade of American ships had ended when Britain's war with France ended and was not mentioned in the treaty. The Treaty simply restored diplomatic relations between the United States and Great Britain. They agreed to return prisoners and recognize pre-war boundaries, and allowed Americans to have their shipping rights in the Gulf of St. Lawrence.

3-3) C. In 1807 Jefferson persuaded the Republican majority to pass the Embargo Act. The measure prohibited American merchant ships from sailing to foreign ports. Jefferson hoped that his policy of peaceful coercion would convince Great Britain to stop violating the neutral nations like the United States rather than lose U.S. trade. The Embargo backfired and brought economic hardship to the United States rather than to Britain. The embargo severely hurt the economy, especially the New England shipbuilders and merchant marine. Jefferson called for the repeal of the Embargo Act in 1809. Jefferson had been successful in all the other achievements listed as the different options but his Embargo Act was a failure.

3-4) D. The "Era of Good Feeling" (1817–25) was a period in U.S. political history where the Democratic-Republican Party was the dominant political party. James Monroe ran unopposed and received all of the electoral votes but one. It was a time when on the surface partisan bitterness ended and there was a renewed sense of nationalism in the country. The term "Era of Good Feeling" is an oversimplification because the national mood was beginning to change over financial issues and the issue of slavery in Missouri which affected the North and West differently. The controversy over the Election of 1824 would end the "Era of Good Feeling."

Chapter 4

4-1) C. During the Jacksonian period voting rights were extended to all white men over twenty-one years of age regardless of their religion or property qualifications. Western states recently admitted to the Union adopted state constitutions allowing all white males to vote and hold office. Eastern states soon followed suit. The Progressive movement in the twentieth century introduced the primary system and the direct election of Senators. The Pendleton Act of 1881 set up the Civil Service system to replace the Spoils System. The nomination convention in 1830 replaced the caucus system to select candidates for political office.

4-2) A. In 1828 Congress passed what became known as the "Tariff of Abominations," a very high protective tax that increased duties as high as 50 percent. John C. Calhoun wrote *Exposition and Protest* to express South Carolina's opposition to the tariff. According to Calhoun's theory of nullification, each state had the right to decide whether to obey a federal law or to declare it null and void. In the Tariff of 1832, Congress lowered the tariff to avoid any conflict with South Carolina. Henry Clay of Kentucky was angry at Jackson's Maysville veto of internal improvement for the state. The Specie Circular of 1836 dealt with land speculation. The Worcester Case involved the right of Cherokee nations.

4-3) C. Charles G. Finney was a Presbyterian minister who was an important figure in the Second Great Awakening. The Second Great Awakening was a religious revival movement in the early nineteenth century emphasizing personal piety over schooling and theology. Finney's dynamic style of preaching attracted believers of this movement to his revival meetings. The Second Great Awakening stimulated the establishment of many reform movements designed to remedy the evils of society. Jonathan Edwards and George Whitefield are identified with the First Great Awakening of the eighteenth century. George Ripley launched a communal experiment at Brook Farm in Massachusetts. Joseph Smith founded the Church of the Latter-Day Saints or Mormons.

4-4) E. The American System proposed by Henry Clay in 1816 was based on expanding the size of the federal government, not limiting its role. The Federal government was expected to spend federal funds on road building, setting up national banks, providing a uniform currency, and helping industries by instituting a protective tariff. All of these steps required more, not less, government intervention.

Chapter 5

5-1) D. Andrew Jackson and Martin Van Buren put off Texas' request for annexation primarily because of political opposition among northerners to the expansion of slavery and the potential addition of up to five new slave states out of the Texas territories. The United States was not concerned about a war with Mexico or rival claims about Texas by either France or Britain. Texas did not have debt or education problems.

5-2) B. The issue of slavery in the territories gained in the Mexican War became the focus of the Election of 1848. Lewis Class, the Democratic nominee, adopted a platform pledged to popular sovereignty. Popular sovereignty maintained that the people who settled the territories should determine whether to allow slavery in the new western territory or state. Zachary Taylor, the Whig nominee, did not take a position on slavery in the territories and the Free-Soil Party led by Martin Van Buren opposed the extension of slavery in the territories. The Bank, the Missouri Compromise, extension of the railroad, and the Indian Removal Policy were not issues in the Election of 1848.

5-3) A. The Know-Nothing or the American Party was a nativist political movement in the 1840s and 1850s. It was feared that the country was being overwhelmed by German and Irish immigrants. They supported a number of anti-immigration laws and anti-Catholic policies. None of the other political parties focused on immigration in the 1840s and 1850s.

5-4) E. In 1860 the Democrats failed to present a united front against the Republicans. Northern Democrats supported Douglas on the platform of popular sovereignty. The southern Democrats broke from their party and nominated John C. Breckinridge. The combined popular vote of Douglas and Breckinridge was higher than the number of votes for Lincoln. Lincoln carried only the northern and western states and he was chosen because other Republicans like William H. Seward were considered too radical.

Chapter 6

6-1) C. The Tenure of Office Act of 1867 was enacted over the veto of President Andrew Jackson. The Act required the president to secure the consent of the Senate before he could remove his appointees once they had been approved by the body. The one purpose was to freeze into the cabinet the Secretary of War, Edwin M. Stanton, a holdover from the Lincoln administration. Johnson's firing of Stanton led to his trial for impeachment. Johnson survived the impeachment by one vote. The Tenure Act was passed to control the president and was not designed to control Reconstruction in the South.

6-2) E. The Copperheads were a group of northern Democrats who opposed the Civil War. They wanted an immediate peace settlement with the Confederates. They were opposed to the emancipation of American slaves. The name Copperheads was given to them by the Republicans to refer to copper liberty-head coins which many wore as badges. None of the other options describe the Copperheads.

6-3) B. On July 4, 1863, General Grant forced the surrender of Vicksburg, a city on the Mississippi River. This victory allowed federal warships to control the full length of the Mississippi and cut the Confederacy in half. The three Confederate states in the West, Texas, Louisiana, and Arkansas, were separated from the rest of the Confederacy. Gettysburg in 1863 ended any hope of the South invading the North. Shiloh in 1862 demonstrated that the war was going to be a drawn-out conflict and not a quick southern victory. Antietam in 1862 convinced foreign powers not to support the Confederacy. The First Battle of Bull Run in 1861, in which the South defeated the North, ended the hope of a quick victory for the North.

6-4) E. In 1876, Samuel Tilden won the popular vote but needed one more electoral vote to win. The Democrats had won the southern states except that the Republicans were contesting the voting returns of South Carolina, Florida, and Louisiana. A special commission, not the Supreme Court, determined who was entitled to the disputed vote of the three states. In a straight party vote, 8–7, Hayes, the Republican, was awarded the votes and became President.

Chapter 7

7-1) C. Political commentators have referred to differences between the Republicans and Democrats as "Tweedle Dee" and "Tweedle Dum." The two major parties agreed on all the major issues except for the inflation of the currency. The Republican Party supported the Gold Standard which meant that every dollar in circulation should be backed by an equal amount of gold. The Democrats and farmers supported the inflation of the currency by unlimited coinage of silver on a 16 to 1 ratio to gold. Farmers believed that by increasing the monetary supply with silver it would help them pay off their debt because it would lead to higher prices for farm products. In the Election of 1896, William Jennings Bryan, the Democratic candidate, ran on a platform that demanded the unlimited coinage of silver at a ratio of 16 ounces of silver to 1 ounce of gold. McKinley and the Republicans supported the Gold Standard. McKinley's voting ended any attempts at unlimited coinage of silver.

7-2) E. Ghost Dance was a set of dances and rites that arose on Indian reservations in South Dakota. It was an effort of Native Americans to resist U.S. domination and drive whites from their ancestral land. In December 1890, the U.S. Army outlawed the dance and the refusal of the Native Americans to stop led to the massacre at Wounded Knee in South Dakota. Over two hundred Native Americans were killed. The Battle of Wounded Knee marked the end of the Indian wars. The Battle of Little Big Horn occurred in 1876 and the Dawes Act was passed in 1887. Chief Joseph's attempt to escape from the U.S. Army to Canada ended in defeat and his surrender in 1877. Sitting Bull had been killed prior to Wounded Knee.

7-3) B. Although Mary Ellen Lease was an advocate of the suffrage and temperance movements, she is best known for her work with the Populist Party. She believed that big business had destroyed the farmers and their way of life. She exhorted Kansas farmers to "raise more hell than corn" as a way to improve their economic conditions during the late 1880s and 1890s. James Weaver was the Populist presidential candidate in 1892. William Jennings Bryan and Thomas Watson headed the Populist presidential ticket in 1896. Benjamin Tillman was the governor of South Carolina from 1890 to 1894.

7-4) D. William D. Haywood was a founding member and leader of the Industrial Workers of the World (IWW) and a member of the Executive Committee of the Socialist Party of America. Haywood favored organizing all workers in one union regardless of trade or skill level. This was different from the AFL, which was organized according to craft. Unlike the Knights of Labor, Haywood actively promoted labor strikes over arbitration or political tactics. His strong position alienated him from the Socialist Party and contributed to his dismissal in 1912. Convicted for violating the Espionage Act of 1907, he fled to Russia to avoid being sent to prison. The ILGU founded in 1900 was a very conservative union that supported skilled workers. The CIO was proposed by John L. Lewis in 1932 during the Great Depression.

Chapter 8

8-1) A. Alfred T. Mahan's *The Influence of Sea Power Upon History* (1890) argued that the United States needed colonies in order to insure control of the markets of the world. He prescribed an imperialist strategy based on the command of the seas. It said that the security of the United States depended on a strong navy. Josiah Strong was a Protestant minister who justified American expansion. Based on spreading the Anglo-Saxon civilization, Mahan's book strongly influenced Senator Albert J. Beveridge and Presidents McKinley and Roosevelt to support an aggressive foreign policy.

8-2) A. The annexation of Hawaii was not part of the Treaty of Paris (1898). The United States had been interested in Hawaii for decades before the Spanish-American War. American settlers in 1893 had petitioned it for annexation and were instrumental in overthrowing the Hawaiian Queen. When the Spanish-American War broke out, the United States used it as an excuse to annex Hawaii and made it a territory in 1900. All the other options were provisions of the Treaty of Paris.

8-3) A. Upton Sinclair wrote *The Jungle* in 1906, describing the unsanitary and unhealthy working conditions of the meatpacking industry. His book was instrumental in the passage of the Pure Food & Drug Act. Frank Norris wrote about the abuses of the railroad. Lincoln Steffens exposed the corruption of municipal government. Ida Tarbell and Henry Demarest Lloyd wrote about the Standard Oil Company.

8-4) B. Women played a major role in the Progressive movement and they were instrumental in persuading Woodrow Wilson to support women's suffrage. In 1920, the Nineteenth Amendment guaranteed women the right to vote. The other issues were not specifically addressed by the Progressives.

Chapter 9

9-1) D. The National War Labor Board was a federal agency created in April 1918. It was composed of representatives from business and labor and chaired by former President William Howard Taft. Its purpose was to prevent strikes by arbitrating disputes between workers and employers in order to ensure labor reliability and productivity during the war. It was disbanded after the war in May 1919.

9-2) A. Frederick W. Taylor was an American mechanical engineer who sought to improve industrial efficiency. He is regarded as the Father of Scientific Management. He carefully observed and analyzed the time and energy for each job, then set standards for each worker. His method improved mass production and contributed to the dramatic increase of productivity in the 1920s. Taylor died in 1915 and was not alive to work with the leaders listed as the other choices.

9-3) B. The Republican candidate Herbert Hoover ran for president in 1928 with this campaign slogan. The slogan symbolized the belief that Republican prosperity would continue to increase the wealth of the country. Hoover carried 58.2 percent of the vote, easily defeating the Democratic rival Alfred E. Smith. Within six months, the Great Depression would destroy the economic prosperity of the 1920s. In 1928, Calvin Coolidge decided not to run for the presidency. Warren Harding, who died in 1923, ran on the slogan of "Return to Normalcy." The Democrat Franklin D. Roosevelt ran on the slogan of a "New Deal" in 1932 and Harry Truman ran on the slogan of a "Fair Deal" in 1948.

9-4) D. The Harlem Renaissance refers to a period in the 1920s and early 1930s when Harlem became the intellectual and cultural center of the African American community. Black writers and poets like Langston Hughes, James Weldon Johnson, Countee Cullen, and Zorn Neal Houston wrote about the diversity of their culture, and the joy and frustrations of being African American in a white-dominated society. These writers did not focus on Harlem's educational community nor did they see their future in Africa. Jazz was the musical expression of the Harlem Renaissance but musicians like Louis Armstrong and Duke Ellington were not active in Marcus Garvey's United Negro Improvement Association.

Chapter 10

10-1) E. The National Labor Relations Act (Wagner Act) was part of Roosevelt's Second New Deal. The NLRA was enacted by Congress in 1935 after the Supreme Court had ruled that the National Recovery Act, which had given labor the right to organize collectively, was unconstitutional. The Wagner Act has been hailed as the Magna Carta of American labor. The NLRA guaranteed workers the right to join unions without the fear of management reprisal. All the other legislation was passed in the hundred days between March 9 and June 16, 1933.

10-2) C. The Reconstruction Finance Corporation was an independent agency of the United States Government chartered during Herbert Hoover's administration in 1932. The agency gave $2 billion in aid of emergency loans to local governments that would be used to help faltering banks, railroads, life insurance companies, and other financial institutions. The President expected these loans to stabilize key businesses which would trickle down to help the smaller businesses. The Reconstruction Finance Corporation did not provide help for individuals, farm boards, and public works nor did it provide bonuses for Army veterans.

10-3) C. John Maynard Keynes, the British economist, thought that Roosevelt had made a mistake in trying to balance the budget. He rejected the Republican philosophy of trickle-down economy or deregulation of business and insisted that deficit spending in difficult times was necessary to give the economy a jumpstart. Keynes believed that deficit spending would be like "priming the pump" to increase investments and create jobs. Keynes never discussed bloc grants but focused on deficit spending on public works and relief in order to spur industrial production.

10-4) B. The Indian Reorganization Act, informally the Indian New Deal, reversed the Dawes Act of individuals owning property and stressed tribal ownership and tribal authority. This reversal returned Native Americans to local self-government on tribal bases. The IRA was designed to restore local rule to the Native Americans who had become citizens in 1924. The Federal Government did not institute any educational or religious programs under this New Deal legislation.

Chapter 11

11-1) C. The Manhattan Project was set up to develop the first nuclear weapon (atomic bomb) during World War II by the United States, the United Kingdom, and Canada. Formally designated as the Manhattan Engineer District (MED), it specifically refers to the period of the project from 1941–1946 under the control of the U.S. Army Corps of Engineers during the administration of General Leslie R. Groves. The scientific research was directed by American physicist J. Robert Oppenheimer.

11-2) E. During World War II, Civil Rights organizations like the NAACP encouraged African Americans to adopt the "Double V" slogan—V for victory over fascism abroad and V for victory for equality at home. All the other options are not related to the Double V campaign.

11-3) B. In December 1943, Stalin, Churchill, and Roosevelt met for the first time in Teheran. At the conference they agreed to open a second front to liberate France in 1944. The Big Three also met at Yalta in February 1945. Only Churchill and Roosevelt met at Casablanca. The Dumbarton Oaks and Potsdam meetings took place after Roosevelt's death in April 1945.

11-4) A. The Kellogg-Briand Pact, also called the Pact of Paris, was negotiated by Frank B. Kellogg, U.S. Secretary of State, and the French Minister Aristide Briand. The Pact denounced war but made no provision for enforcement. The Four and Nine Power Treaties and Washington's Naval Conference were designed to reduce the military arms race, not war. The Four Freedoms was a statement of U.S. war aims in 1941.

Chapter 12

12-1) D. The McCarran Walters Act of 1952, which Congress passed over President Truman's veto, contained these provisions. At the end of World War II, many in the United States were fearful that communism was spreading to America and the public wanted the government to restrict immigration of potential subversives. The Loyalty Oaths and the McCarran Internal Security Act required the government to investigate the background of federal employees and the McCarran Internal Security Act forced communist groups to register their names with the Attorney General. The Refugee Act allowed the government to admit immigrants who had been displaced from their countries because of World War II. The Espionage Act was passed during World War I.

12-2) E. In 1961, John Kennedy changed Eisenhower's policy of brink-manship, secret covert operations to overthrow communism, and massive retaliation. He adopted the doctrine of "Flexible Response" which focused on using Special Forces like the Green Berets to fight insurgent forces in Third World countries. Kennedy rejected the Eisenhower belief in rolling back communism and recognized the Soviet sphere of influence in eastern Europe.

12-3) C. Historians have noted that this was the first election greatly influenced by television. Nixon, who was Eisenhower's vice president, appeared tired and pale and Kennedy seemed calm and self-confident. Polls during the following weeks revealed a sharp increase in those who liked Kennedy. Lightly regarded by Democratic leaders, Kennedy used the debates to his full advantage. As a Roman Catholic, he was extremely popular with ethnic Americans and his selection of Johnson as his running mate shored up his support in the South. However, the tipping point in the election was the televised debates. Nixon's Checker Speech occurred in 1952 and had no relevance to the election of 1960.

12-4) D. The Tet or Lunar Offensive was a surprise attack launched in January 1968 by the Vietcong on the occasion of their Lunar New Year on almost every province and American base in South Vietnam. The U.S. military counterattack inflicted heavy damages on the Vietcong and recovered the lost territory. However, it was a political defeat for President Johnson. The Tet Offensive turned American public opinion against the war. The sight of American forces fighting to regain their own embassy and the ineffectiveness of the South Vietnamese Army convinced Americans that the war was a lost effort. President Johnson's and the military's focus on "body counts" and an impending victory did not hold up after the Tet Offensive. The aftermath of the Tet Offensive forced Johnson from the White House.

Chapter 13

13-1) D. To limit the president's war-making power in the future, Congress enacted the War Powers Act in 1973 over President Nixon's veto. The president was required to inform Congress within forty-eight hours of sending troops into combat. The president also needed Congress' approval if American troops would be involved in fighting abroad for a period of more than ninety days. Without Congressional approval, the president would be forced to bring the troops home. The War Powers Act did not end the draft.

13-2) A. The Iran Hostage Crisis of November 1979 dragged out through the last year of Carter's presidency. In April of 1980, Carter approved a rescue mission, but the breakdown of the helicopters over the Iranian desert forced Carter to call off the effort. Carter's failure to rescue the hostages became a symbol of his presidency. The Hostage Crisis, which lasted 444 days, hurt his public image and contributed to his decisive defeat in the Election of 1980. The "Malaise Speech," the Soviet Invasion of Afghanistan in 1980, and the OPEC Oil Embargo, helped to reinforce the image created by the Hostage Crisis of an inept president. The Amnesty for Draft Evaders was the least damaging event of Carter's administration.

13-3) B. In 1983, Ronald Reagan proposed the SDI, popularly called "Star Wars," a space-based missile defensive system that would destroy enemy missiles before they could reach American territory. None of the other presidents are associated with this program.

13-4) C. As the economy soured and federal deficits soared in 1988, Bush was forced to reverse his "no new taxes" pledge and agreed to accept the Democratic Congress proposal of $133 billion in new taxes. The unpopular tax did not help Bush, but the most damaging event was a recession that started in 1990. With the economy growing at a meager 1 percent annually, Bush's perceived strength in dealing with the collapse of the Soviet Union and the war in Iraq were not as significant. As the White House was unable to improve the economy, Clinton's mantra, "It's the economy, stupid," was successful in convincing the voters that the Democrats would alleviate the economic crisis if they recaptured the White House.

Glossary of
Terms, People, and Events

While rote memorization will not be that helpful to you for the AP U.S. History Exam, you must become familiar with certain terms in order to answer questions quickly and efficiently. The following terms are organized chronologically and are grouped into major eras in U.S. History.

Origins of a New Nation, 1450–1789

Puritanism The Puritans were a religious group who disagreed with the Church of England's theology, which they believed was too lenient. They came to the New World to form a "purer" church and began arriving at Plymouth Colony in 1620.

Mercantilism Practiced by most European states in the late 1600s, mercantilism was an economic theory in which a nation's power depended on its wealth; thus, a nation should go to any lengths necessary to build up its wealth.

Triangular Trade The trade relationship that developed in the late seventeenth century among the Americas, Europe, and Africa. Europeans purchased slaves from Africa; those slaves were resold in the Americas; and the Americas provided raw materials to Europe, who used them to manufacture goods that were then exported to the Americas for sale.

Great Awakening The first American Great Awakening happened in the 1730s and 1740s and was a revival that brought a renewed interest in religious ideas and practices. It led to changes in American colonial society, especially along the Western Frontier and the South, and it may have also had a democratizing effect on colonial America.

French and Indian War Often called the Seven Years War in Europe, this was the conflict between the British and the French from 1756 to 1763. Both countries wanted to expand their colonial interests in the Americas. Colonists and Native Americans fought for both sides; the English ultimately won and received French Canada.

Albany Plan of Union Proposed by Benjamin Franklin at the 1754 Albany Conference, this was the idea of uniting the colonies under one government, to better protect the interests of the colonies. It was rejected by the colonies.

Declaration of Independence Adopted by the Continental Congress on July 4, 1776, this statement announced that the thirteen colonies were independent states and no longer under British control. Written primarily by Thomas Jefferson, it was the formal reasoning for the colonies' decision to go to war with Britain.

Treaty of Paris Signed on September 3, 1783, this treaty officially ended the Revolutionary War and recognized the United States as a sovereign nation.

Articles of Confederation This document, ratified in 1781, established the United States' first official government, which gave most power to the states rather than the federal government. The Articles were replaced by the Constitution in 1788.

Shays' Rebellion Named after Daniel Shays, this was a violent rebellion that took place in 1786 in western Massachusetts. It was provoked by poor farmers angry at the American government's unwillingness to help them with their crushing debts.

Northwest Ordinance In 1787, this law provided the framework for how western territories of the United States would be admitted to the Union. It guaranteed that new states would receive equal status with the older states and that they would have the same rights as citizens of the original thirteen colonies.

Great Compromise of 1787 This plan determined that one house of the U.S. government would be based on population (House of Representatives) while the other would allow equal representation to all states (Senate). It was drafted by Roger Sherman of Connecticut and was instrumental in expediting the ratification of the Constitution.

Federalists/Anti-Federalists Federalists pushed for a strong national government with strong financial credibility. Alexander Hamilton was one of the best-known Federalists, and he sought to establish a national bank that would take on all debts incurred by the Revolution. Anti-federalists opposed this policy.

Important Figures

Jonathan Edwards An eighteenth century theologian who was one of the most important figures in the First Great Awakening. Edwards's "Sinners in the Hands of an Angry God" is one of the most influential sermons in U.S. History.

John Locke One of the most influential of the Enlightenment philosophers, this British scholar's writings were instrumental in shaping the ideas behind the American Revolution. He believed that people should be involved in government rather than oppressed by it.

Thomas Paine A radical recent immigrant to the colonies who, in 1776, published a pamphlet titled *Common Sense*, which became a bestseller in the American colonies. He argued vigorously that the colonies should become independent states and break their ties with the British monarchy. The pamphlet helped convince the colonists to break away from the rule of King George.

John Winthrop He led the Puritans to the New World and became the first governor of the Massachusetts colony.

John Peter Zenger This German-born publisher was prosecuted for printing criticisms of the governor of New York in 1734. Although his statements were harmful, they were based on fact. Thus he was found not guilty. This case is seen as influential to the Bill of Rights and the rights of individual citizens to have free speech.

Founding and Settlement, 1789–1861

Washington's Farewell Address Published in 1796, it outlines Washington's words of advice to the recently formed United States. He warned that unity would be the biggest issue confronting the new nation, and that any attempts to undermine unity among the states would prevent the country from becoming a true power.

XYZ Affair This was a diplomatic episode that damaged the relationship between the United States and France and led to an undeclared naval war from 1798 to 1800. It involved three French agents' (XYZ) demand for bribes before they would negotiate with the United States

Jeffersonian Revolution This refers to Jefferson's philosophy of government, emphasizing a tightly restricted federal government, states' rights, and individual rights and liberties. It also refers to Jefferson's election in 1800, in which the Democratic-Republicans replaced the Federalists.

Louisiana Purchase This 1803 purchase, engineered by Thomas Jefferson, nearly doubled the size of the United States Sold by Napoleon for $15 million, the territory stretched from the Mississippi River to the Rocky Mountains.

Era of Good Feeling A period lasting from approximately 1817 to 1825, in which partisanship took a back seat in American politics. James Monroe was president during this time.

American System A comprehensive plan proposed by Representative Henry Clay of Kentucky in the 1820s to promote industry. The plan consisted of a protective tariff, a national bank, and federally funded internal improvements.

Monroe Doctrine Devised by Secretary of State John Quincy Adams and articulated by President James Monroe in 1823, this doctrine stated that any attempt by European nations to colonize the Americas would be considered an act of aggression. Europe should leave the Western Hemisphere alone, and the United States would not interfere with or colonize Europe.

Missouri Compromise Passed in 1820, it regulated slavery in the western territories. The compromise prohibited slavery in the former Louisiana Territory, north of the 36/30 parallel, except within the borders of the proposed state of Missouri. It also admitted Maine as a non-slave state.

Peculiar Institution This euphemism for slavery and its ramifications became popular during the first half of the nineteenth century, as it was considered inappropriate to use the word slavery.

Abolitionists People dedicated to the abolition of slavery, abolitionists were both black and white and were based primarily in the North. William Lloyd Garrison was one of the most famous abolitionists of the nineteenth century.

Corrupt Bargain This refers to the results of the 1824 presidential election, in which no candidate secured the required number of votes and the House of Representatives was responsible for deciding the outcome. The House elected John Quincy Adams over his rival Andrew Jackson. Henry Clay, the Speaker of the House, convinced Congress to elect Adams, who then made Clay his Secretary of State. Jackson supporters denounced this as a "corrupt bargain," since Jackson had won a plurality of both the popular and electoral votes.

Era of the Common Man During this period from 1829 to 1837, also called the era of Jacksonian democracy, voting qualifications such as the literacy test and property ownership were eliminated, so that all free white males could vote except in six states. Also, nominating conventions replaced Congressional caucuses as a way of selecting presidential candidates.

Trail of Tears Refers to the forced 1838 relocation of more than twenty thousand members of the Cherokee tribe to a new "homeland" in Oklahoma. One out of every five Native Americans died from hunger, disease, or exhaustion during the march.

Manifest Destiny A phrase first used in the 1840s to convey the idea that America had the right and destiny to expand westward without regard for indigenous people's relationship to the land.

Treaty of Guadalupe Hidalgo This 1848 treaty ended the Mexican-American War. For $15 million, it added to the United States the Texas territory (to the Rio Grande), New Mexico, and California.

Compromise of 1850 This complex agreement was meant to appease the North and the South and prevent the South's secession. The strengthening of the Fugitive Slave Act was meant to make the South happy; the North was appeased by the admission of California to the Union as a free state.

Bleeding Kansas Refers to the impact of the 1854 Kansas-Nebraska Act, which allowed residents of the Kansas territory to decide whether slavery would be allowed. As both pro- and anti-slavery groups flooded the territory, violence ensued.

Dred Scott Case Dred Scott had been born a slave but he lived in both slave and non-slave territories; his petition to the court for his freedom was denied. The Supreme Court ruled that slaves were property and thus had no legal right to petition the court. It also declared the Missouri Compromise unconstitutional.

Election of 1860 This election set the stage for the Civil War. Abraham Lincoln was elected president without the support of a single southern state. Less than a month later, the first southern states seceded.

Important Figures

Abigail Adams Wife of the second president, John Adams, and mother to John Quincy Adams, the sixth president, Abigail Adams was a trusted advisor to her husband during the Revolution and over the course of his entire political career. Her correspondence with John Adams provides keen insight into the progress of the American Revolution.

John Brown An American abolitionist from Ohio, he advocated violence as a means to end slavery. In 1856, he led the Pottawatomie Massacre, which helped spark Bleeding Kansas, and he became famous for his unsuccessful raid at Harpers Ferry in 1859.

Henry Clay The Speaker of the House during the 1824 election, he convinced the House to elect John Quincy Adams over Andrew Jackson. He then became Adams's Secretary of State. He was a big supporter of the American system and favored tariffs and a strong national bank.

William Lloyd Garrison A well-known abolitionist who published the anti-slavery newspaper *The Liberator*, he also founded the American Anti-Slavery Association. Later he was a proponent of women's suffrage.

Alexander Hamilton The first Secretary of the Treasury, a Founding Father, and an economist, Hamilton was also an author of the *Federalist Papers*, which advocated for a strong centralized government, including the formation of a nationalized bank that would absorb the new nation's debt.

Andrew Jackson The seventh president of the United States, Jackson was a polarizing political figure who presented himself as a protector of the common man against the power of the privileged, but also supported slavery and advocated for the forced removal of Native Americans from America's expanding territories. He is seen as the quintessential symbol of the frontier life in America.

James Madison One of the Founding Fathers of the United States, he was also one of the principal authors of the *Federalist Papers*, which is among the most influential essays on American government and republicanism. He is also considered the father of the Bill of Rights (the first ten amendments to the Constitution), and he later served as the fourth president of the United States, from 1808 to 1812.

Horace Mann Often considered the "father of modern public American education," Mann was instrumental in developing public schools in Massachusetts. His system spread to other states. He believed that all children should have access to the same type of education, and he advocated for large-scale curriculum changes, longer enrollment in school for children (up until sixteen years old), and better pay for teachers.

John Marshall Chief Justice of the Supreme Court from 1801 through his death in 1835, Marshall made the Supreme Court a center of power in American government. He advocated a strong national government and made several decisions that favored the Federalist viewpoint.

James K. Polk Known as Young Hickory because he was a protégé of Andrew Jackson, Polk was elected president in 1844 on a platform that supported Manifest Destiny. During his presidency, the United States acquired Oregon and seized California through the Mexican War. Historians have criticized Polk for purposely provoking war with Mexico as a way of gaining the southwestern part of the United States.

Elizabeth Cady Stanton A well-known abolitionist, she eventually became a key figure in the women's suffrage movement. Her address at the first women's rights convention in 1848, in Seneca Falls, New York, is seen as the start of the first organized women's and women's suffrage movements.

Tecumseh A Native American leader and member of the Shawnee tribe, he fought against the United States in the War of 1812 and during its subsequent expansion. He was regarded as a hero for his defense of Native American rights.

Civil War and American Imperialism, 1861–1914

Anaconda Plan A key component of the Union's attempt to win the Civil War, it called for the capture of critical Southern ports and control of the Mississippi River, to create logistical and economic difficulties for the South.

Emancipation Proclamation Abraham Lincoln's 1863 edict abolished slavery in the Confederate states. It did not include the four slave states in the Union, for fear of provoking them to join the Confederacy.

Civil War Amendments Also known as the Reconstruction Amendments, the Thirteenth, Fourteenth, and Fifteenth Amendments were adopted in the five years immediately following the Civil War. The Thirteenth Amendment abolished slavery; the Fourteenth included due-process and equal-protection clauses; and the Fifteenth established voting rights for all men, regardless of "race, color, or previous condition of servitude."

Reconstruction The period after the Civil War during which newly freed slaves were granted additional economic, social, and political rights. Many Southerners resented these changes, and organizations such as the Ku Klux Klan were formed in response. This period ended with the Compromise of 1877.

Black Codes These codes refer to laws passed mainly in the South to restrict the rights of newly freed slaves. In some states, blacks could not own property, move, or perform any labor but farming.

Jim Crow Laws These state and local laws allowed for "separate but equal" treatment for blacks, primarily between 1876 and 1965. These laws usually resulted in much worse conditions and treatment for blacks, and were a way of fostering segregation. Under Jim Crow, schools, transportation, and even water fountains were segregated.

Compromise of 1877 This political agreement ended the contested presidential election of 1876. Representatives of the Southern States agreed not to fight the official election of Republican Rutherford B. Hayes, despite major election irregularities. In exchange, the Union army stopped enforcing Reconstruction legislation in the South.

Plessy v. Ferguson A landmark 1896 Supreme Court decision, it upheld the constitutionality of "separate but equal" segregation, which remained the law until 1954, when *Brown v. Board of Education* declared "separate but equal" unconstitutional.

Robber Barons This negative term was used in the nineteenth century to refer to businessmen and bankers who dominated industry and accumulated massive personal fortunes. Some of them included Andrew Carnegie, J. P. Morgan, and John D. Rockefeller.

Social Darwinism A philosophy that evolved from the writings of Charles Darwin, it held that since people inevitably compete with one another, the strongest will survive. "Survival of the fittest" was used to explain the wealth disparity in the United States and the colonization of other parts of the world by the United States and Europe. A British social philosopher, Herbert Spencer, helped to popularize this term.

Gilded Age Taken from the title of a Mark Twain novel, this refers to the late nineteenth century, a time when great prosperity concealed many fundamental tensions in society, including wealth disparity and social inequity.

New Immigration This refers to Southern and Eastern European immigrants, who made up a majority of the post-1900 immigrants. They were called new immigrants because their culture was different from those of the earlier immigrants from northern and western Europe.

Tammany Hall This Democratic political machine ran New York City's politics, beginning in 1870. This model of corruption and greed—best epitomized by William Tweed, known as "Boss Tweed," who ran Tammany Hall in the 1860s—became the norm in many cities.

Populist Party This party represented farmers and won a major political victory in the 1890s when they influenced the election of several U.S. Representatives and a Senator. Populist principles included a more democratic government and more direct involvement by the government to help the working class.

Wounded Knee The last battle between the Great Sioux Nation and the United States, ended the American/Indian Wars. This 1890 conflict was exacerbated when a deaf Sioux did not surrender his weapon, igniting violence that resulted in approximately 150 Sioux deaths.

Yellow Journalism A journalistic style that uses lurid and sensational events to sell newspapers. Yellow journalism was key in shifting public perception of the events in Cuba leading up to the Spanish-American War.

Spanish-American War Beginning in 1898, this war stemmed from American discord over the way the Spanish were treating Cubans. Yellow journalism fostered a sense of outrage against Spain. As a result of the war, the United States acquired the Philippines, making the country a major player in the Pacific. Also, Theodore Roosevelt, the future president, made his reputation as a war hero.

Big Stick Policy This phrase used to describe Theodore Roosevelt's approach to foreign policy refers to the approach of negotiating peacefully while using the threat of a strong military to achieve dominance overseas.

Muckrakers Journalists of the Progressive Era, they wanted to expose the evils of big business and government. They covered topics such as corruption in local and city government and the poor working conditions in factories. Lincoln Steffens, Ida Tarbell, and Upton Sinclair were some of the most influential muckrakers.

Progressivism This movement pushed for large-scale social and political reform that resulted in less corruption, more equal treatment among classes, regulation of big business, and better conditions for laborers.

Square Deal This was Theodore Roosevelt's philosophy of regulating big business, protecting the consumer, and conserving the nation's natural resources.

National American Woman Suffrage Association Founded in 1890 by two of the country's best-known suffragists, Susan B. Anthony and Elizabeth Cady Stanton, it was the largest and most important suffragette organization in the United States, and it was the primary promoter of women's right to vote, pushing for a constitutional amendment that would guarantee that right.

Nineteenth Amendment Passed in 1920, this amendment gave every citizen—regardless of sex—the right to vote.

Niagara Movement This black civil rights organization was founded in 1905 by a group led by W. E. B. Du Bois and William Monroe Trotter. The Niagara Movement opposed racial segregation and did not support conciliation, a method promoted by Booker T. Washington and other black leaders.

Important Figures

William Jennings Bryan A late nineteenth-early twentieth-century politician who made three unsuccessful bids for the presidency, his famous "cross of gold" speech in 1896 garnered his first nomination for the presidency. He served as secretary of state under Wilson and was a devout populist and advocate against big business. Due to his religious beliefs, he opposed evolution and famously defended his views in the Scopes Trial of 1925.

Andrew Carnegie A Scottish immigrant who came to the United States when he was thirteen, Carnegie became one of the late nineteenth and early twentieth centuries' wealthiest businessmen and biggest philanthropists. His ruthless business methods helped him build a major steel company.

Ulysses S. Grant Grant was the eighteenth president of the United States and the general who led the Union Army to victory in the Civil War. His presidency was tarnished by bribery and corruption scandal.

Abraham Lincoln The sixteenth president of the United States, he issued the Emancipation Proclamation and is widely regarded as one of the country's best presidents because of his performance during the nation's worst crisis, the Civil War.

Theodore Roosevelt Roosevelt was the twenty-sixth president of the United States and was famous for his outdoorsman image and his model of masculinity. He was also a leader of the Progressive movement, which attempted to regulate abusive and monopolistic practices by big corporations. As President, his "big stick" policy was instrumental in America's growth as a superpower.

Thaddeus Stevens A radical Republican from Pennsylvania, Stevens fought vigorously for the protection of African American rights after the Civil War. He was also instrumental in drafting the Fourteenth Amendment to the Constitution, guaranteeing minorities equal protection under the law.

Booker T. Washington A former slave who established a black industrial college in 1881 in Tuskegee, Alabama, Washington believed that southern blacks could achieve economic equality with whites by learning skilled trades. He did not oppose the Jim Crow laws of the late nineteenth century, believing that blacks would achieve social equality when they gained economic equality. Other black leaders, particularly W. E. B. Du Bois, strongly opposed his viewpoints.

The World at War, 1914–1945

Neutrality This was the policy/philosophy adopted by the United States following World War I. The country was eager to isolate itself from European conflicts and passed the Neutrality Act of 1935, preventing America from trading arms with any country at war.

Fourteen Points Woodrow Wilson's Fourteen Points outlined the ideas he wanted to see incorporated into the Treaty of Versailles, which ended World War I. They included the end of secret treaties, arms reduction, national self-determination, and the creation of a League of Nations. Of these, only the League of Nations became a reality, and the United States never joined.

Versailles Treaty Signed on June 28, 1919, between Germany and the Allied Powers, the Treaty of Versailles officially ended World War I. It placed blame for the war solely on Germany and required it to pay reparations to the Allied Powers. This set off a chain of events and reactions that eventually led to World War II.

Red Scare This is the period after World War I when radicals, immigrant groups, and perceived political subversives were repressed and, in many cases, jailed in the United States. Nearly seven thousand "radicals" were sent to jail, many of whom were never charged with a crime, and five hundred immigrants were deported.

Return to Normalcy The campaign slogan of Warren Harding, who ran for the presidency in 1920 and won, promised the weary, post–World War I nation a break from Progressive Era social upheaval and reform.

Lost Generation A group of American intellectuals who did not want to support what they perceived to be the overwhelmingly shallow culture of the 1920s. Disillusioned with American life and values, many became ex-pats and relocated to Paris.

Scopes Trial In this 1925 trial in Tennessee, John Scopes, a teacher in a public school, was charged with violating state statutes for teaching evolution. Clarence Darrow was hired by the American Civil Liberties Union (ACLU) to defend Scopes, while three-time presidential candidate William Jennings Bryan prosecuted the case. Scopes technically lost the case and had to pay a fine, but Darrow won in the court of public opinion.

Harlem Renaissance Lasting from the 1920s to the early 1930s, this was the black literary and artistic movement that both celebrated and lamented black life in America. Langston Hughes and Zora Neale Hurston were two of the best-known writers of this period.

Prohibition The period between 1920 and 1933 when the sale, manufacture, and transportation of alcohol for consumption was forbidden, as per the Eighteenth Amendment. The law was often violated, and speakeasies—clubs where people purchased and consumed alcohol— sprang up throughout the United States. As the Depression progressed,

Prohibition became increasingly unpopular. It was eventually repealed by the Twenty-first Amendment in 1933.

National Origins Act This 1924 legislation took an extremely strict stance against immigration and allowed only immigration to the level indicated by the 1890 census. This lowered immigration overall, and it nearly eliminated immigration from Eastern and Southern Europe.

Great Depression The severe, worldwide economic decline began roughly in 1929 and lasted until the early 1940s. In the United States, the Depression began with the stock market crash of 1929. Unemployment and economic crisis spread and created economic hardship for almost all Americans.

Hoovervilles Collections of "houses," usually made of crude materials sprang up on the outskirts of many American cities as the Depression continued. The unemployed and destitute lived in these shacks. Their name indicates the disgust many felt towards President Hoover for not doing more to revive the American economy.

Brain Trust This term was used to describe the group of advisors to Franklin D. Roosevelt during his political career, particularly during his presidency. Roosevelt's Brain Trust was instrumental in crafting New Deal legislation and policies. They were often ridiculed in the media for being idealistic and impractical.

Hundred Days The first one hundred days of Franklin D. Roosevelt's New Deal, lasted from March to June of 1933. Programs were implemented to combat economic crises in farming, banking, and employment. Prohibition was also repealed.

America First Committee This group was dedicated to protesting U.S. entry into World War II. Established in 1940 by a Yale University law student, the AFC included many prominent politicians and public figures who wanted Roosevelt to uphold the United States' isolationist policy. The group disbanded after the Japanese attack on Pearl Harbor on December 7, 1941.

Lend Lease Act Adopted by Congress in 1941, this legislation allowed the United States to sell or lease arms and other equipment to nations whose security was vital to America's long-term survival. This was a direct rebuttal to the Neutrality Act of 1935. Shortly after it was passed, the United States began selling arms to England to help with their World War II campaign.

Big Three The Big Three refers to Joseph Stalin of the Soviet Union, Winston Churchill of Great Britain, and Franklin D. Roosevelt of the United States. These three men and nations were the key players in World War II events and post-war negotiations.

Yalta Conference This was a meeting of the Big Three a few months before the fall of Nazi Germany in 1945. Stalin pledged to assist the American campaign against Japan; Germany was to be divided into zones (each controlled by a WWII victor); and Stalin agreed to allow free elections in Eastern European nations that had been liberated from the Nazis. Critics of the agreement believed that Churchill and Roosevelt essentially gave control of Eastern Europe to the Soviet Union.

Hiroshima On this Japanese city, the United States dropped the first-ever atomic bomb on August 6, 1945, immediately killing almost 80,000 people. By year's end, nearly 150,000 people had died. Almost 70 percent of the city's buildings were destroyed, and the health effects of the bomb have lingered on for generations in Japan.

Important Figures

John Maynard Keynes A British economist, Keynes's ideas influenced Roosevelt's economic policies during the Depression. He believed that deficit spending was necessary during difficult financial times, because it would jumpstart the economy by creating investments and jobs.

Henry Cabot Lodge This Republican senator from Massachusetts, as Chairman of the Senate Foreign Relations Committee, led the opposition to the Versailles Treaty because it contained the League of Nations. His opposition contributed to the Treaty's defeat.

Huey Long Nicknamed "The Kingfish," he was the controversial governor of Louisiana from 1928–1932, during the early years of the Great Depression. He was a strong advocate for government intervention in lifting the country out of the Depression, and he advocated for public works and other plans to stimulate the economy, especially in his home state. His critics viewed him as deeply corrupt.

Franklin D. Roosevelt The thirty-second president of the United States, he was credited with pulling the country out of the Great Depression and leading the country through World War II. Elected to four consecutive terms, Roosevelt died during his fourth term, not long before the end of the war.

Woodrow Wilson The twenty-eighth president of the United States, Wilson was a leading figure in the Progressive Movement. He pushed for the creation of the League of Nations at the conclusion of World War I, but the country's growing isolationism led Congress to withhold its support.

The Cold War to the War on Terrorism, 1945–Present

Cold War This is the period of extreme tensions between the Soviet Union and the United States between the end of World War II and the fall of the Berlin Wall in 1989. Nuclear war was an ever-present threat, and the struggle between democratic and communist ideals colored every aspect of political, economic, and social life.

Containment This U.S. policy, formulated by diplomat George Kennan, advocated forcibly opposing communist aggression anywhere it occurred in the world.

Domino Theory This theory, popular during the Cold War, suggested that if one nation became communist other nations would quickly follow suit. This theory led to the belief that American involvement in Vietnam was crucial to saving Southeast Asia from becoming communist.

Korean War In this war American and other United Nations forces fought to stop communist aggression against South Korea from 1950 to 1953, as consistent with the policy of containment. Korea was eventually divided along the 38th parallel, and it remains so today.

McCarthyism Named after Senator Joseph McCarthy of Wisconsin, this movement of the 1940s and 1950s refers to a period when some politicians tried to root out any potential communist influences within the government. Investigators called people to testify at Congressional hearings, which harmed or ruined many careers, since even the suspicion of communist associations was extremely damaging.

Fair Deal A series of domestic programs proposed by Harry Truman in 1948, it included fair employment opportunities, public-works projects, and an extension of Social Security.

Beat Generation This 1950's literary movement criticized the conformity of American society and responded to the perpetual threat of atomic war. Jack Kerouac, Allen Ginsberg, and William Burroughs were key authors of the movement.

Brown v. Board of Education In 1954 this Supreme Court decision reversed the 1896 *Plessy v. Ferguson* decision, which allowed for *de jure* segregation. Schools could no longer be "separate but equal." This decision kicked off the long process of desegregating public schools.

Sit-in Movement That tactic used by civil rights advocates in the 1960s was designed to disrupt the normal flow of business and affect profits. Activists would "sit in" on segregated areas, typically lunch counters, and refuse to leave.

New Frontier John F. Kennedy's attempt in 1960 to revitalize and reenergize America, the New Frontier is summed up by Kennedy's statement, "Ask not what your country can do for you—ask what you can do for your country," reflecting a desire for more Americans to serve in organizations like the Peace Corps.

Great Society The 1965 program was announced by Lyndon Johnson, who wanted to attack major social problems like poverty and health care. He introduced Medicare and Medicaid, civil rights legislation, and increased funding for education, especially in poorer communities. He had difficulty balancing his vision for a Great Society with the costs and impact of the Vietnam War.

Black Power This mid-1960's movement emphasized pride in African American racial heritage and economic and political self-reliance. The term was coined by the black civil rights leader Stokely Carmichael.

Counterculture This 1960's youth movement advocated for a lifestyle that included drug use, free love, and a rejection of adult authority.

Gulf of Tonkin Resolution This 1964 Congressional resolution gave President Johnson the authority to "take all necessary measures to repel" attacks against American military forces stationed in Vietnam. Critics said this resolution gave him excessive power to expand the Vietnam War without oversight from Congress.

Détente A lessening of tensions between nations, the policy of détente between the United States, the Soviet Union, and China began during Nixon's presidency. Henry Kissinger, Nixon's secretary of state, was behind the policy.

Watergate This was a criminal conspiracy by several high-ranking Republicans to help Richard Nixon's re-election campaign in 1972 by stealing documents from Democratic campaign offices at the Watergate Hotel in Washington, D.C. Many government and campaign officials served jail time for their crimes, in the end, and Nixon was forced to resign in 1974.

OPEC The Organization of Petroleum Exporting Countries is a coalition of countries that sets the price for crude oil and determines how much will be produced. OPEC raised oil prices in 1973, creating economic turmoil in the United States and across the globe.

Religious Right The mostly Protestant movement began in the 1970s and sought to return "morality" to American life. The religious right actively opposed abortion rights, and in the 1980s moved into the political sphere by endorsing candidates and campaigning for them.

Stagflation This is a specific economic condition of the early 1970s in which inflation occurred during a recession, which had not been the norm economically. President Nixon used price and wage controls and increased government spending to fight it.

Supply Side Economics An economic theory adopted by Ronald Reagan in 1980, it holds that lowering taxes for wealthy businesses and investors will immediately spur economic growth, because they will have more money to invest—and this investment will stimulate the economy. What came to be known as "Reaganomics" went against the grain of economic policy dating back to the New Deal, which focused on consumer spending as the source of economic growth.

Evil Empire Ronald Reagan used this term for the Soviet Union, in his efforts to counter its growing military and weapons capabilities.

Ethnic Cleansing This term has come to describe ethnically motivated violence, including the rape, murder, and forcible relocation of ethnic groups. In the twentieth century, ethnic cleansing occurred in Iraq, Rwanda, Sudan, and many other nations.

New World Order After the Cold War ended in 1989, many believed that a peaceful "new world order" could be established, involving more collaboration between the USSR and United States.

Axis of Evil This term was used by President George W. Bush to describe Iran, North Korea, and Iraq, all of which wanted to develop weapons of mass destruction.

Operation Iraqi Freedom Also known as the Iraq War, this was the invasion of Iraq by the United States in 2003 in an effort to stop dictator Saddam Hussein from accumulating weapons of mass destruction. Subsequently, it was discovered that Iraq had ended its weapons program in 1991, and no weapons of mass destruction were found.

Important Figures

Jimmy Carter The thirty-ninth president of the United States, Carter saw the country through a period of stagflation, which lasted his entire term and detracted from his political agenda. One of his greatest accomplishments was negotiating the Camp David Accords between Israel and Egypt.

Betty Friedan Credited with sparking the "second wave" of feminism in the 1960s, Friedan wrote the *Feminine Mystique*, and sought to bring women's issues to the forefront and establish true equality between the sexes.

Barry Goldwater Goldwater was a five-term senator from Arizona who rejected the legacy of the New Deal and ran against Johnson in the 1964 election. He lost in a landslide. He was painted as a reactionary by his opponents, but his supporters appreciated his stance against labor unions and what they viewed as the dangers of the welfare state.

Mikhail Gorbachev Gorbachev was the leader of the Soviet Union when it dissolved in 1989. Both before and after the breakup, he attempted to implement dramatic economic reforms and a new policy of openness toward the West, as well as a new spirit of openness and tolerance within Soviet society.

Martin Luther King, Jr. An American civil rights hero, King advocated for nonviolent ways to end racial inequality in the United States. In 1964, at the age of thirty-five, he won the Nobel Peace Prize for his efforts. He was assassinated in 1968.

Richard Nixon The thirty-seventh president of the United States, Nixon resigned in disgrace as the Watergate scandal came to a head. Nixon was instrumental in escalating the Vietnam War and in opening diplomatic relations with China.

Rosa Parks A civil rights activist, Rosa Parks became famous when she refused to give up her seat on a public bus for a white passenger. Her act of defiance became a powerful unifying symbol of the struggle for racial equality.

THE BIG PICTURE: HOW TO PREPARE YEAR-ROUND

E ven if the AP U.S. History Exam is months away, the time to start preparing is now. This section will help you register for the test, prepare for the test in class and out, and manage the stress that an AP test brings. As the test gets closer, you can use the materials throughout this book to help you review what you've already learned. When the night before the exam arrives, you'll be ready to earn a top score.

Registering for the Test

The AP U.S. History test is offered once a year on a date early in May. If unusual circumstances make it impossible for you to test on that date, you may be able to take the test during the late-testing period later in the month.

If you are enrolled in an AP U.S. History course, the test will probably be offered in your school. In that case, your AP teacher or an AP coordinator at your school will make the arrangements and supervise the test registration process.

However, you can take the exam even if you are not enrolled in the AP course. Each year hundreds of students who are home-schooled or who study independently take the exam. If you wish to take the AP exam but are not enrolled in a course at a school, contact the College Board to locate a nearby school offering the test and then contact the test coordinator at that school to make arrangements.

Here are some important tips for the registration process:

1. **Get the right information.** Refer to the College Board's official Web site for the information you need about the test, including eligibility for late testing, special accommodations for students with disabilities, and reduced testing fees for students who can't afford the fee ($87 in 2011). This site also has information about sending your score on the AP exam to colleges and universities. Go to www.collegeboard.com.

2. **Start the registration process early.** You don't want to miss the one opportunity each year to take the test. If you are enrolled in an AP course, ask your teacher in January or February about registering for the test if this hasn't already been explained and discussed in class. If you are not enrolled in an AP class in a school, you will need to take the initiative and contact the College Board before March 1 to find out what school nearby is administering the AP U.S. History Exam and then contact the school's AP coordinator to register.

3. **Register for the correct test.** Make sure to register for U.S. History, not U.S. Government and Politics (or something else). You don't want to find out too late that you've wasted months of valuable study time.

Thinking About Not Taking the Test?

You have little to lose if you score poorly on the test, and a lot to gain if you do well. You may do better than you expected, especially if you are able to study and review before the test. If you don't do well, you can cancel your score and the score will not appear on AP score reports the College Board sends to colleges. A low test score means you won't get college credit, but it will generally not hurt your admission chances. Colleges still value the fact you chose to challenge yourself by taking an AP course. Of course, you won't get the testing fee back.

But if you do well, you will have made one of the best investments of your life, considering the cost of college credits at both public and private institutions of higher learning.

Taking Effective Notes

To do well on the exam, you must maximize your ability to retain information both in and out of class. Taking good notes will help you remember key points from class and your books. Here are some tips on how to take notes both from class lessons and from reading either a textbook or review book such as this one.

Active Listening

The first key to taking class notes is to practice active listening—which does not mean writing down every thing the teacher says. Here are some key points on active listening in class:

Listen for the main ideas. Don't just write everything down. Before taking notes, listen to what the point of the lecture is and organize your notes around that.

Pay attention to cues. Certain words and phrases will reflect the organization of the lecture. The introduction will indicate to you how you should set up your notes—for example, "Today we will talk about the impact of World War I on the American economy." Listen for transition words such as "next," "the following," and numbered/bulleted lists.

Don't stare at your notebook. Keep an eye on your teacher's body language and expressions—you will be able to tell what is important by following non-verbal cues.

Taking Notes in Class

Once you've started to listen actively in class, you need to focus on how to take effective notes. This does not mean that you write down every piece of information your teacher says. It's unrealistic and ineffective. Here are tips on how to take efficient and effective notes.

Write down the date and the topic. This will jog your memory when you go to study your notes.

Don't copy notes word for word. Do not get so focused on putting every word from a slide or overhead into your notes. Once you start doing that, you stop listening actively—and that's a sure way to miss important information. Instead, jot down a few key ideas and focus on absorbing what your teacher is saying. If your teacher says something is important, write it down.

If you don't understand something, ask. A lot of information is given to you in class, and even your favorite teacher will sometimes go too fast or be unclear. It's better to ask than to write down notes that won't make any sense to you later.

Using Your Notes

You've mastered active listening and note taking in class—so you're set, right? Not exactly. Many people don't review their notes, which is the way to bring all the information together. Here are tips on how to bring your new skills together to set you up to master the AP exam.

Once class is over, rewrite or type your notes. Repeating the information right away will help drill it into you. Plus, you will have a neater version to study from in the future.

Read over your notes before class. This will put you in the right frame of mind. Plus, you are learning history in chronologically—it makes sense to refresh what came before each new unit.

Get help if necessary. Your teacher wants you to succeed and do well on the exam—make sure you use him as a resource, and take any extra help you might need to maximize your studying.

Taking Notes from a Book

Taking notes from the books you read will help you distill the most important ideas for yourself. Here are some tips for how to take effective notes from textbooks or review books.

Don't dive right in. The biggest mistake people make is to start writing once they begin reading the book. Don't fall into this trap! Before you take a single note, you should read, read, and then read some more.

Read to understand. If you don't understand what you are reading, your notes will not be effective, since you will just be re-writing what's already been written.

Map out the main ideas. Once you've read through the material and have an overall understanding, write down the main ideas of what you have just read, and leave space for yourself to fill in details.

Find your own words. Wherever possible, do not copy text exactly from the book you are reading. This will not help you learn anything, and you will likely forget what you've just spit back out onto the page. Paraphrasing the material helps you engage with the material and it will make a lasting impression on you.

Re-read the material. Once you have the main ideas mapped out, you should re-read the material with an eye towards filling in details under each of the main ideas.

Fill in the details. Now that you've re-read, write details under each main idea—again, do not copy the words exactly from the book, but use your own words so that you retain the information

Put the book aside, and read through your notes. Make sure you understand what you've written, and that you've accurately represented the main ideas and filled in the appropriate level of detail.

Review your notes. In order to make the information stick, review the notes as you study.

Creating a Study Plan

If you're like many students with challenging classes, extracurricular activities, and other priorities, you may have only limited time to review for the AP U.S. History Exam. This section will help you get the most out of your limited test preparation time and make it really count.

You need a plan specifically for you—one that addresses your needs in the time you have available. The following strategies are designed to help you create a plan that meets your needs. No two people will have exactly the same plan or use this book in exactly the same way. To develop a personalized test prep plan, you'll need to identify your weak points and then allocate time to address them efficiently and effectively. Here are the three basic steps to creating a personalized test prep plan:

1. **Identify your weak points.** Start by taking an AP U.S. History practice test. This will let you know what you're up against. It will also help you get a feel for the exam and identify the subject areas that you most need to focus on. Based on your performance on the practice test, you can prioritize what subjects you need to review, starting with the areas in which you are weakest. If your time is limited or you feel you're not ready to take a complete practice test, focus your review by skimming the terms in the glossary and identifying those areas where you have the most difficulty understanding the terms.

2. **Develop a review plan and a schedule.** Figure out how much time you can devote each week to test preparation and reserve specific blocks of time for this purpose. Next, create a written schedule that includes specific time slots and activities or content areas you want to review in each time slot. This will help you pace yourself to get through all the material you want to review. There are probably content areas or question types you want to focus on more than others. But make sure your plan includes time to not only review content, but also to master the strategies and take practice tests.

Use the Last-Minute Study Guide or the Comprehensive Strategies and Review as a starting point, adding time for areas of weakness and skipping over areas you are confident you know. There is no right or wrong plan. Your test prep plan should be unique because it should reflect the time you have, the content areas you want to review, and the way you like to study.

3. **Marshal your self-discipline.** The hard part about a test prep plan is making sure you stick to it. Schedule your test prep time and then schedule other things around it so it doesn't get pushed aside by other activities. You've come a long way; now don't blow the test by not being prepared. Develop a plan for your needs and the time you have available and then stay with it.

For some people, it helps to have a study partner. This may make it easier to hold to the schedule and it may also help you study better. You and your study partner can quiz each other, share information, and exchange ideas. However, for other people, having a study partner makes it harder to stay on topic and focus on studying. Try to figure out, based on past experience, how you can best enforce your study plan and most effectively use your time.

Resources for Further Study

Test Prep Books

United States History by AMSCO provides a good comprehensive review of the subject most likely to appear in an AP exam.

Barron's AP U.S. History provides strong, comprehensive coverage of the most common topics tested in the exam. The book includes two practice tests, and two more practice tests can be found in an optional CD-ROM.

Online

www.mymaxscore.com/aptests—At this site, you can take another free AP practice test. Detailed answers and explanations are provided for both the multiple-choice and essay sections.

www.collegeboard.com/student/testing/ap/sub_ushist.html—At the College Board site, you can find sample tests, advice, and general information about the exam. You'll find it particularly useful to review the last several years' worth of essay prompts, which are provided for free on the site. Full tests are available for purchase.

This book contains one practice test. Visit mymaxscore.com to download your free second practice test with answers and explanations.

AP U.S. History Practice Exam

Section 1: Multiple-Choice Questions
Allotted Time: 55 minutes
Questions: 80
Percent of Total Grade: 50%

Directions: Each of the questions or incomplete statements is followed by five choices. Select the one that best answers the question or completes the statement. In answering these questions, use Strategies 1 to 11.

1.   The Mayflower Compact can be described as

    A. a plan to determine a form of economy for the colonies

    B. an agreement to follow the dictates of Parliament

    C. a plan to elect the leaders of Plymouth Colony

    D. a promise to establish self-government that would abide by the will of the majority

    E. a settling of issues over landownership in the colonies

2.   Which of the following was NOT a result of the Navigation Acts of 1660 and 1663?

    A. Colonial trade was limited only to British merchants.

    B. The thirteen colonies were provided protection from Spanish and French forces.

    C. England was the only place where specific colonial goods could be sold.

    D. The thirteen colonies were not allowed to develop their own currency.

    E. Colonists were forced to pay higher prices for manufactured goods from England.

3.   John Winthrop's vision of Massachusetts as the "city upon the hill" was his hope that the colony

    A. would be the center of cultural life for the colonies

    B. would be the commercial center of the English colonial economy

    C. would serve as a model society that combined the religious tenets of Calvinism in guiding government

    D. would provide an opportunity for all people to participate in colonial government

    E. would serve as the representative of the British Crown in the New World

4.   The *Zenger* case of 1734–35 is important because it

    A. established freedom of the press

    B. provided for lowering the property requirements for voting

    C. allowed each town to put aside land for education

    D. ended virtual representation of the colonies in Parliament

    E. enabled governors of each colony to suspend laws in cases of national emergency

5.   "They are a mixture of English, Scotch, Irish, French, Dutch, German, and Swedish. From this promiscuous breed, that race now called Americans have risen."

This passage best expresses the ideas of

A. Alexis de Tocqueville
B. J. Hector St. John de Crevecoeur
C. Thomas Jefferson
D. Horace Kallen
E. Israel Zangwill

PLAN FOR NUMBERING TOWNSHIPS					
36	30	24	18	12	6
35	29	23	17	11	5
34	28	22	16	10	4
33	27	21	15	9	3
32	26	20	14	8	2
31	25	19	13	7	1

6.   The chart above relates to an essential provision of the

A. Missouri Compromise
B. Proclamation of 1763
C. Northwest Ordinance
D. Compromise of 1850
E. Pinckney Treaty

7.   A major strength of the Articles of Confederation was

A. it provided unity to the country during the Revolutionary War
B. it established a uniform currency
C. it granted the government the ability to collect taxes
D. it provided a well-developed court system
E. it funded the internal improvements of roads and canals in order to spur the economy

8.   Which of the following was NOT included in the Treaty of Paris (1738)?

A. The American government would compensate Loyalists for property confiscated during the war.

B. American independence was recognized.

C. British had to evacuate their forts in the Northwest.

D. The Mississippi River was established as the western boundary of the United States.

E. The British promised to pay reparations to the United States.

9.   The Declaratory Act of 1766

A. guaranteed the right of colonial Parliament to control their local militia

B. required the colonists to provide troops to enforce the Proclamation of 1763

C. punished the colonists for their boycott of British goods

D. stated that Parliament had the power to make laws that were binding on all colonists

E. gave the East India Company the exclusive right to ship tea to the colonists

10.   The Three-Fifths Compromise was created in response to which conflict encountered by the Constitutional Convention delegates?

A. how to establish rules of taxation and representation among slaves in the states

B. how to regulate interstate trade in the states

C. how to divide power between the three branches of government

D. how to regulate foreign trade in the states

E. how to elect the president

11.   "The assumption of laying direct taxes does, of itself, entirely change the confederation of the states into one consolidated government…The very idea of converting what was formerly a confederation to a consolidated government is totally subversive of every principle which has hitherto governed us."

What delegate at the 1787 Constitutional Convention would agree with the above quote?

A. Alexander Hamilton
B. Patrick Henry
C. James Madison
D. George Mason
E. Samuel Adams

12.   The *Federalist Papers* were written

A. to protect states' rights
B. by opponents who feared the new government would be too tyrannical
C. for an improvement of the Articles of Confederation, not a replacement of the government
D. as a demand for the inclusion of a Bill of Rights
E. to stress the need for a strong central government and calm anxieties about the powers granted to the central government under the Constitution

13.   Parliament passed the Coercive or Intolerable Acts in response to

A. the Declaratory Act
B. the Non-Importation Agreement
C. the Boston Massacre
D. the meeting of the First Continental Congress
E. the Boston Tea Party

14.   Which of the following views would Alexander Hamilton find the most difficult to support?

    A. the creation of a national bank to serve as a source of credit for the federal government

    B. a protective tariff for American manufacturers

    C. the belief that the federal government possessed implied powers, which were not specifically restricted by the Constitution

    D. a foreign policy that was primarily pro-British

    E. a belief that an agrarian society was the backbone of America, and the masses should provide leadership in the new government

15.   A significant result of the Whiskey Rebellion in 1794 was

    A. Congress prohibited the import of illegal whiskey

    B. farmers in western Pennsylvania were allowed to build their own distilleries without paying the excise tax on alcohol

    C. it demonstrated the strength of the newly formed government of George Washington

    D. it allowed wealthy farmers to have a monopoly of the sale of liquor between Massachusetts and Pennsylvania

    E. the government arrested and jailed many of the rebelling farmers in order to end the rebellion

16.   Washington's Farewell Address warned against all of the following EXCEPT

    A. entangling or permanent alliances with European powers

    B. avoiding involvement in European affairs

    C. maintaining national unity in view of growing factionalism in the country

    D. limiting westward expansion to avoid conflicts with Native Americans

    E. creating political parties

17.   Which is one of the reasons why historians refer to Jefferson's election as the Revolution of 1800?

   A. Jefferson increased the size of the military budget to deal with the rise of Napoleon in France in spite of his opposition to increasing the size of government.
   B. The election began the peaceful transition of power from the Federalists to the Democratic-Republicans.
   C. The Federalists disappeared as a national party.
   D. Jefferson destroyed the national bank created by Alexander Hamilton.
   E. Jefferson established the two-term tradition in American politics.

18.   Which of the following was NOT a cause of the War of 1812?

   A. The British turned to impressment of American sailors.
   B. War hawk leaders from the South and West supported the war as a way to gain control of Canada.
   C. Settlers in the West believed that the British were inciting Native Americans to attack them.
   D. Many Americans supported the war as its "Second War of Independence."
   E. New England merchants and shipbuilders blamed the British for the decline in trade and loss of profits in their region.

19.   John Marshall's Supreme Court decisions from 1805 to 1835 and his interpretation of the Constitution established

   A. the supremacy of the national government over the state government
   B. the principle of executive privilege
   C. the expansion of states' rights
   D. the supremacy of the legislative branch of government
   E. a weakened system of checks and balances

20. Which was one of the main results of the Missouri Compromise?

    A. The free states gained a political advantage over the slave states.
    B. The Southern states gained a political advantage over the free states.
    C. People in the Louisiana Territory could determine whether they would be free or slave.
    D. It preserved the balance between free and slave states.
    E. The Supreme Court approved the federal government to have the power to regulate slavery in the Louisiana Territory.

21. "It is to be regretted, that the rich and powerful too often bend the acts of government to their selfish purposes...Every man is equally entitled to protection of law; but when the laws undertake...to make the rich richer and the potent more powerful, the humble members of society—the farmers, mechanics, and laborers—who have neither the time nor the means of securing like favors to themselves, have a right to complain of the injustice of their Government."

    This statement best reflects the view of

    A. Andrew Jackson
    B. Daniel Webster
    C. John C. Calhoun
    D. Henry Clay
    E. Nicholas Biddle

22. In *Cherokee Nation v. Georgia*, the Supreme Court ruled that

    A. Native Americans could not sue in the Supreme Court
    B. the Cherokee nation had the right to sue in court and to remain on their land
    C. the laws of Georgia had no force within the boundaries of the Cherokee territory
    D. the Cherokee Tribe had to sell their land and move west
    E. Georgia had to grant citizenship to the Cherokees living within its borders

23. Which was a basic belief of Transcendentalism?

    A. The importance of reason was the basis of understanding.
    B. Organized learning was the best guarantee for success.
    C. They rejected efforts to reform society.
    D. Individuals could transcend the limits of the intellectual world by striving for emotional understanding.
    E. They accepted the materialism of American society.

24. The Seneca Falls Convention is best identified with

    A. education reform
    B. the women's rights movement
    C. reforms for the mentally ill
    D. the temperance movement
    E. labor reform

25. Which of the following did NOT enable the North to industrialize in the mid-nineteenth century?

    A. completion of the Erie Canal
    B. a large influx of immigrants from Germany and Ireland
    C. technological improvements that enhanced production and made it easier to transport goods
    D. a protective tariff that enabled industry to prosper
    E. legalization of labor unions that prevented strikes in major factories

Courtesy of the Library of Congress

26.   Which of the following individuals would have supported the main ideas contained in the above painting?

A. John L. O'Sullivan
B. Henry Thoreau
C. Tecumseh
D. Andrew Carnegie
E. Samuel Clemens

27.   "Those, for whose emancipation we are striving,—constituting at the present time at least one-sixth of our countrymen,—are recognized by the laws, and treated by their fellow beings, as marketable commodities—as goods and chattels—as brute beasts... We...maintain—that no man has a right to enslave or imbrute his brother—to hold or acknowledge him, for one moment, as a piece of merchandise."

Which of the following individuals delivered this above speech at the Anti-Slavery Convention in Philadelphia in 1833?

A. Frederick Douglass

B. William Lloyd Garrison

C. Sojourner Truth

D. William Harper

E. William Still

28.   Which of the following developments had the greatest impact on the farmers in the early nineteenth century?

A. John Deere's steel plow

B. the combine

C. Eli Whitney's cotton gin

D. Cyrus McCormack's reaper

E. the threshing machine

29.   The majority of immigrants who came to America during the first half of the nineteenth century were from

A. Great Britain and Germany

B. France and Italy

C. Germany and Ireland

D. Russia and Italy

E. China and Japan

30.   Which of the following was NOT a part of the Compromise of 1850?

A. California was admitted as a free state.

B. A stringent fugitive slave law was adopted.

C. Popular sovereignty would determine whether western states were free or slave states.

D. Slavery was abolished in the District of Columbia.

E. The Mexican cession was divided into Utah and New Mexico.

31.   Harriet Beecher Stowe's novel *Uncle Tom's Cabin*

   A.   was prompted by the passage of the Kansas-Nebraska Act
   B.   was a firsthand account of slavery
   C.   exposed the cruelties of slavery to a generation of Northerners
   D.   presented a false picture of the plantation system
   E.   forced Southerners to reexamine their attitude toward the "peculiar institution" of slavery

32.   Which was a result of the Kansas-Nebraska Act?

   A.   Whigs and Democrats united in opposition to the doctrine of popular sovereignty.
   B.   Many Southerners were outraged and demanded secession.
   C.   The Republican Party was formed.
   D.   Stephen Douglas became the leading candidate among Northern Democrats.
   E.   Abraham Lincoln became leader of the Republican Party.

33.   In the *Dred Scott* decision of 1857, the Supreme Court ruled that

   A.   the Missouri Compromise was constitutional
   B.   Scott was a citizen and free because he had lived in the free states of Illinois and Wisconsin
   C.   the Compromise of 1850 was unconstitutional
   D.   the doctrine of popular sovereignty was constitutional
   E.   Congress did not have the authority to exclude slavery from the territories

34.   The candidate who supported the unrestricted extension of slavery into the territories in 1860 was

   A.   Stephen Douglas
   B.   John Bell
   C.   Abraham Lincoln
   D.   John Breckinridge
   E.   Jefferson Davis

35.   The main reason Lincoln opposed the Crittenden Compromise was

A. President Buchanan refused to support it

B. Northern Democrats believed it violated the Constitution

C. it established popular sovereignty as the mechanism for determining if a state were free or slave

D. it violated the Republican position against the extension of slavery into the territories

E. he was unable to convince Republican stalwarts like William Seward and John C. Fremont to accept it

36.   The above illustration shows the reaction of the citizens of New York during the Civil War to

A. passage of the Conscription Act of 1863

B. Lincoln's signing of the Emancipation Proclamation

C. Northern defeat at the Battle of First Bull Run

D. Lincoln's call for volunteers from New York to fight the war

E. the suspension of the writ of habeas corpus and the establishment of military tribunals

37.   President Lincoln's plan of Reconstruction developed in 1863 allowed Southern states to be readmitted into the Union once

A. freed slaves were allowed to vote

B. a majority of Southern voters took an oath of allegiance to the Union

C. Southern states repealed the black codes

D. ten percent of Southern voters declared their loyalty to the Union and abolished slavery

E. the states agreed to the establishment of the Freedmen's Bureau

38.   Which of the following industrialists is associated with the Gospel of Wealth?

A. John D. Rockefeller

B. Cornelius Vanderbilt

C. Andrew Carnegie

D. James Hill

E. J. P. Morgan

39.   Which of the following is NOT an accurate statement about the Knights of Labor?

A. They supported an eight-hour workday.

B. They admitted women and African Americans into the union.

C. They supported a workers' cooperative.

D. They supported the abolition of child labor.

E. They stressed the use of strikes over arbitration as a way to resolve labor disputes.

40. In which way did trolley cars, elevated trains, and cable cars transform the cities?

A. They ended the use of horse-drawn transportation to the cities.
B. They enabled cities to devote land specifically for recreational use.
C. They allowed cities to use more land to build skyscrapers.
D. They provided for the building of tenements along transportation routes.
E. They contributed to the growth of suburbs.

41. The Dawes Severalty Act of 1887

A. allowed Native Americans to retain their cultural heritage
B. provided immediate citizenship for Native Americans
C. enabled speculators to buy land directly from Native Americans
D. forced Native Americans to relinquish their tribal lands and assimilate into American society
E. provided funds for the Carlisle School in Pennsylvania where Native Americans were given a Christian education

42. The single tax as a solution to the poverty created by the Industrial Revolution was associated with

A. Edward Bellamy
B. Henry George
C. Frank Norris
D. Henry Demarest Lloyd
E. Lincoln Steffens

43. Which of the following was NOT a part of the Populists' 1892 Omaha Platform?

    A. the creation of a national banking system with regional banks established in major cities across the country
    B. government ownership of railroads and telegraph companies
    C. a graduated income tax
    D. the free and unlimited coinage of silver
    E. immigration restrictions

44. A significant achievement of the Granger movement for farmers was that it

    A. convinced the government to support an inflationary monetary policy
    B. enabled the farmers to obtain state subsidies to offset the decline in farm prices
    C. allowed for the formation of cooperatives for the growing of crops for the market
    D. demonstrated that the farmers were political forces whose needs were being ignored by the Democratic and Republican parties
    E. helped to create a working alliance with the needs of the urban labor force in the industrial North

45. The Progressive movement of the twentieth century can best be described as a movement that

    A. represented the interests of farmers and rural America
    B. saw the need to regulate business because of the abuses created by the industrialization and urbanization of America
    C. wanted to nationalize the major industries in the country
    D. sought to ban immigrants from eastern and southern Europe
    E. united workers, farmers, and African Americans to promote economic and social justice

46. Which of the following was NOT a major achievement of the Square Deal?

   A. Pure Food and Drug Act
   B. Hepburn Act
   C. U.S. Forest Service
   D. Clayton Anti-Trust Act
   E. Meat Inspection Act

47. The most controversial issue at the 1945 meeting of Joseph Stalin, Winston Churchill, and Franklin D. Roosevelt at Yalta was

   A. Germany would be divided into occupation zones
   B. the Soviets agreed to enter the war against Japan, which they did on August 8, just a few weeks before Japan surrendered
   C. a peace organization would be formed at a conference in San Francisco
   D. there would be free elections in the liberated countries of eastern Europe
   E. The Soviets would control the southern half of Sakhalin Island and the Kuril Islands in the Pacific.

48. Which of the following was NOT a result of the Neutrality Acts of 1935, 1936, and 1937?

   A. prohibition of all arms sales and shipments to belligerent nations
   B. abandonment of the traditional U.S. policy of freedom of the seas
   C. allowing the cash-and-carry sale of nonmilitary goods to belligerents
   D. prohibition of the extensions of loans and credits to belligerent nations
   E. a distinction between aggressor and victim in deterring the sale of arms to countries

49.   In 1942, President Roosevelt signed Executive Order 9066, which resulted in

A. allowing women to serve in armed forces but not combat units
B. the establishment of the Office of Price Administration
C. the relocation and internment of first- and second-generation Japanese Americans
D. the banning of discrimination against the hiring of African Americans in defense industries
E. requiring all noncitizen adults to register with the government

50.   The primary purpose of the National Origins Act of 1924 was to

A. restrict Chinese immigration to the United States
B. limit immigration from the Western Hemisphere
C. institute a literacy test for all immigrants coming to the United States
D. set up a quota system based on the 1890 census that restricted immigration from eastern and southern Europe
E. improve the processing centers at Ellis and Angel islands so the Federal government could keep more detailed records

51.   "It must be the policy of the United States to support free people who are resisting attempted subjugation by outside pressures... We must assist free people to work out their destinies in their own way."

Which of the following contains the ideas expressed in the above passage?

A. Truman Doctrine
B. Marshall Plan
C. Eisenhower Doctrine
D. North Atlantic Treaty Organization
E. Alliance for Progress

52.   The Servicemen's Readjustment Act (or the GI Bill of Rights) was passed

    A. to encourage veterans to reenlist

    B. to integrate the armed forces

    C. due to the fear of postwar protests by veterans

    D. to fulfill the need of business communities for a more educated workforce

    E. because of the concern that returning veterans could not find jobs

53.   The main reason for the collapse of the Paris Summit Conference in 1960 was

    A. the Bay of Pigs invasion

    B. the U-2 incident

    C. U.S. support of the French in Indochina

    D. the Quemoy episode

    E. the Suez crisis

54.   Which was NOT one of the main reasons why President Kennedy's New Frontier social program became bogged down in Congress?

    A. A conservative coalition of Southern Democrats and Republicans blocked its passage.

    B. Republican majorities in the Senate opposed his legislative proposals.

    C. A sluggish economy prevented government funding of these programs.

    D. The emerging civil rights movement contributed public support for Kennedy's social program.

    E. The Bay of Pigs invasion, the Cuban missile crisis, and problems in Vietnam distracted his attention from his domestic policies.

55.   The goal of the Niagara Movement founded by W. E. B. Du Bois
       in 1905 was to

       A. promote economic self-sufficiency among African Americans
       B. acquire political power by forming a third party that would
           force Democrats and Republicans to end racial segregation
       C. encourage African Americans to settle in the West where
           there were more economic opportunities
       D. seek equality before the law as well as equal economic
           opportunities
       E. provide training programs for African Americans to gain
           access to higher education

56.   Which of the following ideas is NOT expressed in Frederick
       Jackson Turner's essay *The Significance of the Frontier in
       American History?*

       A. The frontier promoted a spirit of individualism.
       B. Political democracy and self-improvement could be traced to
           the frontier.
       C. The availability of cheap land in the West provided a safety
           valve for those who wanted to start over again.
       D. The frontier forced Americans to be creative and innovative
           as they expanded westward.
       E. The frontier promoted social and economic equality among
           Native Americans and white settlers.

57.   Which of the following men reinforced the business philosophy
       of the 1920s?

       A. Frederick W. Taylor
       B. Bruce Barton
       C. F. Scott Fitzgerald
       D. Ernest Hemingway
       E. Sinclair Lewis

58.   Which of the following men did NOT support American expansion overseas at the beginning of the twentieth century?

A. Alfred T. Mahan
B. Andrew Carnegie
C. Josiah Strong
D. William Howard Taft
E. William Randolph Hearst

59.   "Chronic wrongdoing, or an impotence which results in the general loosening of the ties of civilized society may...ultimately require the intervention by some civilized nations and in the Western Hemisphere...may force the United States...in flagrant cases of such wrongdoing or impotence to the exercise of an international police power."

The ideas expressed in the above passage can be best associated with

A. James Monroe
B. Franklin D. Roosevelt
C. Woodrow Wilson
D. Theodore Roosevelt
E. William McKinley

60.   In the Teller Amendment approved by Congress in response to McKinley's war message against Spain in April 1898, the United States pledged to

A. grant self-determination to the Philippines
B. guarantee independence to Cuba once Spain was defeated
C. support the Open Door Policy
D. provide aid to Filipino rebels in their struggle against Spain
E. investigate Spain's brutal treatment of the Cuban rebels

61.　Mark Twain's novel *The Gilded Age*

A.　describes changing social patterns of the nineteenth century as a result of rapid economic growth

B.　depicts the ordeal of immigrants as they were forced to adjust to life in America

C.　documents the social changes in the South as a result of the Reconstruction era

D.　satirized the economic growth and political life in the United States from the end of Reconstruction to the beginning of the twentieth century

E.　analyzed the plight of farmers and Native Americans who were seriously affected by the expansion of railroads across the United States

62.　The strength of the Democratic Party in the late nineteenth century was built upon

A.　farmers in the Midwest

B.　the emerging urban middle class

C.　the white South and the growing immigration population controlled by big-city machines

D.　Northern blacks and immigrants in the industrial areas

E.　labor unions and the small towns of the Northeast

63.　All of the following made it difficult for the United States to remain neutral in World War I from 1914 to 1917 EXCEPT

A.　U.S. loans to allies of over $3 million

B.　the ethnic population of the United States

C.　British propaganda

D.　the rise of Bolshevism in Russia

E.　the Zimmerman telegram

64.   In *Schenck v. United States*, the Supreme Court ruled that

   A. the Sedition Act was unconstitutional
   B. the president can issue an executive order that necessitates the suspension of free speech
   C. Congress can prohibit or limit free speech during wartime
   D. free speech can be revoked if an individual is not a citizen of the United States
   E. the government can suspend habeas corpus during wartime

65.   Which of the following was NOT a result of the Great Migration north by African Americans?

   A. African Americans who remained in the North experienced permanent economic improvement.
   B. Race riots broke out in cities across the North.
   C. African Americans in the North fared better economically than those who lived in the South.
   D. Northerners, especially returning veterans, resented competition with African Americans for low-paying jobs.
   E. Many African Americans continued to face discrimination in housing, jobs, and schools.

66.   Senator Henry Cabot Lodge and a majority of conservative Republicans opposed the League of Nations because

   A. public opinion in the United States opposed the country's involvement in the League of Nations
   B. they wanted to ensure that Congress, not the League of Nations, had the final authority to decide war authorizations
   C. they believed that the United States should not be involved in any more European wars
   D. Democrats and Republicans disagreed over the reparations provision of the treaty
   E. they feared that France and Great Britain would control the voting in the League of Nations

67.   Which is the LEAST accurate description of political and eco-
       nomic life in the United States from 1920 to 1928?

       A. Republicans dominated the government and supported a
          protective tariff.
       B. Andrew Mellon's tax plan benefited the wealthy.
       C. Buying stock became the American way of life.
       D. The agricultural sector did not benefit from the economic boom.
       E. Productivity in major industries declined during the decade.

68.   Which of the following was NOT a cause of the Great Crash?

       A. the uneven distribution of income
       B. excessive stock speculation
       C. installment buying
       D. a decline in farm prices
       E. excessive federal regulation of banks

69.   What was one main difference between the First and Second
       New Deal?

       A. The First New Deal was more successful than the Second
          New Deal.
       B. The Second New Deal did not rely on Keynesian economics.
       C. The First New Deal had the overwhelming support of
          Republicans.
       D. The Second New Deal sought to establish permanent reforms
          to help workers and farmers to ensure against further eco-
          nomic downturn.
       E. The First New Deal made no provision for the right of unions
          to organize.

70. Which of the following was NOT a critic or opponent of the New Deal?

A. Frances Perkins

B. Huey Long

C. Al Smith

D. Francis Townsend

E. Charles Coughlin

71. In *Schechter Poultry Corp. v. United States* (1935), the Supreme Court

A. upheld the constitutionality of the Agricultural Adjustment Act (AAA)

B. declared that labor unions had the right to bargain collectively

C. supported the Federal Deposit Insurance Corporation that guaranteed bank deposits

D. declared that the National Industrial Recovery Act (NIRA) was unconstitutional

E. ruled the Emergency Banking Act of 1935 violated the principles of checks and balances because it was Congress, not the president, who had the right to reorganize the banks

72. Which of the following had the greatest influence on the "Beat Generation"?

A. C. Wright Mills, *White Collar*

B. Jack Kerouac, *On the Road*

C. Norman Mailer, *The Naked and the Dead*

D. F. Scott Fitzgerald, *The Great Gatsby*

E. Michael Harrington, *The Other America*

73. One result of the passage of the Gulf of Tonkin Resolution was

   A. it ended permanent hostilities between the United States and North Vietnam
   B. it reaffirmed the exclusive right of Congress to declare war
   C. the United States committed troops to Asia for the first time
   D. Congress gave President Johnson unlimited power to wage war in Vietnam
   E. Congress outlined the specific goals of U.S. involvement in Vietnam

74. Which of the following was NOT a part of Lyndon Johnson's Great Society program?

   A. federal bloc grants
   B. the Medicare Act
   C. the Immigration Act of 1965
   D. the Elementary and Secondary Education Act
   E. the Appalachian Regional Development Act

75. In the book *The Feminine Mystique*, Betty Friedan

   A. advocated the passage of the Equal Rights Amendment
   B. supported the Supreme Court decision of *Roe v. Wade*
   C. argued that the government should establish extended maternity leave care for women
   D. asserted that middle-class society prevented women from using their individual talents
   E. outlined a political platform encouraging women like Shirley Chisholm and Geraldine Ferraro to run for Congress

76.   The Freedom Riders in the 1960s were

A. a group of veterans who opposed the war in Vietnam

B. a group of Northern white and African American students who tried to register black voters in the South

C. young Americans who provided educational help to poor African Americans living in the South

D. an integrated group of people who rode buses to the South to integrate interstate traveling facilities like bus stations and waiting rooms

E. organized by the Southern Christian Leadership (SCLC) to achieve social justice

77.   Which of the following economic issues was NOT one of the major economic issues during the Carter administration from 1977 to 1981?

A. energy shortages

B. low interest rates

C. poor economic growth

D. high inflation rates

E. massive layoffs

78.   Nixon's policy of Vietnamization referred to

A. a gradual withdrawal of American troops from Vietnam and the handover of the ground war to the South Vietnamese

B. the introduction of more American forces to ensure stabilization of South Vietnam

C. an end to all American aid to Vietnam unless the government became more democratic

D. using more Green Beret forces to work with American troops in Vietnam

E. working with China to help establish stability in Southeast Asia

79.   The Saturday Night Massacre of October 20, 1973, involved

A. the resignation of Vice President Spiro Agnew and his staff
because of bribery charges

B. protesters being fired upon at Kent State University

C. Nixon's firing of independent prosecutor Archibald Cox

D. the release of the Pentagon Papers by the *New York Times*

E. the U.S. invasion of Cambodia to cut off the supply lines of
the North Vietnamese

80.   Which of the following was NOT a result of the "Reagan Revolution"?

A. more conservative Supreme Court decisions

B. the dismantling of the welfare state and elimination of enti-
tlement programs

C. the emergence of the Religious Right or Moral Majority as a
major force in American politics

D. fewer government regulations on businesses and the economy

E. the removal of government interference in people's private
lives, such as abortion and pornography

Section 2, Part A: Document-Based Question
Allotted Time: 45 minutes
Percent of Total Grade: 22.5%

Directions: The following question requires you to construct a coherent essay that integrates your interpretation of Documents A–J and your knowledge of the period referred to in the question. High scores will be earned only by essays that both cite key pieces of evidence from the documents and draw on outside knowledge of the period.

Discuss and analyze how American society reacted to the influx of "New Immigrants" to the United States during the late nineteenth and early twentieth centuries.

Historical Background: In the first seven decades of the nineteenth century immigration came largely from Britain, Ireland, and Germany. However, between 1880 and 1914, streams of "New Immigrants" arrived from Italy, Greece, Poland, and Russia.

Document A

> Source: Emma Lazarus, "The New Colossus," 1888.
> Here at our sea-washed, sunset gates shall stand
> A mighty woman with a torch, whose flame
> Is the imprisoned lightning, and her name
> Mother of Exiles. From her beacon-hand
> Glows world-wide welcome; her mild eyes command
> The air-bridge harbor that twin cities frame.
> "Keep, ancient lands your storied pomp!" cries she
> With silent lips. "Give me your tired, your poor,
> Your huddled masses yearning to breathe free,
> The wretched refuse of your teeming shore.
> Send these, the homeless, tempest-tost to me,
> I lift my lamp beside the golden door!"

Document B

Source: Prescott F. Hall, *The North American Review*. January 1912.
Since 1820, we have received from Europe and Asia some twenty-eight millions of people. About one-third of these came prior to 1880 and were of races kindred to those already here; in other words, they had a common heritage of institutions if not of language, and were assimilated into the general population with comparative ease. The other two-thirds, the eighteen million who have come since 1880, have been on the other hand, of entirely different races—of Alpine, Mediterranean, Asiatic, and African stocks. These races have an entirely different mental make-up from the Baltic race; they bring with them an inheritance of widely differing political and social ideals, and a training under social and political institutions very different from ours...The South Italian which constitutes the largest element in our present immigration, is one of the most mixed races in European and is partly African, owing to the negroid migration from Carthage to Italy...The Hebrew, which constitutes the next largest element of immigration, in spite of long residence in Europe is still, as it always has been, an Asiatic race.

Document C

Source: *The Ram's Horn*. April 25, 1896.

Ohio State University Billy Ireland Cartoon Library & Museum

Document D

Source: John Mitchell, *American Federationist*. October 1909.

The standard of wages for both skilled and unskilled labor in the United States has been built up as a result of years and years of energetic effort, struggle, and sacrifice. When an immigrant without resources is compelled to accept work at less than the established wage rate, he not only displaces a man working at the higher rate, but his action threatens to destroy the whole schedule of wages in the industry in which he secures employment, because it not infrequently occurs that an employer will attempt to regulate wages on the basis of the lowest rate paid to any of the men in his employ. Any reduction in wages means a lowering of the standard of living, and the standard of living among a civilized people can not be lowered without lowering in the same ratio the physical standard and the intellectual and moral ideals of that people.

Document E

Source: Harris Weinstock, "Immigration and American Labor." *The Annals of the American Academy of Political and Social Science.* January 1917.

We are told that immigration tends to beat down wages; but the fact remains that wages have advanced more rapidly and hours of labor have been shortened more during the period of our greatest European immigration than in any previous period in our industrial history. It has been pointed out that eighty-five per cent of all labor in the slaughtering and packing industries is done by alien laborers. They mine seven-tenths of our bituminous coal…The immigrant, by furnishing the needed labor opens out new productive possibilities that otherwise would remain closed, so that instead of robbing these here of work, his presence makes new and still more abundant work possible.

Document F

Source: Henry Cabot Lodge. Congressional Record, 54th Congress, 1st Session. March 16, 1896.

It is found, in the first place, that the illiteracy test will bear most heavily upon the Italians, Russians, Poles, Hungarians, Greeks, and Asiatics, and very lightly, or not at all, upon English-speaking emigrants or Germans, Scandinavians, and French. In other words, the races most affected by the illiteracy test are those whose emigration to this country has begun within the last twenty years and swelled rapidly to enormous proportions, races with which the English-speaking people have never hith-erto assimilated, and who are most alien to the great body of the people of the United States...Statistics show that the change in the race character of our immigration has been accompanied by a corresponding decline in its quality...If a lower race mixes with a higher in sufficient numbers, history teaches us that the lower race will prevail...The lowering of a great race means not only its own decline but that of human civilization...The gates which admit men to the United States and to citizenship in the great Republic should no longer be left unguarded.

Document G

Source: Jane Addams, "Pen and Book a Test of Character." *Journal of Constructive Philanthropy*. January 4, 1913.

Literacy is neither a test of character nor of ability; it is merely an index of the educational system of the community in which a man has been reared. The literacy test will always work in favor of the man from the city and discriminate against the man from the country. On the face of it, it would seem safer to admit a sturdy peasant from the mountains of Calabria than a sophisticated Neapolitan, familiar with the refined methods of police graft which have made the Camorra famous. In addition to that, the peasant finds work waiting for him, the educated man "above manual labor" often has a pitiful struggle to keep himself from starvation.

Document H

Source: President Woodrow Wilson. Congressional Record, 63rd Congress, 3rd Session. January 28, 1915.

This bill embodies a radical departure from the traditional and long established policy of this country...It seeks to all but close entirely the gates of asylum which have always been open to those who could find nowhere else the right and opportunity of constitutional agitation for what they conceived to be the natural and inalienable rights of men; and it excludes those to whom the opportunities of elementary education have been denied, without regard to their character, their purposes, or their natural capacities...The laws here embodied are not tests of quality or of character or of personal fitness, but tests of opportunity. Those who come seeking opportunity are not to be admitted unless they have already had one of the chief of the opportunities they seek, the opportunity of education.

Document I

Source: Statistical Abstract of the United States. Government Printing Office, 1929.

NORTHWEST EUROPE & SCANDINAVIA		EASTERN & SOUTHERN EUROPE		OTHER COUNTRIES	
Country	Quota	Country	Quota	Country	Quota
Germany	51,227	Poland	5,982	Africa (except Egypt)	1,100
Great Britain and Northern Ireland	34,007	Italy	3,845	Armenia	124
Irish Free State (Ireland)	28,567	Czechoslovakia	3,073	Australia	121
Sweden	9,561	Russia	2,248	Palestine	100
Norway	6,453	Yugoslavia	671	Syria	100
France	3,954	Romania	603	Turkey	100
Denmark	2,789	Portugal	503	Egypt	100
Switzerland	2,081	Hungary	473	New Zealand & Pacific Island	100
Netherlands	1,648	Lithuania	344	All Others	1,900
Austria	785	Latvia	142		
Belgium	512	Spain	131		
Finland	471	Estonia	124		
Free City of Danzig	228	Albania	100		
Iceland	100	Bulgaria	100		
Luxembourg	100	Greece	100		
Total	142,483		18,439		3,745
Total %	86.5		11.2		2.3
Total Annual Immigrant Quota:					164,667

Document J

Source: Edith Terry Bremer. *Survey*. May 15, 1924.

No set of immigration laws can be smoothly, justly, and humanely administered, which are not built upon an international philosophy in regard to this vast human phenomenon. The Immigration Bill has no discernible social philosophy. If it becomes law, in spite of its rigidly mechanical devices for execution and its laudable intent to prevent unnecessary distress to immigrants in certain instances, it is bound to increase the exploitation of immigrants, to create new strife among groups already domiciled here, to bring disaster to individuals, and to be as irritatingly difficult to administer exactly as our immigration laws have ever been.

Section 2, Parts B and C: Standard Essay Questions
Allotted Time: 70 minutes
Percent of Total Grade: 27.5%

Part B

Directions: Choose ONE question from this part. You are advised to spend 5 minutes planning and 30 minutes writing your answer. Cite relevant historical evidence in support of your generalizations and present your arguments clearly and logically. In answering the question, use Strategies 18 to 20.

1.   Assess the validity of this statement: Historians have referred to the Constitution as a "Bundle of Compromises."

2.   Discuss and evaluate the impact of Manifest Destiny on national unity in the United States in the 1840s.

Part C

Directions: Choose ONE question from this part. You are advised to spend 5 minutes planning and 30 minutes writing your answer. Cite relevant historical evidence in support of your generalization and present your arguments clearly and logically. In answering the question, use Strategies 18 to 20.

1.   Compare and contrast Booker T. Washington's and W. E. B. Du Bois' objectives for African Americans in the late nineteenth and early twentieth centuries.

2.   Few years in U.S. history were as troubled or as violent as 1968. Evaluate to what extent this statement is accurate.

Answers for Multiple-Choice Questions

1. **D:** In 1620 Pilgrim leaders drew up and signed the Mayflower Compact. The document was not a constitution but a simple agreement to form a crude government and to submit to the will of the majority. The compact was signed by forty-one adults and was a promising step toward genuine self-government. The Mayflower Compact did not provide direction for the election of leaders of Plymouth colony, did not address issues of landownership, and did not determine the economy of the colonies.

2. **D:** The British regulation of colonial trade through the Navigation Laws controlled all aspects of their economy as each choice describes, except the printing of currency. Each colony printed its own currency, and the British did not attempt to regulate currency in controlling the colonies. It was not until the Constitution was ratified in 1789 that the thirteen colonies adopted a uniform currency.

3. **C:** John Winthrop, the first governor of the Massachusetts Bay Colony, believed that he had a calling from God to lead a new religious experiment in America. Like many Puritans, he saw the Massachusetts colony as establishing a new covenant with God that would be a beacon to humanity. Massachusetts was not founded to represent cultural, economic, or political freedom but as "the city upon a hill" that would be a holy society and a model for the rest of the world.

4. **A:** John Peter Zenger was a German-born American printer and journalist. In 1733, he began publishing the *New York Weekly Journal*. He was arrested in 1734 for his attacks on the policies of the colonial governor. He was acquitted on the grounds that his charges were based upon fact. It was the first important victory for freedom of the press in the American colonies and pointed the way to open discussion, which is the backbone of a democracy. None of the other options are associated with the Zenger trial.

5. **B:**   The French American settler and writer J. Hector St. John de Crevecoeur published the essay *Letters from an American Farmer* in 1782. In this essay, he describes an America in 1770 that was an ethnic mixture that could not be found in any other country. He notes that all the different groups melt into one race, "the new American," which laid the foundation for a multicultural American identity not known in Europe. Alexis de Tocqueville wrote *Democracy in America* to describe the United States during the Jacksonian era. Thomas Jefferson wrote the Declaration of Independence. Horace Kallen and Israel Zangwill were twentieth-century writers who wrote about immigration.

6. **C:**   In May 1785 the Articles of Confederation adopted the Northwest Land Ordinance of 1785, which laid the foundation of land policy in the United States until the passage of the Homestead Act in 1862. The Land Ordinance established the basis for a public land survey system. Land was to be systematically surveyed into square townships, six miles each. Each of these townships were subdivided into thirty-six sections of one square mile or 640 acres. The ordinance was also significant for establishing a mechanism for funding public education. Section sixteen in each township was reserved for the maintenance of public schools. Many schools today are still located in section sixteen of their respective townships. The Missouri Compromise of 1820 and the Compromise of 1850 dealt with the issues of slavery and representation in Congress. Great Britain issued the Proclamation of 1763, which prohibited colonists from settling beyond the Appalachian Mountains. The Pinckney Treaty between the United States and Spain allowed the United States to use the port city of New Orleans.

7. **A:**   The Articles of Confederation did not have a court system or a uniform currency or the ability to collect taxes and make internal improvements. In spite of these defects, the Articles of

Confederation, as the first written Constitution, kept alive the ideal of unity and held the states together until they were ready for a stronger government. The articles provided a steppingstone from boycotts in 1774 to the Constitution's adoption in 1789.

8. **E:** The treaty contained each of the listed options except the provision for war damages. However, the thirteen states agreed that they would put no lawful obstacles in the way of preventing British creditors from collecting debts owed to them by the colonists. The British even insisted that Loyalist territory be restored. Neither one of these provisions was carried out in a way that satisfied Great Britain.

9. **D:** The British Parliament passed the Stamp Act of 1765, which put a tax on newspapers, legal documents, deeds, and playing cards. The colonists protested the Stamp Act by boycotting British goods. In 1766 Parliament repealed the Stamp Act but also passed the Declaratory Act, which reaffirmed Parliament's right to make laws that bound the colonies. Parliament asserted that it had absolute power over its North American colonies. The Declaratory Act did not refer to colonial militia, stationing of troops, or punishing the colonists for boycotting British goods. The Tea Act of 1773 gave the East India Company exclusive control of all tea imported to the colonists.

10. **A:** The Three-Fifths Compromise was reached because the South wanted slaves to count for representation but not for taxation. The Three-Fifths Compromise stated that a slave would count as three-fifths of a person for the purpose of taxation and representation. The Constitution also guaranteed that Congress would not pass laws banning the slave trade for twenty years. The Connecticut Compromise dealt with the issue of representation. The Commercial Compromise focused on control of interstate and intrastate commerce. The Electoral College Compromise addressed the issue of direct election of the president.

11. **D:** George Mason, a Virginia delegate at the Constitutional Convention, claimed that the power to tax would destroy the individual states. Mason argued that the Constitution did not represent the interests of the people and the states and that the new government would produce a monarchy or tyrannical aristocracy. He opposed the ratification of the Constitution. Patrick Henry and Samuel Adams did not attend the convention. James Madison of Virginia and Alexander Hamilton of New York supported a strong central government with the power to levy taxes.

12. **E:** The *Federalist Papers* were written by James Madison, John Jay, and Alexander Hamilton to stress the need for a strong central government. They were a series of eighty-five articles or essays advocating the ratification of the Constitution. These authors outlined cogent reasons for supporting the Constitution and implied that the Constitution contained specific provisions that prevented the government from becoming too powerful. These authors did not believe it was necessary to add a Bill of Rights to the original Constitution and thought that the Articles of Confederation was too weak to be effective.

13. **E:** Parliament passed the Intolerable Acts, as they were called in the colonies, in 1774, in response to the Boston Tea Party. On December 16, 1773, a hundred Bostonians loosely disguised as Indians dumped 342 chests of tea into Boston Harbor. The Intolerable Acts took away many of the chartered rights of colonial Americans and closed the port of Boston until damages were paid and order could be ensured. The Declaratory Act of 1766 reaffirmed Parliament's right to tax the colonists. The Boston Massacre occurred in 1770, and the First Continental Congress was called by the colonists to protest the Intolerable Act. The Non-Importation Agreement was an agreement not to import goods from Great Britain.

14. **E:** Jefferson, not Hamilton, believed that the future of America depended on building an agrarian society. Hamilton, the first secretary of the treasury, supported a commercial society with a large industrial base. This view included the creation of a national bank and a protective tariff to help American industry, which required a close working relationship with Great Britain. Hamilton also thought a strong central government would have "all the necessary powers" needed to achieve these goals.

15. **C:** The Whiskey Rebellion occurred when rebelling farmers refused to pay a tax on distilled liquor. Washington raised an army of fifteen thousand men and placed them under the control of Alexander Hamilton. The show of force led to the collapse of the rebellion without any bloodshed on either side. Washington was applauded for his strong actions in enforcing the law, unlike the inaction of the government of the Articles of Confederation during Shays' Rebellion.

16. **D:** Washington's Farewell Address did not counsel the American people about westward expansion. In 1796, Washington was concerned about the survival of the nation. He was tired of the political bickering and believed the creation of political parties could destroy the country. He also believed that it was in our national interest to avoid involvement in European affairs. Washington's address contained no references to Native Americans living in the United States.

17. **B:** The election of 1800 was the first peaceful transition of power from one party to another. Politics had become more partisan between the Federalists (led by President John Adams) and the Democratic-Republican party (led by Thomas Jefferson). Adams and Jefferson had been opponents in the previous election. By 1800 the country was deeply divided over the wars in Europe, relations with France and England, Adams's crackdown on dissent, and whether there should be a strong or weak federal

government. The peaceful transfer of power showed that the U.S. constitutional system could endure various strains. Federalists quietly accepted their defeat and relinquished their control of the federal government to Democratic Republicans. Jefferson cut the size of the budget. Andrew Jackson destroyed the Bank of the United States. The Federalists declined after the War of 1812. George Washington established the two-term tradition.

18. E: New England merchants were opposed to the war. After the repeal of the Embargo Act at the end of Jefferson's second term in 1809, these merchants were making sizable profits from the Napoleonic War, and they considered the impressments a minor problem. Americans in the South and West considered British impressments a major issue and an attack on the national honor. War hawks like Henry Clay and John C. Calhoun saw the war as an opportunity to gain control of Canada and a way to end British support of Native American attacks on settlers in the Ohio Valley.

19. A: The Marshall Court became strongly identified with judicial nationalism over states' rights. Marshall's opinion in the case *Marbury v. Madison*, which established the principle of judicial review, implied that the judicial branch had the power to determine the constitutionality of state and federal legislation. This decision strengthened the system of checks and balances. In cases like *Fletcher v. Peck*, the Supreme Court ruled that the states could not invalidate a contract, and in *McCulloch v. Maryland*, Marshall ruled that the federal law of national banks is absolute over the state banks. These decisions demonstrated the supremacy of the federal government and did not increase the power of the executive or legislative branches of government.

20. D: The Missouri Compromise preserved the balance of power between free and slave states. In 1819 there was a balance of eleven free and eleven slave states. The admission of Missouri as a

slave state would have shifted the balance of power in the Senate. Henry Clay of Kentucky proposed the Missouri Compromise. Missouri would become the twelfth slave state and Maine would be admitted as a free state. The Missouri Compromise maintained the balance of power and prohibited slavery from extending north of the 36 degrees 30 minutes N line. The question of popular sovereignty in the new territories and federal control of slavery would become a hot issue in the 1850s.

21. **A:** Andrew Jackson expressed these views in his veto of the 1832 Second Bank Bill. Jackson objected to the control of the government by the rich and powerful. He asserted that the bank benefited the wealthy at the expense of the poor. Jackson criticized the National Bank because it gave preference to the rich at the expense of the common man. Daniel Webster and Henry Clay attacked Jackson's veto message for promoting class warfare between the rich and poor and supported Nicholas Biddle, the president of the Second National Bank. John Calhoun had resigned as Jackson's vice president over the Tariff of 1828.

22. **B:** In the Cherokee nation case the Supreme Court ruled that the United States could not remove the Cherokees from their land. The Cherokees legally owned the land and had the right to sue in court and thus prevent Georgia from forcing them to migrate West. The Supreme Court ruled in the *Worcester* case (1832) that Georgia could not force its laws on the Cherokee nation since it was an independent nation. Native Americans were not granted citizenship until 1924.

23. **D:** Transcendentalists like Ralph Waldo Emerson argued for a mystical and intuitive way of thinking as a means of discovering one's inner self. They stressed the importance of intuition over reason. Transcendentalists were extremely individualist and viewed organized institutions as unimportant. They supported a variety of reform movements, especially the

antislavery movement. They challenged the materialism of American society by focusing on artistic achievements over the importance of wealth.

24. **B:**   In 1848, leading feminists such as Susan B. Anthony and Lucretia Mott met at Seneca Falls, New York. This was the first women's rights convention in U.S. History. They issued the Declaration of Sentiments (which they modeled after the Declaration of Independence) and demanded the right of suffrage as well as property rights. Following the Seneca Falls Convention, feminists campaigned for equal voting as well as legal and property rights. The abolition movement eventually overshadowed all other reform movements by the 1850s.

25. **E:**   The legalization of labor unions did not contribute to the industrialization of the North. Labor unions in the United States would not begin to grow until the late 1880s. Labor unions were formed because workers complained of long hours, poor wages, and unsafe working conditions. The North experienced industrial growth because the Erie Canal provided a continuous trade route from New York to the West. Technological improvements like steamboats, the influx of immigrant workers, and the protective tariff instituted by Clay's American System enabled the North to prosper. American labor unions would be legalized in 1935 during the Great Depression.

26. **A:**   The painting shows Manifest Destiny, the religious belief that the United States should expand from the Atlantic Ocean to the Pacific Ocean in the name of God. John L. O'Sullivan, a journalist, wrote in 1839 that it was America's duty to spread westward because it was ordained by God that the United States would spread civilization from coast to coast. In 1848, the term *Manifest Destiny* would be used to justify the annexation of Texas and the Mexican War. Neither Henry David Thoreau nor Andrew Carnegie supported American expansion. Tecumseh

was a Native American who resisted the advancement of settlers westward. Samuel Clemens (Mark Twain) criticized the idea that the United States had a unique mission to spread civilization.

27. **B:** William Lloyd Garrison set forth the case for the abolitionists against slavery at this antislavery convention in 1833. Garrison advocated the immediate abolition of slavery in every state and territory without compensating the slave owners. In 1831, the first antislavery society was established in New York, and in 1833 it held its first convention, where Garrison emerged as the organization's main figure. Frederick Douglass was an abolitionist and early follower of Garrison who founded the antislavery journal *The North Star* in 1847. Sojourner Truth and William Still organized efforts to help fugitive slaves escape to freedom in the North. William Harper was a Southerner who contended that slavery was justified because of the laws of nature.

28. **D:** Cyrus McCormack's mechanical reaper in 1830 reduced the amount of manual labor used to produce grain and dramatically increased grain production in the United States. The mechanical mower and reaper improved the efficiency of wheat farmers. John Deere's steel plow allowed farmers to till more soil in less time, but the reaper is often credited as the cotton gin of the West, because it allowed farmers to grow large quantities of wheat instead of less-profitable corn. It also shifted the farmer from subsistence farming to commercial farming in the 1830s. The threshing machine and the combine improved grain production, but the reaper made grain production profitable.

29. **C:** The majority of immigrants came from Germany and Ireland. They are usually referred to as Old Immigrants in order to distinguish them from the New Immigrants from Russia and Italy who immigrated primarily between the 1880s and 1914. Chinese and Japanese migration was not substantial until 1850, and that was restricted primarily to the West Coast. Between

the 1830s and 1850s, nearly four million people came from northern Europe to the United States.

30. **D:** The Compromise of 1850 allowed California to become a free state, adopted a stringent fugitive slave law, and stipulated that slavery issues in the territories of Utah and Mexico would be decided by popular sovereignty. The compromise banned the slave trade in the District of Columbia, but it did not abolish slavery.

31. **C:** Harriet Beecher Stowe wrote *Uncle Tom's Cabin* in 1853 in response to the stringent fugitive slave law of the Compromise of 1850. Stowe had never seen a plantation, but her fictional account of Uncle Tom and overseer Simon Legree exposed Northerners and Europeans to the cruelty of slavery in the South. The book sold over three hundred thousand copies within a year. Southerners condemned the "untruths" in the novel and began to vigorously defend their institution from Northern attacks.

32. **C:** The Republican Party was founded in Wisconsin in 1854 as a direct reaction to passage of the Kansas-Nebraska Act. The membership was entirely Northern and Western. Its basic goal was to prevent the expansion of slavery in the territories. Many Northern Democrats and Whigs split from the party and joined the Republicans. Northern Democrats opposed Stephen Douglas's popular sovereignty doctrine, while Southerners saw Kansas as fertile ground for a slave state. John C. Fremont, not Abraham Lincoln, was the first Republican candidate for president in 1856.

33. **E:** A majority of the Supreme Court under the leadership of Chief Justice Roger Taney ruled that Dred Scott was not a citizen and could not sue in federal court. Slaves were property, and the Missouri Compromise was unconstitutional because it excluded slavery. Congress did not have the power to pass laws that deprived people of their property. The Court did not address the Compromise of 1850 or the doctrine of popular sovereignty.

34. **D:** In the 1860 presidential election, John Breckinridge, vice president under James Buchanan, ran as one of the two candidates of the fractured Democratic Party. He represented Southern Democrats and supported the unrestricted extension of slavery in the territories. He came in third in popular votes behind Lincoln, who opposed the extension of slavery, and Douglas, the Northern Democrat who supported popular sovereignty. Bell ran on the Union ticket, and Davis was not a candidate.

35. **D:** The Crittenden Proposal contained a constitutional amendment that would have guaranteed the existence of slavery south of the 36 degree 30 minute parallel. Lincoln (much less any Republican) could not accept it because it violated his position against the expansion of slavery into the territories. Lincoln's opposition was not based on Buchanan's or the Northern Democrats' position on the compromise.

36. **A:** In 1863 Congress passed the Conscription Act, which authorized the president to draft citizens between the ages of eighteen and thirty-five for a three-year term of military service. At the beginning of the war, Lincoln called for a volunteer army, but by 1863 more soldiers were needed. The Conscription Act provoked opposition from the poor, who feared that they would not get their jobs back when they returned to civilian life, because the newly freed slaves would take them. Lincoln signed the Emancipation Proclamation in January 1863. From July 13 to July 16, riots broke out in New York City to protest the draft. Most of the mob, which were primarily Irish immigrants, attacked African Americans and wealthy whites. Many African Americans were killed, and federal troops were called in to restore order. New York was placed under martial law until the rioting ended. Lincoln had already set up the practice at the beginning of the Civil War.

37. **D:** Lincoln's plan of Reconstruction required that only 10 percent of the Southern population swear allegiance to the Union and that

slavery be abolished. The Fifteenth Amendment was passed in 1868 and guaranteed African Americans the right to vote. The Radical Republicans wanted 50 percent of the South to pledge allegiance to the Union, and the Freedmen's Bureau was part of their program. Southern states introduced black codes at the end of the Civil War to restrict the rights of newly freed slaves.

38. C: Andrew Carnegie argued in his essay *The Gospel of Wealth* that the wealthy had a responsibility to contribute to society through philanthropic programs. Carnegie distributed over $350 million of his fortune to libraries, schools, and other civic projects. Rockefeller, Vanderbilt, Hill, and Morgan justified their success by applying the laws of Social Darwinism. They did not agree that they had an obligation to support civic projects.

39. E: The Knights of Labor, under Terence Powderly, preferred arbitration over strikes. Powderly believed that collective bargaining would be a more effective weapon in winning public support for the union's programs. The union supported the eight-hour day, abolition of child labor, workers' cooperatives, Blacks, and women into the union. The Knights of Labor declined in membership after the Haymarket riots in 1886, when the union's call for a general strike for an eight-hour day led to uprisings that resulted in the deaths of seven police officers. Americans, as Powderly feared, were horrified by these events and turned against the union.

40. E: Improvements in transportation made it possible for people to move away from the cities. Prior to the Civil War, cities were small, and people worked within walking distance of their jobs. Cable cars in San Francisco and trolley cars in New York made it easier for people to commute from their work in the cities to residential areas known as suburbs. This transportation revolution created distinct neighborhoods devoted to manufacturing and commerce as well as residential areas. The lack of land contributed to the need for skyscrapers. Tenements were located

next to factories rather than along transportation routes, and recreational areas like Central Park and Prospect Park were designed to improve outdoor activities for the working poor, not because of the development of trolley or cable cars.

41. **D:** The Dawes Severalty Act divided tribal lands into plots of 160 acres where Native Americans were forced to farm. They would be granted citizenship if they stayed on the land for twenty-five years and adopted civilized lives. The best lands would be sold by the government to railroads and white settlers over a number of years. The Carlisle School was founded by the Dawes Act.

42. **B:** Henry George wrote *Progress and Poverty* in 1879 and called for a single tax on land. He claimed that the government should finance all of its projects from the proceeds of this single tax. George believed that speculators reaped huge but unearned profits from rising land prices. By taxing this unearned income, the government could improve conditions created by industrialization. Bellamy wrote a futuristic novel about life in the year 2000, and Norris exposed the corruption of the railroad tycoons. Lloyd wrote about the evils of Standard Oil, and Steffens described the corruption of the municipal bosses.

43. **A:** The Populist Party did not address the issue of a national banking system. The Democratic Party under the leadership of Woodrow Wilson created the Federal Reserve System in 1913, which established twelve regional banks and provided for greater control of the economy. The Populists' main concern was to inflate the currency by limiting coinage of silver to gold by a ratio of 16 to 1. They also supported all of the other proposals.

44. **D:** The Grangers were founded in 1867 as a social organization to help bring families together. By the mid-1870s, their membership had risen to over one million, and they were focused on economic issues, like falling grain prices and rising railroad shipping rates. They used their political clout to pass state Granger laws

to regulate freight and storage. The Grangers did not support an inflationary monetary policy, state subsidies, cooperatives, or an alliance with urban labor forces. However, the discontent of rural America did force Congress to pass the Interstate Commerce Act (1886) to regulate railroad rates.

45. **B:** The Progressives, unlike the Populists who represented rural America, were urban middle-class Americans who were disturbed by the economic changes brought about by the rise of large business corporations. They were not radicals but reformers who wanted the government to regulate business. They believed that by eliminating corruption in politics and business, democracy would function better. Many thought that society would be improved by increasing public participation in government. They were not radicals and did not support the nationalization of industries. Woodrow Wilson vetoed the Immigrant Bill of 1917 that contained the literacy test. Yet many Progressives agreed on the need to restrict immigration and insisted on the "Americanization of Immigrants." Progressives sought to protect workers and farmers, but they provided little help for African Americans.

46. **D:** The Clayton Antitrust Act (1914) was part of Woodrow Wilson's New Freedom program, not Theodore Roosevelt's Square Deal. The Clayton Antitrust Act was passed during Wilson's first administration and strengthened the provision in the Sherman Antitrust Act for breaking up monopolies. Congress, as part of Roosevelt's Square Deal, successfully approved all of the other choices for consumers, workers, and the environment.

47. **D:** Some historians believe that the origin of the Cold War can be found in this meeting when a gravely ill Roosevelt was outmaneuvered by the deceitful Stalin. They contend that FDR handed over the countries of eastern Europe, and Stalin had no intention of holding free elections anywhere. Others argue that Soviet troops controlled these territories, and the Soviets—who

had been invaded twice in less than twenty-five years—were not going to give up this buffer zone without a war. The question of German occupation, the United Nations, and the Soviet Union's entrance into the war against Japan were important to the United States and the Soviet Union, but these were not as controversial as why the countries of Eastern Europe became Soviet satellites.

48. **E:** The Neutrality Acts of 1935, 1936, and 1937 never distinguished between victims and aggressors. These laws basically stated that the United States could not sell arms to countries that were at war. To avoid the problem that occurred in World War I, when 128 American lives were lost on the British luxury liner *Lusitania*, the Neutrality Acts forced the United States to give up its traditional policy of freedom of the seas. In 1939, the neutrality laws prevented the United States from helping Loyalists or Republicans during the Spanish Civil War.

49. **C:** This executive order directed one hundred thousand Japanese Americans on the West Coast to leave their homes and reside in internment camps. Japanese Americans living in other parts of the United States, including Hawaii, were not affected by this order. There was no executive order regarding women in noncombat units. An executive order was not necessary to establish an Office of Price Administration. Executive Order 8802 ended discrimination in hiring in defense industries, and the Smith Act of 1940 required the registration of immigrants in the United States.

50. **D:** The National Origins Act was designed to severely limit immigrants by setting quotas based on nationality. Quotas were based on the 1890 census, because that was the year before the arrival of the New Immigrants from eastern and southern Europe. Nativists considered immigrants undesirable. By 1927 the quota for immigrants from Asia and eastern and southern Europe was 150,000. The Chinese Exclusion Act of 1882 restricted the number coming to the United States, and Congress instituted a

literacy test in 1917. The National Origins Act exempted immigrants from the Western Hemisphere from restrictions and did not include any provisions for improving the processing centers.

51. **A:** In 1947, President Harry Truman pledged to assist any free peoples who were fighting communist or armed revolutionaries. The Truman Doctrine provided Greece and Turkey with $400 million in aid. The Marshall Plan provided economic aid to Europe, and NATO was a military alliance to protect Western Europe. The Eisenhower Doctrine was set up to protect the Middle East, and the Alliance for Progress was designed to help Latin America.

52. **E:** In 1944, Congress passed the GI Bill partly out of fear that the employment market would never be able to absorb the fifteen million veterans returning to civilian life at the end of World War II. The bill made generous provisions for sending soldiers to school. In the postwar decade some eight million veterans advanced their education at the government's expense. The GI Bill was not designed to encourage reenlistment or to integrate the armed forces. It was not a response to the fear of postwar protests by veterans, nor was it created to fulfill the need of business communities for a more educated workforce.

53. **B:** On the eve of the Paris Summit Conference in May 1960, an American U-2 plane was shot down in the heart of the Soviet Union. The incident exposed a secret U.S. tactic for gaining information. After denials by Washington bureaucrats, President Eisenhower took full responsibility for the flight. Soviet leader Nikita Khrushchev called off the summit. The Bay of Pigs invasion occurred in 1961. The other options took place before 1960.

54. **A:** Kennedy entered the White House with fragile Democratic majorities in Congress. Southern Democrats controlled key congressional committees, such as the House Ways and Means Committee. They joined with Republicans to ax New Frontier proposals that included medical assistance for the elderly and increased federal

aid to education. Kennedy turned to foreign policy mainly because his domestic program was blocked. The conservative Southern Democrats, not the sluggish economy or the civil rights movement, prevented passage of the New Frontier programs.

55. **D:**   W. E. B. Du Bois was an African American graduate of Harvard. In 1905, Du Bois met with a group of black intellectuals in Niagara Falls, Canada, to discuss programs of action and protest to secure equal rights for blacks. Du Bois criticized Booker T. Washington's approach and asserted that it was necessary for African Americans to secure their economic bases before they sought to gain political and social equality. Du Bois and the Niagara Movement argued that political and social rights were prerequisites for economic independence. The members of the Niagara Movement did not want to form a third political party or provide training programs for African Americans. However, Du Bois and other members of the Niagara Movement founded the National Association for the Advancement of Colored People (NAACP) to abolish all forms of segregation in the United States and increase education opportunities.

56. **E:**   Turner used the frontier thesis to explain the American character of individualism, faith in democracy, and a sense of optimism, which were based on the availability of cheap land, which created hope for a better future. The changing nature of the frontier also necessitated that Americans be creative and innovative to solve their daily problems. However, Turner failed to point out that American settlers massacred large numbers of Native Americans, which violated the basic principles of democracy. The frontier created conflict, not equality, between the two groups as white settlers expanded westward and infringed on the rights of Native Americans.

57. **B:**   In 1925 Bruce Barton wrote *The Man Nobody Knows* in which he compared Jesus to a successful businessman. For Barton,

Jesus was a modern advertising executive who was able to use the Apostles as an effective sales force in spreading the gospel. Frederick Taylor implemented scientific management on a large scale to increase productivity. The other authors were critical and unsympathetic to the business world.

58. **B:**   In 1898, Andrew Carnegie, Mark Twain, and William Jennings Bryan formed the Anti-Imperialist League, which opposed the acquisition of the Philippines. Carnegie believed that taking possession of the Philippines violated the principles of the Declaration of Independence and the foundation of the Constitution. Alfred T. Mahan's *The Influence of Sea Power upon History* (1890) argued that the United States needed to expand to prevent European rivals from dominating Asia and Latin America. Josiah Strong's *Our Country* (1885) argued that the United States had an obligation to spread civilization to Asia and Latin America. Newspaper publisher William Randolph Hearst's "yellow journalism" vigorously pushed expansion into Cuba, and William Howard Taft promoted economic imperialism (Dollar Diplomacy) in Latin America.

59. **D:**   In 1904, Roosevelt announced the Roosevelt Corollary to the Monroe Doctrine, which stated that the United States had the right to intervene in any Latin American country that was unable to pay off debts or acted contrary to the interests of the United States. Unlike the Monroe Doctrine, which warned Europe to stay out of Latin America, the United States became the big brother to Latin America. Over the next twenty years, the United States sent troops to Haiti, Nicaragua, the Dominican Republic, and Honduras. Franklin D. Roosevelt's Good Neighbor Policy opposed intervention in Latin America, while Woodrow Wilson's Moral Diplomacy sought to promote democracy in Latin America. McKinley was assassinated in 1901.

60. **B:** Congress passed a joint resolution authorizing war with Spain, and part of the resolution, the Teller Amendment, declared that the United States had no intention of taking political control of Cuba once peace was restored to the island. The Cuban people would control their own government. Unfortunately, the United States remained in Cuba from 1898 until 1901, and Cuba was subjected to U.S. oversight and control for many years. The Teller Amendment did not address the Philippines or the treatment of Cuban rebels.

61. **D:** *The Gilded Age* is a novel written by Mark Twain in 1873 that satirized the greed and political corruption in post–Civil War America, especially in Washington, D.C. The term "Gilded" commonly given to this era comes from the title of this book. "Gilded" refers to a thin layer of gold over baser metal, so the title takes on a derogatory term to symbolize graft, materialism, and corruption in public life. *The Gilded Age* does not address any issue that deals with social patterns, immigrant life, or the plight of farmers or Native Americans.

62. **C:** Democrats built their political base on the Solid South that would remain loyal throughout the late nineteenth century until the election of 1928. In the North, immigrants who crowded into ethnic neighborhoods became victims of political machines. In New York, Tammany Hall served the needs of the immigrants by finding them jobs, apartments, and food. In return, the politicians were guaranteed their votes. Democrat machines dominated politics in all major U.S. cities. Farmers, the emerging middle class, Northern blacks, and residents of small towns in the Northeast supported the Republican Party. This coalition would remain intact until the election of 1932.

63. **D:** The communists did not take power in Russia until November 1917. The overthrow of the czar had taken place in March 1917, and the United States declared war on Germany in April 1917,

eight months before communism gained control of Russia. Economic interests, the split among ethnic groups in the United States, British propaganda, and the Zimmerman Telegram (in which Germany promised to return lands to Mexico that it had lost in 1848) made it difficult for the United States to remain neutral in thought and action.

64. **C:** In 1919, the Supreme Court upheld the constitutionality of the Espionage Act involving a man who had been imprisoned for distributing antidraft pamphlets. Oliver Wendell Holmes concluded that the right to free speech could be lifted when there was a "clear and present danger" to public safety. The Sedition Act prohibited anyone from making disloyal remarks about the U.S. government. The *Schenck* case allowed for the revoking of free speech, not the suspension of habeas corpus, nor the right of the president to issue an executive order banning free speech or prohibiting freedom of speech for noncitizens.

65. **A:** Although 20 percent of the African American population lived in the North, they did not achieve permanent economic improvement through better-paying jobs. Returning veterans were given priority in getting back to their old jobs. African Americans were still the last hired and the first fired. Race riots broke out in many cities across the North after World War I because Northerners resented the migration of over six hundred thousand African Americans, believing they threatened their neighborhoods and their lifestyles. African Americans earned more money by working in the North rather than the South, but they still received less than their white counterparts and lived in the less-desirable neighborhoods in the cities.

66. **B:** Henry Cabot Lodge was a Reservationist. Unlike the Irreconcilables who opposed any membership in the League of Nations, Lodge wanted restrictions on U.S. membership in the league. He was not opposed to involvement in European affairs,

nor did he fear the league would be dominated by France and Great Britain. Public opinion was not opposed to the league, but the public agreed with Lodge that Congress would have to approve any U.S. actions on the league and that the Monroe Doctrine superseded the decisions of the League of Nations.

67. **E:** The prosperity of the 1920s rested upon technological innovations. The business boom was led by a 64 percent increase in manufacturing output between 1919 and 1929. New machinery and assembly lines resulted in impressive gains in productivity. The pro-business attitude of the Republican Party, which controlled all branches of government and supported lowering taxes, protective tariffs, as well as the stock market fever, resulted from increased productivity. This development enabled workers to earn higher wages. Mellon's tax plan benefited those in the upper tax bracket. The agricultural sector was the only area in which income declined.

68. **E:** There was no federal regulation of banks in the 1920s, and many banks bought stock on margin with their customers' savings. When the market crashed, customers lost their money because there was no federal guarantee of their deposits. During the 1920s, the government had complete faith in business and did little to control it. Congress enacted high protective tariffs that protected U.S. industries but hurt farmers and international trade. All the other choices were major underlying reasons for the Great Crash.

69. **D:** The Second New Deal lasted from the summer of 1935 to the summer of 1938. Its goal, unlike the First New Deal, which focused primarily on recovery over reform, was to establish permanent economic reforms. The Second New Deal relied heavily on Keynesian-style deficit spending to stimulate the economy. Permanent reforms introduced during the New Deal to protect workers were the Social Security Act for old-age pensions and

unemployment insurance and the Wagner Act, which gave labor the right to organize. In the First New Deal, the National Recovery Act had granted labor the right to organize, but the Supreme Court declared the NRA unconstitutional. Most Republicans opposed the First and Second New Deals, and it is difficult to determine which New Deal was more successful.

70. **A:** Franklin D. Roosevelt appointed Frances Perkins as the first woman to hold a cabinet position (secretary of labor). She had worked with him when he was governor of New York. Huey Long's Share the Wealth Program and Francis Townsend's Old Age Revolving Pension Plan were proposed because Long and Townsend believed Roosevelt was too conservative. Al Smith and the American Liberty League attacked Roosevelt for being too radical. Charles Coughlin opposed Roosevelt because he thought the New Deal was under the influence of Jewish bankers.

71. **D:** In 1935 the Supreme Court ruled that the National Industrial Recovery Act was unconstitutional, because it gave legislative power to the president to organize an industry code. The states, not the federal government, had the right to control businesses exclusively involved in intrastate commerce, and the federal government did not have the power to recognize the right of unions to bargain collectively. The Supreme Court declared the Agricultural Adjustment Act unconstitutional in 1936. The Supreme Court never ruled on the constitutionality of the insurance of bank deposits or the Emergency Banking Act.

72. **B:** *On the Road* is a 1951 novel by Jack Kerouac. It is largely auto-biographical, based on the spontaneous road trips of Kerouac and his friends across America. It is often considered a defining work of the postwar Beat Generation, which was inspired by jazz, poetry, and drug experiences and encouraged rebellion against traditional society. Sociologist C. Wright Mills'

book *White Collar* portrays the dehumanizing corporate world. Norman Mailer's *The Naked and the Dead* is 1948 novel based upon his experiences with the 112th Cavalry Regiment during World War II. *The Great Gatsby* is a novel about the upper class in the 1920s. *The Other America* influenced the war on poverty.

73. **D:** With only two dissenting votes, Congress passed the Gulf of Tonkin Resolution, which empowered the president to use further force in Southeast Asia to protect U.S. soldiers from attack. President Johnson wanted congressional approval for committing troops to Vietnam in order to avoid President Truman's difficulties in Korea, when he ordered armed forces to that country without congressional support. Congress relinquished its war power to the president without any specific directions on the purpose of U.S. involvement. The United States would withdraw from Vietnam in 1975.

74. **A:** Federal bloc grants are associated with President Richard Nixon's program of New Federalism, which was designed to shift the responsibility for the federal programs of the Great Society (such as Medicare, elementary and secondary education, and aid to Appalachia) to the states. The Great Society also changed the immigration laws to end the quota system that had existed since 1924.

75. **D:** In 1963, Betty Friedan's *The Feminine Mystique* became a classic of feminist protest literature by exploring the boredom of middle-class suburban women who were beginning to question the traditional roles of women in society. Friedan challenged women to pursue professional careers rather than be homemakers. Her book ignited the women's movement in 1963 and transformed the social fabric of the United States. The proposed Equal Rights Amendment, *Roe v. Wade*, extended maternity leaves, and the emergence of women in politics largely occurred after the publication of Friedan's book.

76. **D:** The Freedom Riders were white and African American civil rights activists who rode interstate buses into the segregated South to test whether these states were complying with the Supreme Court decision that had outlawed racial segregation in restaurants and waiting rooms in terminals servicing buses that crossed sate lines. The Freedom Riders began in May 1961 and were sponsored by the Congress of Racial Equality (CORE). They were not involved in voting registration or providing economic help to the poor in Southern states.

77. **B:** During the 1970s, the biggest domestic issue was the growing inflation rate that by 1979–80 had reached 13 percent. Paul Volcker, chairman of the Federal Reserve Board, tried to break inflation by pushing rates as high as 20 percent. Throughout the Carter administration, interest rates were at historic highs. The high interest rates hurt the automobile and building interests and resulted in the layoffs of thousands of workers. Stagflation was the economic problem faced by the Carter administration. It was an era characterized by high inflation at a time of slow economic growth.

78. **A:** Nixon's policy of Vietnamization was to withdraw 540,000 U.S. troops from South Vietnam over an extended period. The United States was not going to rely on more special forces or end all aid to Vietnam or work with China to establish stability. Nixon hoped that, with American money, weapons, training, and advice, Vietnam could gradually take over the burden of fighting their own war.

79. **C:** Archibald Cox Jr. had been appointed special prosecutor in charge of investigating the Watergate scandal. When he insisted upon receiving secret tapes that President Richard Nixon had made in the Oval Office, Nixon ordered Cox to be fired. On October 20, 1973, after both Attorney General Elliot Richardson and Deputy Attorney General William Ruckelshaus

resigned their positions rather than fire Cox, Nixon assigned the task to U.S. Solicitor General Robert Bork, who also considered resigning, but Richardson convinced him that his resignation could leave the Justice Department in chaos, and Bork agreed to follow Nixon's order to remove Cox from his position. The affair became known as the Saturday Night Massacre. Spiro Agnew had resigned on October 10, 1973, and the protest at Kent State University occurred on May 4, 1970. The release of the Pentagon Papers was in 1971. Nixon ordered the invasion of Cambodia in April 1970.

80. E: The Reagan Revolution refers to the conservative mood of the country in the 1980s. The Moral Majority of the Religious Right emerged in the 1980s as supporters of Ronald Reagan and the Republican Party. They wanted the government to pass legislation that overturned the *Roe v. Wade* decision that legalized abortion and wanted restrictions on issues concerning pornography, homosexuality, as well as prayers in school. Reagan appointed conservative judges to the Supreme Court, reduced the welfare state, and proposed few government regulations on businesses and the economy.

Answers for Document-Based Questions

Until the late nineteenth century, U.S. policy regarding immigration remained largely open to receive not only the wealthy but the oppressed and persecuted of all nations and religions. American-born poet Emma Lazarus best summarized this approach in the sonnet "The New Colossus" in 1883, in which she saw America welcoming Europe's "huddled masses yearning to breathe free, the wretched refuse of your teeming shore" (Document A). Her sonnet is inscribed on the pedestal of the Statue of Liberty, which was dedicated in 1886 in New York Harbor.

However, by the mid-eighteenth century, America had begun to question whether the door should be open to everyone. Movements of various kinds attempted to get Congress to restrict entrance to the country. In 1875, Congress prohibited the immigration of convicts and prostitutes. In 1882, Congress further barred "idiots, lunatics, and persons likely to become public charges." More important, in that year Congress passed a law discriminating against immigrants on the basis of race. The Chinese Exclusion Act of 1882 forbade the further immigration of Chinese laborers.

In the East, Americans objected to the new waves of southern and eastern European immigrants. Many of these people were Italians, Jews, Poles, Greeks, and Russians with dark complexions who spoke foreign languages and were mostly Catholics and Jews. Editorial cartoons complained that there were no laws to keep out poor and undesirable immigrants (Document C).

Prescott Hall and five Harvard graduates founded the Immigration Restriction League in 1894. The league was founded in Boston but quickly gained support across the United States in New York, Chicago, and San Francisco. The members of the league felt it was necessary to oppose the undesirable immigrants that were coming to the United States from southern and eastern Europe. Prescott Hall served as the general secretary of the league from 1896 to 1921. Hall and other league members used books and journal articles to disseminate information about the inferiority of these New Immigrants.

Hall believed that the New Immigrants had a different "mental makeup from the Baltic race" (Document B). He and other league members claimed that southern Italians presented the most danger to the American way of life because it was "one of the most mixed races in Europe and is partly African" (Document B). The league also used scientific arguments based on a flawed application of Darwinian evolutionary theory to call for immigration restrictions.

The American Federation of Labor (AFL) also proposed stopping all immigration for at least two years. John Mitchell, president of the AFL, asserted that immigrants harmed American workers because they were willing to work for lower wages, which threatened the schedule of wages for all workers in the industry (Document D). Mitchell was critical of the New Immigrants because they were unskilled, did not speak English, and were illiterate. However, some Americans thought that the New Immigrants helped America. Harris Weinstock, who was born in London but moved when he was a young child and became state market director of California, claimed that immigrants did not lower wages for American workers. Immigrants provided the needed labor for such industries as slaughterhouses, coal mines, and wool mills (Document E). By furnishing needed labor, native American workers were able to pursue new productive possibilities or different job options (Document E).

As immigration continued to increase substantially throughout the 1890s, the Immigration Restriction League proposed a literacy test be made part of an immigration bill. The literacy test was designed to prevent immigration from southern and eastern Europe. Senator Henry Cabot Lodge of Massachusetts and a member of the Immigration Restriction League supported a literacy test because it would weed out the worst of the New Immigrants (Document F). He believed that those who passed the test would be able to assimilate more easily into American culture. Lodge also claimed that the values of the New Immigrants mostly from southern and eastern Europe were incompatible with American ideals. In addition, he believed that the mixing of races through interracial marriage would lead to the decline of American civilization (Document F).

Jane Addams, a renowned social worker and founder of Hull House settlement in Chicago to help immigrants, strongly opposed using a literacy test to judge immigrants. She insisted that "literacy is neither a test of character or ability." Addams claimed that the peasants find work quicker than educated workers because they adapt better (Document G). The struggle for the passage of the literacy test lasted twenty years. Congress passed the literacy test for the first time in 1896, which required New Immigrants to read at least forty words in any language for admission. Democratic President Grover Cleveland vetoed the bill in 1897. Republican President William Howard Taft vetoed the literacy test in 1913. In 1915, President Wilson vetoed the literacy test, claiming that it violated the traditional policy of providing asylum and opportunities for those who need help (Document H). In 1917, Congress overrode Wilson's veto and instituted the first literacy requirement for naturalization as part of the Immigration Act of 1917. The law stated that immigrants over sixteen years of age should read at least thirty words and not more than eighty in ordinary use in any language.

The culmination of immigration restriction efforts came in 1921 when the first quota law was enacted. Like the Chinese Exclusion Act of 1882, it restricted immigration based on national origin. The quota limited annual immigration from any European country to 3 percent of the number of its natives based on the 1910 census. However, Restrictionists complained that the new law allowed too many immigrants from southern and eastern Europe to enter the United States. Thus Congress passed the Immigration Act of 1924, which reduced immigration from 3 percent to 2 percent of the foreign-born citizen of each nationality living in the United States in 1890. Using 1890 rather than 1910 or 1920 excluded the new immigrants from southern and eastern Europe truly proportionate to their number in the population. This new law ensured the largest number of immigrants would come from northern and western European countries like Germany, Great Britain, and Ireland rather than Italy, Poland, and Russia. For example, the Italian quota was reduced from 42,057 to 3,845. The maximum total allowed for each year was cut from 357,000 in 1921 to 164,667 (Document I).

Social workers and leaders like Edith Bremer implored the president to veto the bill. They believed the quota system was inhumane. They also believed that the law would increase the exploitation of immigrants and be difficult to administer as well as create strife among the immigrant population (Document J).

The immigration restriction laws reversed earlier practices and became a permanent feature of national policy until 1960. The day of Emma Lazarus's welcoming all people and the indiscriminate acceptance of all races had ended. The American people had narrowed the Golden Door on who could enter the United States.

Answers for Standard Essay Questions

Part B

1. The Constitution is the document that sets up the entire system of government for the United States. It was written by fifty-five delegates from all the states (except Rhode Island) in 1787 and was ratified in 1788. The U.S. Constitution includes how the government is organized, the responsibilities of the federal government and the states, and the rights of citizens. The drafters of the Constitution disagreed about many issues contained within it, and in order to move the process forward, they had to compromise on several key issues, including representation in government, how the executive branch would be elected, slavery, and taxation. In many instances, the solutions in the Constitution attempted to appease both sides. For this reason, it is accurate to call the Constitution a "bundle of compromises," as many historians do.

One of the largest areas of disagreement was on how states would be represented in government. If the size or population of a state determined its representation in government, smaller states would be at a disadvantage. Larger states felt that they should be able to take advantage of their population. If the government were to be truly democratic, then each person should count toward representation in government. This debate led to the Great Compromise, also called the Connecticut Compromise, since it was proposed and brokered by Roger Sherman of Connecticut. As part of the compromise, the Constitution created a bicameral legislature. In the House of Representatives, representation would be determined by population—this gives larger states the opportunity to have their population adequately represented. Every ten years, a census is taken to determine the population of each state and the accuracy of representation in the House of Representatives. In the Senate, all states have the same number of representatives: two.

Issues of representation also came into play when deciding how the executive branch, or the president, would be elected. Some delegates believed the president should be elected directly by the people, while others believed that the people could not be trusted with such a decision.

Opponents of direct election offered a number of alternatives, including election by state legislature. In the end, Sherman's Great Compromise included a provision to solve this problem. The Constitution established the Electoral College, which is a set of elected representatives who ultimately determine who becomes president. The people directly elect members of the Electoral College, but not the actual president.

Slavery was another large source of disagreement during the drafting of the Constitution. Specifically, the drafters disagreed about how slaves should be counted as part of the population, if slaves should be counted for tax purposes, and whether or not the slave trade should be abolished in the United States. Including slaves as part of the population obviously relates to the bicameral structure of the government; if states were part of the population, states with more slaves—traditionally Southern states—would have more representatives in the House of Representatives. Northern states, however, believed that slaves should not count as part of the population but should be counted for taxation purposes. Southern states asserted the opposite—count slaves as part of the population but not for taxation purposes. The Three-Fifths Compromise solved this issue. Each slave counted as three-fifths of a person for both representation and taxation purposes.

The larger issue of slavery and its place in the United States was also a source of compromise in the Constitution, as many felt the issue would be too thorny to solve efficiently and in a way that would preserve the solidarity of the young nation. The divide between the pro- and anti-slave delegates was too wide; as a compromise, the Constitution specifically did not abolish the slave trade and instead gave a twenty-year window during which the importing of slaves was legal and during which no new legislation about importation was allowed. This compromise delayed the more direct decisions about slavery and in many ways contributed to the causes of the Civil War.

Compromise came into play for issues of commerce as well. Southerners opposed tariffs, fearing they would damage the Southern economy, which was heavily dependent upon trade. Northerners thought tariffs would protect their businesses from overseas competition. The Commerce Compromise allowed the federal government to tax imports but not exports.

As the above examples indicate, the Constitution is, in fact, a bundle of compromises, and so to call it that is valid. No one issue was decisively settled in a way that favored either side of an issue. In the end, the Constitution negotiated delegate differences in a way that allowed the process to move forward and allowed the new country to have a foundation for its government.

2. During the 1830s and 1840s the rush of settlers beyond the nation's borders into Texas and Oregon inspired some politicians to call for the annexation of those areas occupied by the migrants. Journalist John L. O'Sullivan, an influential advocate of the Democratic Party, while not using the term Manifest Destiny, did predict a divine destiny for the United States. In 1845, he first used the phrase to state that it was the country's Manifest Destiny to overspread and to possess the whole continent that God had given to the United States for the development of liberty.

The theme of America's Manifest Destiny in the 1840s led to diplomatic confrontations with Great Britain and war with Mexico. In 1841, John Tyler, who had become president after the first Whig president (William Henry Harrison) died in office after serving barely a month, initiated the policy of Manifest Destiny. Texas, which had been settled by Americans who had been encouraged by Mexico in the 1820s to farm its sparsely populated northern province, revolted and gained its independence in 1836. As an independent republic, Texas petitioned for annexation in 1837. Both Democratic presidents Andrew Jackson and Martin Van Buren put off the request for annexation because of political opposition among Northerners to the passion of slavery and the potential addition of slave states created out of the Texas territories.

In 1843, Tyler, who was hoping to be elected president in his own right in 1844, decided to put the full weight of his administration behind the annexation of Texas. He thought that the annexation of the Lone

Star Republic would appeal to the South, who wanted additional slave states, and gain him supporters for the election of 1844. He worked to annex Texas, but the Senate rejected his treaty of annexation in 1844.

In the 1840s, Oregon fever captured the nation. Both the United States and Great Britain claimed Oregon, a vast territory on the Pacific Coast. By the 1840s, however, over five thousand Americans traveled two thousand miles over the Oregon Trail to settle in the area south of the Columbia River. The British had fewer than one thousand settlers living north of the Columbia River. By the election of 1844, many Americans believed it was their Manifest Destiny to take undisputed possession of all of Oregon and to annex the Republic of Texas. Expansionists also hoped to persuade Mexico to give up its province on the West Coast: California. The Mexicans had a small population of less than seven thousand along with a large number of Native Americans, but U.S. citizens were streaming into the region in larger numbers and eventually outnumbered the Mexican population in California as they had done in Texas.

The election of 1844 was fought over the issue of expansion. Before the election of 1844, Whig candidate Henry Clay and the presumed Democratic candidate, Martin Van Buren of New York, declared their opposition to annexation. Angry Southern Democrats refused to support Van Buren at their nominating convention and selected James K. Polk of Tennessee, a protégé of Andrew Jackson, as the nominee. Polk, an avowed expansionist, ran on a platform that tied the annexation of Texas with the occupation of all of Oregon and the acquisition of California. The Democratic slogan of "54'40 or Fight" appealed strongly to Westerners and Southerners, who were in an expansionist mood in 1844. The Democratic platform also provided a sort of regional compromise. Expansionists in the North were inclined to promote the occupation of Oregon, but Southern expansionists focused primarily on the annexation of Texas. Although elected by a very slim margin, Polk interpreted his election as a mandate for expansion. After the election, but before he took office, Congress annexed Texas, which became the fifteenth slave state even though Mexico had never recognized the independence of Texas.

On the question of Oregon, Polk sought to compromise with Great Britain to the dismay of the advocates of Manifest Destiny, who had demanded all of Oregon with the warlike slogan of "54'40 or Fight," referring to the northern border of the region. Polk was willing to settle for the southern half of Oregon rather than all of Oregon. Despite the earlier clamor for all of Oregon, the Oregon Treaty of 1846 was ratified by the Senate. The strong advocates of Manifest Destiny had not prevailed along the northern U.S. border, but Manifest Destiny would be more consequential for Mexico.

In April 1846 war broke out between Mexico and the United States when Polk moved troops to occupy a portion of the Texas border claimed by Mexico. The Mexican army captured an American patrol, killing eleven soldiers. The Mexican War was politically divisive. Northern Whigs opposed the war, and Abraham Lincoln, the young Whig congressman from Illinois, opposed going to war over the incident and doubted that American blood had been shed on Mexican soil. Even Northern Democrats accused the president of misleading the public. As the war dragged on, many Northern Whigs formed the opinion that the war was nothing more than a plot by Southerners to expand slavery. Other northerners asked why Polk was willing to compromise on Oregon but so eager to pursue a war for slave territory. New England transcendentalist writer Henry David Thoreau went to jail rather than pay taxes to support what he believed was an unjust war. The expansionist dreams of Manifest Destiny served to fuel sectional antagonisms.

After the Mexican War ended in 1848, the disagreement over the expansion of slavery made further territorial annexation too divisive to be an official government policy. Many northerners were increasingly opposed to what they believed to be efforts by Southern slave owners and their friends in the North to expand slavery at any cost. The Wilmot Proviso was introduced in 1846 by Pennsylvania congressman David Wilmot, which stipulated that appropriations be amended to forbid slavery in the new territories acquired from Mexico, indicated the degree to which Manifest Destiny had become controversial. The House passed the Wilmot Proviso, but the Senate defeated it.

Manifest Destiny in the 1840s renewed the sectional debate over the extension of slavery and increased tensions between the North and the South. Throughout the 1850s, Congress dealt with the status of the vast western lands acquired during the 1840s. The question of how to determine whether territory should be free or slave would ultimately lead to the Civil War in 1860.

Part C

1. The struggle for equal rights in the African American community has consistently been part of the landscape in the history of the United States. In the late nineteenth and early twentieth centuries, two key figures in this struggle emerged—Booker T. Washington and W. E. B. Du Bois. They both shared the desire for equality for African Americans, but their approach, philosophy, and methods differed greatly.

Booker T. Washington was one of the last civil rights leaders who had been born into slavery. Because of this, his perspective and experience differed greatly from those of W. E. B. Du Bois. He was accustomed to existing in a pre–Civil War society where blacks not only had limited civil rights but were not even considered citizens. Washington's experiences led him to adopt a cooperative and collaborative approach to race relations. He articulated these ideals in 1895 during a speech to the Cotton States and International Exposition. In what came to be known as the Atlanta Compromise, Washington told a primarily white audience that while segregation was not to be tolerated, blacks should not expect to end it forcefully and by rushing the process of assimilating into the white mainstream. Washington supported a slower pace to equality, something that came to be called accommodationism. He did not advocate actively or publicly for civil rights that were already recognized by law. Under this model, blacks did not lobby to have access to the current systems of political power, civil rights, or even higher education.

Washington's thought was that if blacks were able to obtain jobs in industry, they would accumulate wealth that would later serve them well and provide the leverage they needed to gain full equality in the future. In addition, by not forcefully attempting to gain access to mainstream white education and politics, they would pacify whites while they used their industrial education to bring wealth and stability to their communities. Washington believed that this stability was a key part of blacks' proving that they could be reliable and responsible members of American society. Washington lived his ideals as part of the all-black Tuskegee Normal and Industrial Institute. At age twenty-five, Washington took up the leadership of the institute, which focused on technical and industrial skills as well as academics. He expanded the size of the institute, which later became Tuskegee University.

W. E. B. Du Bois had been born free and initially supported the ideas of Washington, but he ultimately broke away from this conciliatory approach and believed that pacifying whites was ill advised. He came to call Washington the "Great Accommodator" and took a much more active approach to obtaining equality in practice and under the law for blacks. Du Bois did not advocate for blacks to stay away from established white systems of education, politics, or society. He strongly encouraged blacks to obtain the same type of liberal arts education afforded to most whites, and in 1905 he founded the Niagara Movement, which believed that no one class or race "owned" education. The Niagara Movement was a civil rights organization that originally supported Washington's accommodation approach; however, in their declaration of principles, written primarily by Du Bois, they took a much more forceful and proactive approach, declaring segregation of any kind intolerable and calling for equal rights both in practice and under the law. The Niagara Movement ultimately disbanded, but Du Bois maintained this stance and approach toward civil rights. He later became president of the National Association for the Advancement of Colored People (NAACP), which criticized Washington's approach to civil rights and equality. Du Bois was a prolific author and wrote many papers on his stance on race relations.

Both Washington and Du Bois wanted to end racial segregation in America. Washington thought the process would take longer and required a less adversarial relationship with whites, while Du Bois thought blacks should aggressively push forward in their struggle for equality. Both men made significant contributions to the civil rights movement in the late nineteenth and early twentieth centuries.

2. The year 1968 proved to be a turbulent time for the United States. The war in Vietnam continued to drag on, and the hopeless stalemate soured the American public on the conflict. The assassination of two revered leaders and riots across the country added to the uneasiness and fear that something was wrong with the country.

On January 30, 1968, on the occasion of their lunar new year (Tet), the North Vietnamese and Vietcong launched a surprise attack on more than one hundred cities and towns in Vietnam, stunning the U.S. military command in South Vietnam. The Vietcong even attacked the U.S. Embassy in Saigon and invaded the embassy grounds, killing five U.S. Marines. The events shocked the self-confidence of the American people, who had been told by President Johnson that the Vietcong and the North Vietnamese were close to being defeated. U.S. troops ultimately halted the offense and inflicted heavy losses on the Vietcong.

Despite America's success, the Tet Offensive proved to be a turning point in the war. The destruction was viewed by millions on their televisions at home and dismayed the public and appeared to be a setback for Johnson's administration. For the first time, polls showed strong opposition to the war, with about 50 percent believing the entire Vietnam War was a mistake. The Tet Offensive opened up a year of political drama. Congress turned down requests for troops. As opinion polls showed the president's popularity sinking to historic lows, President Johnson squeaked to a narrow victory in the New Hampshire primary. The Democratic antiwar candidate, Eugene McCarthy, took 42 percent of the vote against Johnson.

On March 31, 1968, Johnson announced that he would not seek the Democratic Party's nomination. Johnson's stunning withdrawal from the presidential race in 1968 four years after his overwhelming victory in 1964 was followed by the assassination of Dr. Martin Luther King, Jr. In the spring of 1968, King chose to support striking sanitation workers in Memphis, Tennessee, and also picked the city to inaugurate a poor people's campaign for peace and justice. On April 4, 1968, James Earl Ray assassinated King as he stepped out on the balcony of his motel in Memphis. The assassination led to a wave of riots in more than one hundred cities across the nation. In Washington, D.C., U.S. Army units set up machine guns outside the Capitol and the White House. Five days after King's shooting, President Johnson declared a national day of mourning for the lost civil rights leader. A crowd of three hundred thousand attended his funeral. Vice President Hubert Humphrey attended the funeral on behalf of the president. There was fear that Johnson might be confronted with protests and demonstrations if he attended.

Robert F. Kennedy, the younger brother of John F. Kennedy, decided to enter the presidential race after McCarthy's strong showing in New Hampshire. He spoke out forcefully about this senseless murder. Kennedy said the country needed and wanted unity between blacks and whites. On June 2, Kennedy, who was a more effective candidate than McCarthy in mobilizing the traditional Democratic bloc of voters, won the California primary. After his victory speech, he was shot and killed by a young Jordanian assassin, Sirhan Sirhan, who was resentful of Kennedy's pro-Israel view.

When the Democrats met in Chicago for their convention, Vice President Hubert Humphrey, who had faithfully supported Johnson's policies, was the likely nominee. The events surrounding the Democratic Convention from August 21 to August 26 demonstrated how deep the divisions within America had become. Antiwar zealots streamed into Chicago and were intent on making their presence known to delegates at the convention. Chicago mayor Richard Daley was equally determined to showcase his city's achievements in maintaining law and order. Antiwar activists called for a massive demonstration at the delegates' hotel and at the convention center. Mayor Daley responded by arranging for barbed-wire barricades around the convention hall as well as using thousands of police and National Guard reinforcements to prevent violence.

The media, however, focused on the Yippies, or Youth International Party, which called for a Festival of Life on the beaches of Lake Michigan. Daley refused to issue a parade permit, which added to the tensions. Soon clashes occurred between Chicago police officers and demonstrators. Some militants baited the police by calling them pigs and shouting obscenities and hurling bags and cans of excrement at the police lines. As people around the world watched on television, police clashed with protesters and bystanders alike, using clubs and tear gas. Some journalists and reporters were caught up in the violence. Network news reporters like Mike Wallace and Dan Rather were roughed up by the Chicago police while inside the halls of the Democratic convention.

The tragic events of 1968 brought whole sectors of the counterculture into political activism. Many young Americans intensified their protests against the war and many baby boomers became united in their opposition to the establishment, which would have lasting consequences for American society. The election of 1968 would also show that many Americans were turning against New Deal liberalism in favor of the conservatives. For many people, 1968 forever changed American society.

About the Author

Michael Romano has a PhD in U.S. history. He has worked with students at both the high school and college levels. As a high school teacher, he taught AP U.S. history. As a New York state social studies supervisor of K–12, he was a mentor for high school teachers who taught social studies AP classes. Romano was an adjunct professor of various New York colleges and currently teaches at a local university. He has also presented at various local and regional social studies conferences.

Notes

Notes

Notes

Notes

Notes

Notes

Notes

Notes

Notes

Notes

_____

_____

_____

_____

_____

_____

_____

_____

_____

_____

_____

_____

_____

Notes

Notes

Also Available

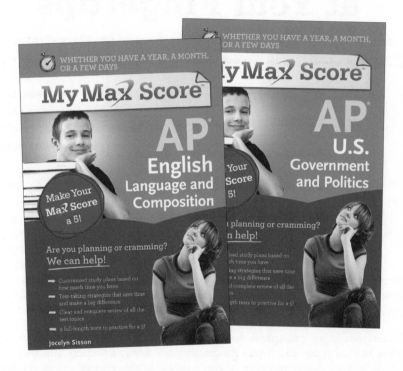

My Max Score AP English Literature and Composition
by Tony Armstrong • 978-1-4022-4311-0

My Max Score AP English Language and Composition
by Jocelyn Sisson • 978-1-4022-4312-7

My Max Score AP Calculus AB/BC
by Carolyn Wheater • 978-1-4022-4313-4

My Max Score AP U.S. Government & Politics
by Del Franz • 978-1-4022-4314-1

$14.99 U.S./ $17.99 CAN/ £9.99 UK

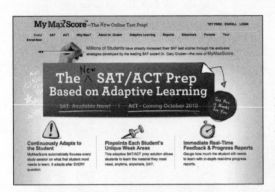

Essentials from
Dr. Gary Gruber
and the creators of My Max Score

"Gruber can ring the bell on any number
of standardized exams."
—*Chicago Tribune*

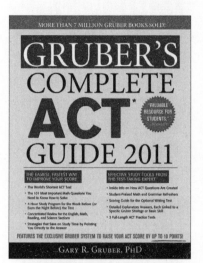

$19.99 U.S./ $23.99 CAN/ £14.99
978-1-4022-4307-3

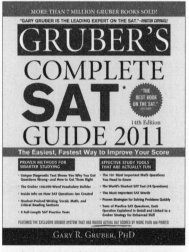

$19.99 U.S./ $23.99 CAN/ £10.99
978-1-4022-3777-5

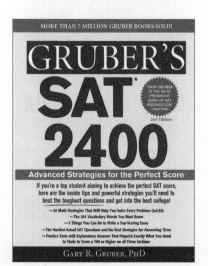

$16.99 U.S./ $19.99 CAN/ £11.99
978-1-4022-4308-0

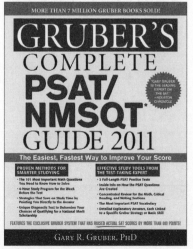

$13.99 U.S./ $16.99 CAN/ £7.99
978-1-4022-3859-8

"Gruber's methods make the questions
seem amazingly simple to solve."
—*Library Journal*

"Gary Gruber is the leading expert on the SAT."
—*Houston Chronicle*

$14.99 U.S./ $15.99 CAN/ £7.99
978-1-4022-1846-0

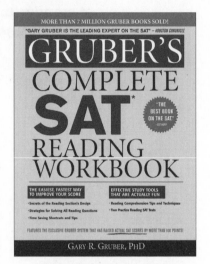

$14.99 U.S./ $15.99 CAN/ £7.99
978-1-4022-1847-7

$14.99 U.S./ $15.99 CAN/ £7.99
978-1-4022-1848-4

$12.99 U.S./ $15.99 CAN/ £6.99
978-1-4022-2010-4